THE COGNITIVITY OF RELIGION

THE COGNITIVITY OF RELIGION
Three Perspectives

J. Kellenberger

UNIVERSITY OF CALIFORNIA PRESS
Berkeley and Los Angeles

University of California Press
Berkeley and Los Angeles, California

Copyright © 1985 by J. Kellenberger

Library of Congress Cataloging in Publication Data
Kellenberger, James.
The cognitivity of religion.
Bibliography
Includes index.
1. Knowledge, Theory of (Religion)   I. Title.
BL51.K415 1985   200′.1   84–27999
ISBN 0–520–05383–4

Printed in Hong Kong

To
Anne

Contents

Preface

To many it has seemed, and to many it seems today, that knowledge of God is the crown of faith, or at least not at odds with depth in religion, and that within limits we can approach such knowledge using our reason. The existence of God can be proved in five ways, St. Thomas Aquinas exultantly proclaims in the *Summa*. But we are also told that those who believe without seeing are blessed, and Kierkegaard, denying absolutely the intuitions of St. Thomas Aquinas, is clear that knowledge of what we must strive to believe destroys depth in religion. There are, it seems to me, two very different religious intuitions about the place of knowledge in religion, and these opposed intuitions extend as well to the cognates of knowledge, including rationality. These opposite intuitions have formed into two antithetical perspectives on the cognitivity of religion. Both perspectives are identifiable as tendencies in early religious reflection and as contenders in contemporary religious thought. Each perspective has impressive strengths, and each has a strong intuitive appeal. Yet they systematically differ at the deepest level of their intuitions.

Though it is not the single locus of their opposition, a crystallizing nub is their difference over the rationality of religion. One champions the rationality of religion. The other denounces the idea that religion should be subject to rationality. However they are in essential agreement on the nature of rationality: for both, as it may be put, rationality is an attribute of proper enquiry. Such a view of rationality is not absurd. In fact it is this concept of rationality that applies when we ask of any belief, including religious belief, 'Is this true?' and 'What supports this?' and proceed to investigate. Regarding religious belief, one perspective welcomes such support and seeks it. The other rejects it and seeking it.

Also, as I shall try to show, there is a third perspective, which, in the West, is embodied in the Psalms. This third perspective differs from the other two perhaps most radically in its tacit rejection of enquiry-rationality as the kind or rationality that is at significant issue for religion. Because it is informed by a very different model of rationality, the third perspective cuts between the other two (though it does not explicitly address them), or better, provides a bridge between them. Moreover, when the implicit self-understanding of this third perspective is formed into a grammar of religious cognitivity, that grammar offers a middle ground of accommodation for the strengths of the first two perspectives. And so, as I hope to show, not only for rationality, but for knowledge and the other cognates of knowledge, the third perspective offers a kind of bridge between the other two.

Thanks are due to many who have helped me in one way or another with this book. I wish to thank Dean Jerome Richfield and the School of Humanities at California State Univesity, Northridge for granting me research reassigned time when it was needed and to thank Daniel Sedey, Chair of the Philosophy Department, for consistently providing me with teaching schedules that enabled me to devote a maximum of time to writing this book. I also wish to thank Alice Ostrem for typing the manuscript, and for her care and patience in dealing with revisions. I owe special thanks to Professor John Hick, the editor of this series, and to John Miles of the University of California Press, both of whom suggested various ways that I might improve the book. My happiest debt is to my wife Anne, in part for some stylistic help, but mainly for her understanding and general support during the months of writing and revision.

Some of the material in this book has appeared previously in *Studies in Religion/Sciences Religieuses*, the *International Journal for Philosophy of Religion*, and *Philosophical Investigations*. In the last two cases, where permission was required, I would like to thank the editors and copyright holders for granting their permission.

Introduction

In this book I intend to address an issue that I shall call the issue of the cognitivity of religion,[1] or more simply, the issue of cognitivity. Really it is not so much a single issue as a nest of issues or, most accurately, a changeable, shifting issue that assumes different forms. Historically there seem to be two fundamentally opposed perspectives on this issue. The issue of the cognitivity of religion pre-eminently has to do with the place of knowledge in religion. However it also extends to associated or cognate concepts, such as rationality, religious understanding, and evidence for religious belief. Sometimes the issue centres on one cognate, sometimes on another. For this reason the issue of cognitivity has elicited different and opposite reactions in many periods and settings. As a consequence, while two perspectives on the place of the cognitive in religion have emerged at various times, and while an opposition between two perspectives has steadily been maintained, that opposition has not always been the same in focus. It seems that there are in religious reflection two profoundly different intuitions about knowledge and its cognates, one positive and one negative, and that the opposition between these intuitions takes various forms depending upon the circumstances of the religious context.

In one form the opposition is between the mystical intuition (the intuition of some mystics, at least) that the truths of religion are 'beyond knowledge' and the viewpoint of those natural theologians who allow that religious truths, some of them, can be known because they can be proven. For Dionysius (or Pseudo-Dionysius) the 'Unknowable' is approached only after a renunciation of 'all the apprehensions of [the] understanding', while for St. Thomas Aquinas God's existence can be proven and so known with 'scientific knowledge' (*scientia*) without the object of worship thereby being denigrated.[2] In another form the opposition manifests itself after it has been allowed that religious knowledge

1

in some sense is attainable. Those on one side, like St. Bonaventura,[3] stress the role of Divine illumination in attaining knowledge of God; those on the other, like Aquinas again, stress the role of reasoned argumentation.

The opposition in more than one form relates to the character of faith. Faith has been viewed as above and unapproachable by reason, as it was by Tertullian;[4] and it has been viewed as assisted by reason, as in the Thomistic tradition. Again, in opposition to the Thomistic idea that faith is essentially 'intellectual assent',[5] John Calvin saw faith as an affective response, a response of hope and trust.[6] Though Calvin did not deny a cognitive belief in God's existence, he said that it is of no importance: it is held in common with the devils, who believe and shudder (James 2.19).[7] A similar opposition pits faith as inwardness – a matter of disposition and intention, or, for Kierkegaard, 'subjectivity' – against faith as acceptance of doctrine and a rejection of what is doctrinally false.

In its most recent form the opposition focuses on the nature of religious language. For one perspective religious language is and must be cognitive – have a truth-value-bearing element. For the other it seriously misrepresents religious discourse to view it as cognitive.[8]

Perhaps some of these pairs of opposed perspectives can to an extent be resolved. I have neither affirmed nor denied this. Also there may be room for a middle view in some cases. Still we should not fail to see that each pair of opposite perspectives reflects what are very different studied reactions regarding some aspect of religion and knowledge and that these reactions can run deep.

I would not deny that the issues defined by these various pairs of perspectives have implications for one another or that they overlap. Clearly they do bear *prima-facie* implications for one another. And they perhaps should overlap, since all are part of the same general issue. It remains, though, that their foci are different. They are like overlapping circles with different centres. Taken together they at least begin to define the issue of cognitivity, and we can start to get clear on the dimensions of the issue by, as it were, connecting the centres of these overlapping circles. The metaphor is helpful, I think. But it is not perfect. For these several issues do not necessarily comprise all of the general issue.

Another way to present the issue of cognitivity is to break it into its parts. If we focus our attention on the modern issue of cognitivity, we can distinguish the following five interconnected parts or subissues:

1 An issue regarding *rationality*: what value, if any, does rationality have for religion?
2 An issue regarding the cognitive in religious *belief* and *language*: does cognitive belief have a deep place in religion?
3 An issue regarding *understanding*: is religious scepticism coherent? Is it possible to understand religious belief without believing?
4 An issue regarding *evidence*: can religious belief be evidentially grounded and yet be religious?
5 An issue regarding *knowledge*: is religious knowledge the crown of faith or is it incompatible with depth in religion?

Though these subissues are interconnected, each can be formulated as a separable grammatical issue.[9] Of course, while I have broken the modern issue into just five parts, it could have been divided into more or fewer parts by my dividing or combining issues. Also more subissues could have been included; however I believe that these five are the salient issues, and taken together they may be allowed to define the modern issue of cognitivity. From this point on our enquiry will be concerned with the issue of cognitivity in its modern form.

1 The Two Perspectives on the Modern Issue of Cognitivity

I INTRODUCTION

I shall in this chapter bring forward the views of various modern and contemporary proponents of the two perspectives I have identified in order to apply each perspective to the five subissues that together comprise the modern issue of cognitivity. In this book I am concerned to resolve the issue of cognitivity, or at least to mollify the two opposed positions that form the issue. But I do not want to stint the problem. In this chapter I want to set out the opposition in its full force. Accordingly, I shall emphasise those strengths of each of the two perspectives that derive from the differences that divide one from the other. In the final two chapters I shall begin to still the pendulum and as much as possible bring the two extremes together in a unified vision. For now, however, our concern is with the glory of the differences.

It would be surprising, I believe, if each of these opposed and abiding intuitions did not have some bit of the truth. In each case, for each subissue, I shall try to summarise the strengths – the insights, we may say – of each perspective from a more or less neutral but sympathetic viewpoint. However before we get down to presenting the two perspectives on the five subissues perhaps we should try to find proper designations for our two perspectives, which so far have gone nameless. Several candidates, none of which is without merit, present themselves:

Rationalist Perspective   vs. Anti-rationalist Perspective
Knowledge Perspective   vs. Anti-knowledge Perspective
Knowledge Perspective   vs. Faith Perspective

Cognitive Belief Perspective vs. Non-cognitive Belief
Perspective
Intellectualist Perspective   vs. Inwardness Perspective.

But these titles will not do, it seems to me, for each skews the issue by
implying that it is only or primarily about one facet of the general
issue. There are other descriptive designations that might be
considered, but all, I think, are lacking. Thus the best course may
be to adopt a pair of non-descriptive designations. It is precisely
this that I propose to do. One perspective – the one oriented
negatively toward knowledge and the cognitive – I shall label the
First Perspective; the other – the one oriented positively toward
knowledge and the cognitive – I shall label the *Second Perspective*.
These titles of course do not imply logical status or temporal order
of emergence. They are purely labels, or tags, and could be
transposed.

II THE TWO PERSPECTIVES ON THE FIVE SUBISSUES

(1) The Rationality Subissue: What Is the Value of Rationality for Religion?

The issue here is composite. It can be expressed in a series of
questions about the place of rationality in religion: Is trying to be
rational about one's religious belief helpful to religious belief? Is it
compatible with it? Could it even be destructive of religious belief?
And what is the character of rationality as it relates to religion?
  Briefly, one perspective, the First, that which is oriented against
the cognitive, is highly suspicious of rationality in religion.
Initially it tends to see rationality as incompatible with religious
faith. The Second Perspective, which especially for this issue is
closely associated with apologetics, tends to see a positive value
for rationality.

The First Perspective

Several modern and contemporary thinkers hold views on
rationality in religion that are First-Perspective in nature.
Kierkegaard is important among them. So is Wittgenstein and so

are the Neo-Wittgensteinians. I shall present their views in some detail, starting with the views of Kierkegaard.

Kierkegaard in more than one pseudonymous work voices a concern with 'reflection' in religion or with 'reason' (*Forstanden*) being brought to faith. While we have yet to examine fully the character of rationality as it applies to belief in God, we can allow that, on the face of it, whatever else it involves rationality somehow involves holding beliefs on the basis of support. It is to this element (though not to it alone) that Kierkegaard objects. Faith cannot be made 'safe' by trying to ground it in support. Faith, for Kierkegaard, of necessity is 'absurd'.

Kierkegaard employs the category of the absurd differently in different works. Notably there is a difference between the absurd in *Fear and Trembling* and the absurd in the *Postscript*. In *Fear and Trembling* Kierkegaard's paradigmatic believer, the knight of faith, believes and acts 'by virtue of the absurd'.[1] In the *Postscript*, however, the absurd is not that by which one believes, it is that which is believed.[2] It is the *Postscript* conception of the absurd that is particularly relevant to our concerns here. Faith, for Kierkegaard in the *Postscript*, is subjectivity or inwardness. It is, he says, 'an objective uncertainty held fast [with] the most passionate inwardness', and he adds, its object is 'the absurd . . . that the eternal truth has come into being in time'.[3] This is the 'absolute paradox', which Christian faith must believe. For Kierkegaard the passion of faith, the subjective truth of religion, is opposed to and diminishes with support and its rationality. Faith requires risk, and the greater the risk the greater the faith. But, moreover, for Kierkegaard, the object of faith proper, of Christian faith, is the greatest uncertainty, for it is – as he says – the 'contradiction' that God existed in human form at a particular time in a particular place; and as a 'contradiction' it cannot have reasons in its support. Faith *must* confront the 'offence' to reason that belief in the eternal-become-temporal poses. For Kierkegaard, to try to escape the possibility of offence by seeking reasons is to renounce faith. Thus, for Kierkegaard in the *Postscript*, there are three related reasons why faith cannot have reasons in its support. First, to seek reasons is to renounce faith by trying to lessen the passionate subjectivity required by faith. Second, faith logically, or objectively, cannot be supported because its object is a 'contradiction'. Third, to seek reasons is to seek to avoid the possibility of offence. For these three reasons, of necessity for

Kierkegaard in the *Postscript*, faith in its confrontation with 'human reason' must be opposed to reason and not rational.

Faith for Kierkegaard in the *Postscript* is *against* reason, it is not *above* reason. Kierkegaard's view should be distinguished from Tertullian's. For Tertullian we are to believe that the Son of God died *because* it is absurd, and that He was buried and rose again is certain *because* it is impossible. For Kierkegaard faith must embrace the absolute paradox, the object of faith, in the face of uncertainty; and the object of faith is and remains uncertain – indeed the greatest uncertainty – even after faith embraces it. Faith, for Kierkegaard in the *Postscript*, is the continuous struggle to hold fast the absolute paradox with passionate inwardness and to avoid being offended by its opposition to reason. Faith requires the continuing uncertainty of the absolute paradox both for the continuing possibility of the offence to reason and for the continuing passion of inwardness. It is not merely that the absolute paradox is beyond positive proof and has no support from reason – it steadily confronts reason.[4]

Wittgenstein greaty respected Kierkegaard's religious sensitivities,[5] and like Kierkegaard in the *Postscript* Wittgenstein often seems to find no place in religious belief for reason or rationality. However, Wittgenstein has his own reasons for separating religion from the claims and adjudication of reason. In fact Wittgenstein seems to have different reasons at different times. In 'A Lecture on Ethics', which he gave in 1929–30, Wittgenstein said that verbal characterisations of religious experience are nonsense and that all ethical and religious expressions involve a 'misuse of our language'. Those who try to 'write or talk Ethics or Religion', as the religious do, run against the 'boundaries of language' in a perfectly hopeless way. Wittgenstein deeply respects the 'tendency of the human mind' to try to speak of the ultimate meaning of life and of the absolute good, as religious believers do; but he is clear that what they say can only be nonsense and cannot in any way add to our knowledge.[6] In this lecture, it appears, Wittgenstein was still strongly influenced by his *Tractatus* views.[7] In any case, in this lecture, while he is sympathetic to religion (though not religious himself),[8] he has a non-cognitivist view of religious language. For Wittgenstein, then, in 'A Lecture on Ethics', the issue of the rationality of religious belief and support for religious belief cannot arise because religious expressions are neither true nor false and hence are open to neither support nor refutation.

In his *Lectures on Religious Belief*, given in 1938, Wittgenstein's view seems to have changed.[9] (In the next section we shall examine more closely Wittgenstein's early and late views on the cognitivity of religious language.) In these lectures Wittgenstein does not say that religious discourse involves a misuse of language. Instead he says that in religion a different use is involved. And in these lectures he has fairly definite views on the rationality of religion which he does not base upon a non-cognitivist construction of religious belief. Religious believers, he says, are not unreasonable. But, he says, they certainly are not reasonable either. Rather, reasonability does not apply.[10] But the reason he gives for this is not that religious expressions are neither true nor false. The reason Wittgenstein gives has more to do with the way religious belief is held. Religious believers do not try to hold their belief with a conviction proportionate to evidence, and for this reason talk of rationality, or reasonableness, is misplaced. It has no role in religious discourse. Again, indubitability, even the indubitability of our belief that Napoleon existed, is not enough for religious persons to change their whole lives. That is, for Wittgenstein, religious belief is not held in the way beliefs are held when reasonability applies even if there is a superabundance of evidence. Consequently Wittgenstein criticises the effort of apologists to make religion reasonable. Doing so changes the entire nature of religious belief. It makes religious belief into a science, a scheme in which theories are supported and eliminated in accordance with findings. For Kierkegaard in the *Postscript*, if I have him right, faith is against reason and rationality. For Wittgenstein in both his lecture on ethics and his lectures on religious belief neither reasonability nor unreasonability applies to religion, though for different reasons in the different lectures. And for both Kierkegaard and Wittgenstein, or at least the later Wittgenstein, an effort to make religion reasonable would destroy it.

Wittgenstein wrote little specifically on religion. However, following Wittgenstein several Neo-Wittgensteinian philosophers have developed aspects of his religious thought. In doing so they have made their own contribution to our understanding of the general issue of religion's cognitivity, and to our understanding of the issue of religion and rationality in particular. Wittgenstein finds no place for talk of reasonability in religious discourse, but at the same time he allows that in religious discourse expressions like 'I believe . . .' are used differently from the way they are used in 'science'. Following this theme, and applying it to rationality, some Neo-Wittgensteinians have claimed that there is a rationality *internal* to religion.

D. Z. Phillips in his essay 'Faith, Scepticism, and Religious Understanding' allows that the distinction between the rational and the irrational is central to any acount of meaning, but he does not accept it that there is one paradigm of rationality for all modes of discourse.[11] Rather there is a diversity of criteria for rationality, as there is a diversity of 'contexts'. Phillips mentions only religion, but elsewhere he names, in addition to religion, science, morality, art, and politics.[12] The distinction between the real and the unreal does not come to the same thing in every context, he says – and, he implies, by extension the distinction between rational and irrational does not either. To see what rationality comes to in a context one must pay heed to that context: one must look at actual practice. If we do this, he says, we shall find that *coming to see that there is a God* is coming to see the possibility of eternal love; it is not like seeing that an additional being – another planet, say – exists. In the latter context, but not in the religious context, criteria of rationality appropriate to science apply.

For Phillips it is not just that there is a diversity of contexts, and so a diversity of criteria for rationality. Also, for Phillips, there is no overriding criterion by which various criteria can be judged. Every context is in order as it is. As it is a mistake to think that the scientific criterion is the paradigm so too it is a mistake to judge the religious criterion by the scientific or by any other, just as it would be a mistake to judge the scientific by the religious criterion or by any other. Phillips says that there is no general justification for the internal criteria for *what is of God*, and the request for such a general justification has no meaning for him.[13] Trying to give such a general justification amounts to applying one set of criteria to another set when each is appropriate only to its context. And, pretty clearly, Phillips would say the same specifically for criteria for rationality. The job of the philosopher, for Phillips (and here he echoes Wittgenstein), is not to justify whatever criteria he finds in the religious context, it is to try to understand them, to look and to describe them in their own terms without imposing a foreign criterion appropriate to some other context.[14]

For Phillips, then, religious belief is internally rational according to its proper criteria. However what it is that is rational for Phillips is not so much religious belief as it is religious activity.[15] This should not be too surprising, for in essence religious belief *is* religious activity for Phillips. Religious belief, as belief in a religious 'picture', expresses itself in the behaviour of the religious person. It is not a mere propositional belief. In the Neo-Wittgensteinian view, the internal sense of 'rationality' that applies to the religious context applies to religious activity, or if to belief, to belief as expressed in practice.

Peter Winch has developed at somewhat greater length than Phillips what we may call the internal view of religious rationality.[16] In his essay 'Understanding a Primitive Society' Winch develops and defends this view as it applies to belief in the efficacy of magic and to the practice of magic in a 'primitive society', the Zande society of northeastern Africa. However, while in this essay he concentrates on applying this view to divergent cultures (such as Zande culture and twentieth-century Western culture) he also wants it to apply to divergent 'contexts of life' within Western culture (such as religion and science). In a part of this essay Winch is replying to Alasdair MacIntyre's article 'Is Understanding Religion Compatible with Believing?'[17] in which MacIntyre argues that it is not. For MacIntyre both the Zande belief in magic and religious belief fail to come up to our evolved scientific criteria for rationality. For Winch the criteria appropriate to the Zande belief in magic and to religious belief are internal to those 'ways of living'. Winch allows, even insists, that 'men's ideas and beliefs must be checkable by reference to something independent – some reality', and he allows that the very existence of a language requires a concept of rationality and, moreover, that rationality has certain 'formal requirements' relating to consistency.[18] But, for Winch, in order to discover what reality amounts to and what will count as consistency in a specific setting we need to look at the context of life in question. The issue between MacIntyre on the one hand and Phillips and Winch on the other, then, seems to be this: Is it appropriate – logically appropriate – to judge a practice like religion, and the criteria for rationality embedded in that practice, by a criterion taken from another area of life, a criterion taken to be overriding? To some extent the issue is made unclear by both sides not articulating with any care the exact criteria at issue, but perhaps it is naive to think that this could be done once we get beyond such 'formal requirements' as consistency. In any case Winch is clear that there are different criteria for rationality. And clearly he, like Phillips, believes that it is illegitimate to assume that one criterion, the scientific, is more in accord with reality than that of the Azande or that of religious believers. Rather we should heed what the Wittgenstein of the *Investigations* tried to show, which, for Winch, is 'that what counts as "agreement or disagreement with reality" takes on as many different forms as there are different uses of language'.[19]

The rationality issue between Winch and MacIntyre, as far as the Azande are concerned, relates in great part to *belief* in magic, but, as we should expect, it also relates to the practice of magic. In fact, as Winch's discussion in 'Understanding a Primitive Society' progresses, the focus is more and more on the practice or activity that is found in a context of life, the Zande context or the religious context. When Winch explicitly refers to 'Judaeo-Christian cultures', as he does only once or twice, the examples he uses are examples of religious practice: the Mass and prayer.[20] Belief in God, as distinct from religious activity, is not mentioned. Like Phillips, Winch regards religious activity as the expression, if not the substance, of religious belief.

This is not the place for an extended discussion of problems with the internal view of religious rationality; nevertheless two problems might be mentioned. First, there is the problem of relativism. Winch, for one, is aware of the danger of a 'Protagorean relativism' and addresses it in two ways. (i) As I noted, Winch insists that our ideas must be checkable by reference to some independent reality. So, applying Winch's point to religious belief, religious reality is not open to arbitrary changes – it is not a matter of what one feels like saying. Although, he is clear, reality is not something identifiable outside the religious setting that gives religious language and practice sense; rather the distinction between real and unreal and what counts as agreement with reality are embedded in religious language itself. (ii) Winch appeals to what he calls 'limiting notions', such as birth, death, and sexual relations, as notions which 'give shape to what we understand by "human life".' In some manner, then, these notions are to provide objective touchstones for various modes of social life. The second problem that we should mention here is related to the first. As it applies to Phillips and Winch it is this: It seems that, on their view, though different 'contexts of life' and the belief they involve must be related to reality in their own terms, there can be no logical room for questions about the rationality or irrationality of modes of social life as a whole. But it seems that there can be such questions since some modes of life – that centred around belief in trolls and fairies, for instance – have been rejected as irrational.[21] Winch to some extent anticipates this problem by pointing out that at least some forms of life have 'an essential reference to something outside themselves'.[22] Black Magic and the Black Mass have such a 'parasitic' relationship to the orthodox concepts of Christianity, and accordingly can be rejected as 'irrational (in the sense proper to religion)'. A similar relation, he suggests, holds between the practice of astrology and astronomy.

Concerning these problems, let it be sufficient for the present to observe that Winch and Phillips recognise and address them. More positively, Winch and Phillips may be seen as trying to develop the concept of rationality: trying to clarify it some would say, trying to expand it others would say. Whichever it is, they do not deny the application to religion of a concept of rationality internal to religion. They urge that, if we would understand the character of religion's rationality, we must in some manner heed the character of religious life. On the importance of heeding the character of religious life Wittgenstein would agree. And so would Kierkegaard, provided that what is heeded is not merely 'habitual belief' but religious faith in its full subjectivity.

The Second Perspective

For the Second Perspective the value of rationality is axiomatic, although this is not to say that rationality is in any sense put above religion. On the contrary, for the Second Perspective, rationality or reason is felt to be inherently good and so necessarily not at odds with religious belief. this Second-Perspective view on reason and religion of course has a long heritage, reaching back to Aquinas, Anselm, Augustine and beyond. Even some who are counted mystics give a place to reason. St. Francis de Sales says of natural reason that it 'is a good tree which God has planted in us; the fruits which spring from it cannot be but good', even though in comparison with the fruits of grace they are of small value.[23] In this heritage it may be that for some, for instance Augustine and Anselm as they are sometimes understood, reason can be applied only after one believes. For others, notably Aquinas, natural reason, the reason we all have by virtue of being human, can lead those without belief to knowledge of God's existence if not to knowledge of the mysteries of the Godhead. More recently, at the beginning of the nineteenth century, William Paley tried to establish the existence of God, or the high probability of the existence of God, through a rational examination of nature. Again, Paley's appeal was to natural reason, although his vehicle was the design argument, fitted with empirical observations of adaptation in the spirit of a scientific age; and his effort was as much to support faith as to persuade unbelievers to take up belief in God. William Paley qualifies as a modern proponent of the Second Perspective on rationality and religion. So do the 'devout sceptics' of the nineteenth century. And so do a number of twentieth-century philosophers who either defend efforts to prove the existence of God or defend a tentative and hypothetical approach to religious belief. Peter Geach and Alvin Plantinga are examples of philosophers who do the first. H. H. Price, John King-Farlow, and William Christensen are examples of philosophers who do the second.

Peter Geach is at once a defender of Thomism and a follower of Wittgenstein, though he is in nearly complete disagreement with such Neo-Wittgensteinians as D. Z. Phillips and Peter Winch. In general he is sympathetic to efforts to give a causal deductive demonstration of God's existence, even though he thinks that such an effort requires an analysis of the form of causal propositions and we lack such an analysis. Still he is inclined to think it is rational to believe that some causal argument is valid before a complete logical analysis has been developed, as it was rational to believe in the validity of certain mathematical proofs before logicians could give a rigorous account of them. If there is a God, then logic cannot show that there is no God. Logic, as the Logos, was in the beginning with God, and it strikes Geach as blasphemous to say that God is 'above logic'.[24]

Moreover, Geach emphasises a second function of natural theology: it can expose religious errors about God. In his essay 'On Worshipping the Right God'[25] Geach argues that it is possible to direct divine worship to the wrong thing. This, for

Geach, is the nature of idolatry. It is possible to worship the wrong thing because 'to worship', like 'to refer', is an intentional verb, and if one is wrong enough in the way one thinks of God, one's worship will be misdirected. Geach is not sure where the line is to be drawn, but he is sure that there is a line. Thus, for Geach, natural theology, by exposing errors in our thinking about God, not only can correct our understanding but can help worship to be worship of the True God. In this way, in Geach's view, natural theology can save one from sinful errors in religious practice. We perhaps find here a connection to Wittgenstein's thought: as for Wittgenstein philosophically mistaken views are too deep to be merely mistakes, so for Geach logical errors in religion are not merely logical and not merely errors; they have an ethico-religious dimension as well.

Traditionally Second-Perspective philosophers have tried to show the rationality of belief in God by establishing or supporting the truth of the belief in God's existence. Aquinas, Anselm, and Paley all provided arguments for the truth of that belief, and Geach, though he does not formulate such an argument himself, is sympathetic to the effort. Now to the extent that Aquinas, Anselm, and Paley were successful they succeeded in showing that belief in God was supported and, therefore, rational. However, since there is a distinction between showing that a belief is true and showing that a belief is rational, it is possible to argue more directly that belief in God is rational, and some Second-Perspective philosophers have done precisely that. Such an effort seeks a kind of support for belief, but support at one remove, as it were. It seeks to show that religious belief has support to the extent that it is rational to believe it true. As George Mavrodes points out, this is the thrust of Alvin Plantinga's book *God and Other Minds*. In *God and Other Minds* Plantinga sets out to 'investigate the rational justifiability of a particular religious belief – the belief in the existence of God', and at the end of the book he concludes: 'If my belief in other minds is rational, so is my belief in God. But obviously the former is rational; so, therefore, is the latter.'[26] (Plantinga's argument, which it is not our concern to criticise, is, briefly put, that belief in God is as rational as belief in other minds because belief in God and belief in other minds are equally probable on the evidence that supports belief in other minds.) This also is Plantinga's thrust in his more recent book *The Nature of Necessity*, in which he argues, not that the ontological argument is sound, but that, given certain versions of the ontological argument, it is rational to accept its central premise, and so it is rational to accept its conclusion.[27]

Within the Second Perspective, then, some have sought to show the rationality of religious belief by showing that its truth has support, and some have sought to show its rationality more directly. What, however, is the Second-Perspective attitude toward holding religious belief *before* its rationality has been shown? Many if not all with Second-Perspective views tend to be sympathetic toward those who suspend belief until they can believe rationally. What came to be known as 'devout scepticism' belongs to the Second Perspective. Devout sceptics reject or hold back from religious belief, not because they have no religious emotions or reject religious morality, but because on ethical grounds they will not believe where the truth is not clear enough for rational belief. Devout sceptics are acquainted with the Bible and know the naturalistic interpretation which it can be given, and they know Hume's criticisms of miracles. Also they have come to know the various forms of religion and believe that it would be parochial to accept any one of them as their own. Devout sceptics will not accept the religion of their fathers as a convention to be outwardly assumed or something to be piously mouthed while not lived. In this they are like Kierkegaard. For this is essentially a reaction against habitual belief. Kierkegaard saw inwardness as what was missing. The devout sceptic concludes that honesty requires doubt, and doubt requires the suspension of belief. But devout sceptics are as passionate in their scepticism as Kierkegaard is in his inwardness. While they are agnostics, they are not anti-religious agnostics. Anti-religious agnostics are hostile to religion and disposed to reject religious belief but do not feel quite justified in unequivocally denying God's existence. Devout sceptics, however, may be disposed to believe and even long to believe.[28] Even so, despite sympathy and a concern to believe, their honesty requires doubt and that they not believe. Several nineteenth century figures exemplify this ideal, among them Matthew Arnold and Henry Sidgwick, as well as Alfred, Lord Tennyson.

For devout sceptics the best faith may *be* honest doubt. David Hume in the eighteenth century had said that 'to be a philosophical sceptic is, in a man of letters, the first and most essential step towards being a sound, believing Christian.'[29] In the nineteenth

century, however, doubt itself became a kind of faith or surrogate
for faith. So it came to be regarded by Tennyson, who wrote the
lines that best capture the thought:

> There lives more faith in honest doubt,
> Believe me, than in half the creeds.[30]

One thing Tennyson is saying in the poem from which these
lines are taken, *In Memoriam*, is that it is wrong to see doubt as evil.
Doubt is not to be denied as sinful, but faced, measured, and dealt
with, for only this honest facing of doubt will create an enduring
faith.[31] But, beyond this, Tennyson is also saying, in accordance
with the lines quoted, that the best faith in an uncertain universe *is*
honest doubt, as opposed to an unexamined acceptance of a creed
or belief. It is true that Tennyson himself longs to believe: he
wishes to 'faintly trust the larger hope', and we should note here
the role of trust, the affective core of faith. But Tennyson had come
to see nature as 'red in tooth and claw', as denying the law of
love.[32] Try as he would he could not deny this perception. Here is
the 'honest doubt' that Tennyson recognised and sought to
resolve. As for T. H. Huxley, Tennyson's contemporary, the
processes of nature were at odds with the principles of ethics. The
universe was not silent, it spoke against the presence of a God of
love.

Devout sceptics and those existential believers who follow the
Kierkegaard of the *Postscript* are alike in that both have doubts and
both face their doubts. However, they are utterly different in the
ways that they treat their doubts. Existential believers who follow
Kierkegaard seek to overcome their doubts by willing to believe
despite their force. Devout sceptics seek to resolve their doubts
and honestly to lay them to rest. For Kierkegaard in the *Postscript*,
the pitch and commitment of faith are in proportion to the doubt
of the believer. For Kierkegaard, the authenticity of faith is a
function of inwardness and passion, which in turn require the
objective uncertainty of what is believed. For devout sceptics, the
integrity of their faith is a function of their intellectual honesty in
believing or not believing. Their cry of faith, if they have one, is: 'I
affirm my integrity and believe as what I have seen of the truth
allows.' Devout sceptics may wish to believe, but they will believe
only after they have honestly laid to rest their doubts. They prefer
honest doubt to dishonest belief not only as a matter of the ethics

of belief, but also as a matter of what would be most fitting in the eyes of God.[33]

H. H. Price is a contemporary philosopher who would have complete sympathy with the devout sceptic's endeavour to believe only rationally. Price too is aware that serious believers can feel the need to have good reasons for their faith, and in one place he raises such a concern in connection with one for whom it would be acute, namely, a believer who is also a philosopher.[34] As a believer he cannot help believing in God and is thankful that he does. But as a philosopher he recognises a duty to hold beliefs favoured by the available evidence and is concerned about an apparent lack of good reasons for his religious belief. Price's philosopher, while remaining a religious believer, would wish also to be a 'rational believer' in a certain definite sense of that term. He would wish to hold only beliefs that are supported by good reasons that he can present to others, and would wait for such reasons before believing. But he has no adequate reasons for his religious belief. At bottom, the issue for the rational believer (whether he believes already or not) and for the devout sceptic is the same: are there good reasons for belief? The rational believer would find honest support for the belief he already holds or would hold. The devout sceptic would honestly resolve his doubts before he believes. A way open to the rational believer to find such reasons, Price suggests, is to test 'the Theistic hypothesis'.[35] For Price there is no incompatibility between serious religiousness and honestly seeking to test the Theistic hypothesis that there is a God. (Later, in section (4) of this chapter, where we shall examine the two perspectives on the place of evidence in religion, we shall look at the 'devotional experiment' with which, for Price, one can test the Theistic hypothesis.)

Price is not alone in finding the tentative attitude of hypothesis-testing to be compatible with religious attitudes. John King-Farlow and William Christensen do so too. In their book *Faith and the Life of Reason* they develop the concept of 'hypothetical faith'.[36] They are theists, and their hypothetical faith does not come to doubt and suspended belief, as faith did for the devout sceptic, but it does accommodate doubt and tentativeness in belief. Theological statements like 'God exists' and 'God loves mankind', they suggest, should be treated as hypotheses in two primary ways: they should be held and put forward in a tentative spirit, and they should be offered with a view to explaining what we experience. Such a view of faith, they hold, allows faith to be reasonable and makes it compatible with important forms of religious commitment. It surely is compatible with an explicit commitment to the truth, as they say, but moreover it is compatible with commitment to the decalogue and the commandments of love.

Price, King-Farlow, and Christensen stand firmly in that tradition of rational belief in which the believer strives to believe in accord with good reasons that can be articulated and presented to others. In the combined traditions of devout scepticism and this strict rational belief – in opposition to Kierkegaard's 'most passionate inwardness' and First-Perspective intuitions generally – believers *are* prepared to hold a tentative religious belief. They try not to succumb to religious emotion, and they try to see all sides of the issues relating to belief. They are sympathetic toward the idea that we all should hold our beliefs with a firmness proportionate to the weight of our evidence, and until there is support we should try to withhold belief. They are not averse to drawing a close analogy between hypotheses and religious belief. In fact they may see this as a duty. In the present day many philosophers who reflect on religion (following Hume if not Tennyson) are in this combined tradition or see it as the proper tradition of religious belief. Among them, in addition to Price, King-Farlow, and Christensen, are Paul Edwards, Terence Penelhum, Kai Nielsen and many others.

William James, I think it is fair to say, is also in this tradition, even though to some extent James sought to expand – or to clarify – the concept of rationality.[37] In some way, it has been allowed by all parties, rationality involves support for what is believed. This is so for the First Perspective, and it is so for the Second Perspective. Within the Second Perspective, various apologetic efforts are directed toward finding support for religious faith, or for its rationality. And, within the Second Perspective, devout sceptics, as we have seen, would rather remain with their honest doubt than believe before their doubts have been resolved. But what if evidence *cannot* decide an issue – which many would say is just the case with religious belief? It is to this possible state of affairs that William James speaks. W. K. Clifford had said in 'The Ethics of Belief' that it 'is wrong always, everywhere, and for anyone to believe anything upon insufficient evidence'. Clifford's staunchly Second-Perspective pronouncement is put in terms of wrongness, ethical wrongness, and what is wrong, presumably, is to believe upon evidence that is insufficient to justify *rational* belief. James replies to Clifford in a similarly moral or legalistic tone and argues that, sometimes, it is 'lawful' to believe without sufficient intellectual grounds. What, he asks, if evidence cannot decide the issue *and* the issue must be decided? What if we have an option between two beliefs that cannot be decided on 'intellectual grounds' and that option is 'live' (each side makes some appeal to our belief), 'forced' (there is no middle ground), and 'momentous' (we are presented with a unique opportunity)? In such a case we are faced with a 'genuine option', which must be decided, but moreover a genuine option that cannot be decided on the basis of evidence. And, James argues, the option between accepting and rejecting religious faith is a genuine option of just this nature. As a genuine option it must be decided. (Even scepticism, he argues, amounts to choosing one option.) But if it must be decided, and it cannot be decided on the basis of evidence, then it is 'lawful' for our 'passional nature' to decide the issue after consulting our psychological needs.

James of course is not saying that we may lawfully believe anything we like. He is saying that *if* intellectual grounds are insufficient and we are faced with an unavoidable decision in belief, and only if these conditions hold, then it is proper – in accordance with rationality – to decide such issues on the basis of 'passional need'. He is not saying that we can lawfully believe whatever appeals to us despite the evidence against it or that it is proper to use psychological devises to precipitate belief in the face of negative evidence. Nor is he saying that it is proper to believe without adequate evidence when the option is not a forced option. When an option is not forced (as is often the case in science, James allows), then if sufficient evidence is lacking we should remain undecided. Here his judgement coincides with Clifford's. Moreover, even when we are faced with a genuine option for which we have inadequate evidence for a decision, still our decision in order to be lawful must have a basis, namely, our psychological needs, which in such cases become legitimate reasons.

James's analysis, I believe, is wholly Second-Perspective. Like King-Farlow and Christensen he is not trying to develop a notion of rationality that applies uniquely to religion. He is trying to clarify the constraints of rationality as they apply to what he calls genuine options, only one of which is the religious option.

Whether his effort is altogether successful is another question. Whether it is, and whether he is clarifying or instead expanding the concept of rationality, are questions which we shall take up later (in Chapter 2).

George Mavrodes is another philosopher who at times has had a Second-Perspective concern with rationality. He has inasmuch as he has examined various possible avenues to rational religious belief and religious knowledge, such as, the proofs for God's existence and religious experience.[38] He also has reflected on the character of religious rationality, an enterprise which may be either First-Perspective or Second-Perspective in nature. However Mavrodes, while he addresses rationality in religion in particular, reflects on rationality in general. The principles that he proposes, or his grammatical comments on rationality, while they importantly relate to religious rationality, also relate to rational belief in general. Accordingly, since he is seeking to clarify or develop the general notion of rationality, his effort, like that of King-Farlow, Christensen, and James, and unlike that of Phillips and Winch, is Second-Perspective in nature. I shall close this discussion of the Second Perspective on rationality and religion with a brief presentation of a logical point about rationality made by Mavrodes, a point that has a fair claim to be a clarification as opposed to an expansion of the concept.[39] Mavrodes observes that the assertion 'My belief that God exists is rational' is ambiguous. It can mean (i) the belief *God Exists* (what is believed, the proposition) is rational, or it can mean (ii) *my* believing that God exists is rational. And these are different claims. What would make the belief, or the proposition, that *God exists* rational is not very clear, Mavrodes helps us see. (Is it *someone's* having formulated a proof or having found evidence? Is it there being a proof or evidence regardless of whether it has been formulated or found?) On the other hand, what makes a person's own belief that God exists rational is much clearer: in some way that person himself or herself must have appropriated that which makes, not *the* belief, but his or her believing, rational. What Mavrodes brings to our attention is that different persons can share the content of their belief and yet differ in the rationality of their believings. Rationality, we may say following Mavrode's line of sight, is better conceived as an attribute of an individual believer's relationship to his or her belief than as an attribute of the belief's content. This logical insight is often appreciated by those, like John Hick, who look to the individual's religious experience as a basis for the rationality of his or her particular belief in God.[40] However I shall wait until Chapter 3 to develop what I take to be the significance of this insight.

In discussing the two opposed perspectives on rationality and religion we have, without pausing to examine them, touched upon problems in each; and we have as well, I think, found that each perspective has a kind of integrity. Let me now state in a summary fashion what I take to be the strengths of each perspective:

Strengths of the First Perspective. The First Perspective sees the danger of intellectualising religion, and it sees the danger that religion will be transformed into something else if traditional tests of rationality are applied to it. The First Perspective specifically recognises the danger to religious passion and commitment posed by rationality and the pursuit of rationality. When it gives a place to rationality, as it does when it posits an internal religious rationality, it seeks a sense appropriate to religion.

Strengths of the Second Perspective. The Second Perspective insists upon honesty in the faith-attitude. It seeks to avoid any special pleading for religion. It tries to clarify the concept of rationality and to understand better its application to religion, but it does not posit internal and possibly question-begging criteria for rationality.

(2) The Cognitivity-of-Belief Subissue: Is Religion Cognitive at Its Core?

The issue here is whether cognitive belief has a deep place in religion. If religion is not cognitive, then of course cognitive belief will not have a deep place, for it will have no place. On the other hand if religion is cognitive, if there is a true–false element to religious belief, it does not follow from that alone, many feel, that cognitive belief has earned a significant place in the life of religious faith.

Those with the First Perspective either deny that religious belief is cognitive or, if they do not deny this, they deny that belief's cognitivity enters deeply into religion. Those with the Second Perspective assume or argue that religion is cognitive but moreover, they maintain, religion's very significance draws deeply upon its cognitivity.

The First Perspective

On this subissue, as on the others, there are different versions of the First Perspective. Several are worthy of attention. Again we shall start with Kierkegaard.

Though Kierkegaard's view in the *Postscript* is left implicit, it can be drawn out fairly easily. As we saw in the last section, for Kierkegaard faith must confront the possibility of offending reason, and so, for this reason and others, it is not rational. In a similar way, and for related reasons, for Kierkegaard, the Kierkegaard of the *Postscript*, faith must be cognitive. Faith, for Kierkegaard in the *Postscript*, is subjectivity; it is not objectivity. The subjective has to do with HOW one believes; the objective has to do with WHAT one believes. For Kierkegaard, however, the passion of faith arises precisely from embracing and holding fast an 'objective uncertainty', and what is uncertain is the *truth* of WHAT is believed. Indeed, for Kierkegaard, the greater the objective uncertainty the greater the passion of faith, until, finally, faith proper, which embraces the 'absolute paradox', is infinite passion.[41] But in this case the very passion of faith is dependent on there being an objective WHAT, whose truth is supremely uncertain. Secondly, for Kierkegaard the object of faith, faith proper, the 'absolute paradox', is that 'the eternal truth has come into being in time'. That is, for Kierkegaard, the object of faith proper is that: God is eternal *and* God became temporal. The absolute paradox is supremely paradoxical, then, because it contains a 'contradiction', as Kierkegaard says, a tension between the truth of two propositions. If it is true that God is eternal, then it cannot be true, in reason, that God became temporal. Thus Kierkegaard must give a cognitive status to WHAT is believed in faith for two reasons: first, because faith is a passionate embracing of a WHAT the truth of which is objectively uncertain, and second, because the supreme objective uncertainty of faith proper derives from the logical tension between the truth of 'contradictory' propositions.

Nevertheless, for Kierkegaard cognitive belief in the objective WHAT of religion does not have a deep place in religion. For Kierkegaard, the importance of the WHAT of belief, as far as faith is concerned, is not that it is true but that it is objectively uncertain. But beyond this, I want to suggest that, for Kierkegaard, the core of religion is subjectivity to *the exclusion of the objective*, even though an objective WHAT is necessary for that very subjectivity. Let me explain the sense in which the objective is excluded from the core of religion for Kierkegaard by drawing upon a parable that Kierkegaard tells in the *Postscript*. I have in mind his parable of the idol worshipper, in which he invites us to consider two believers.[42] One 'lives in the midst of Christendom [and] goes up to the house of God, the house of the true God, with the true conception of God in his knowledge, and prays, but prays in a false spirit'. The other 'lives in an idolatrous community [but] prays with the entire passion of the infinite, although his eyes rest upon the image of an idol'. 'Where,' Kierkegaard rhetorically asks, 'is there most truth [that is, the greatest subjectivity]?' The answer he expects is clear; and, within his own categories, I believe that he is entitled to that answer. However, for Kierkegaard the infinite passion of faith can have only one object: the absolute paradox. Bearing this point in mind, it seems that there are two ways we can reason regarding his idol worshipper. First, we can reason that since the idol worshipper has infinite passion the object of his faith is in some way the absolute paradox. And second, we can reason that since the object of his faith is an idol, and not the absolute paradox, he must lack infinite passion. But Kierkegaard tells us in the parable that the idol worshipper has 'the entire passion of the infinite'. So we should reason the first way and not the second.[43] Accordingly, even though he misconceives the object of his worship the idol worshipper has true faith. The cognitive has no deep place in religion, and the objective is excluded from the core of religion, for Kierkegaard, then, in this sense: even though religious believers must believe in the Divine to worship the Divine, they can have an utterly wrong conception of the Divine; their beliefs *about* the Divine, true or false, do not affect their faith one way or the other.[44]

This, I believe, is the Kierkegaardian view on the place of cognitive belief in religion that we find in the *Postscript*. Do we find another view in other pseudonymous works? Well, I believe that we do find in other works, in *Fear and Trembling* specifically, a different view of faith. In *Fear and Trembling* the exemplar of faith is Abraham, the biblical Abraham, the father of Isaac. What makes Abraham's faith different from the faith Kierkegaard describes in the *Postscript* is that its object is not presented as the absolute paradox. (At least this is one essential difference.) For Kierkegaard the object of Abraham's faith, its immediate object, is this: even though he will follow God's command to sacrifice his son, since Isaac has been promised to him by God, Isaac will not be required of him.[45] What he believes, then, is beyond the reach of ordinary persons, but it is not the absolute paradox. Abraham as the knight of faith believes by virtue of the absurd, but the absurd is not the object of his faith. Does this difference between the model of faith in the *Postscript* and the model in *Fear and Trembling* affect the depth of the place in religion that Kierkegaard would give to cognitive belief? No, I think not. In *Fear and Trembling* Abraham's trial is a trial of faith and trust in God, and for Kierkegaard Abraham's trust in God, given God's promise, comes to a focus in a single belief: that Isaac will not be taken from him. This is a cognitive belief, of course. So, as in the *Postscript*, we find that Kierkegaard does not hesitate to make the immediate object of faith a specific WHAT, a proposition. But nevertheless, in *Fear and Trembling*, as in the *Postscript*, cognitive belief does not have a deep place in religion. Abraham's belief that Isaac will not be taken from him is the occasion and focus of *his* faith and trust. However, that particular belief is not essential to faith. It plays no role in Job's faith or in the faith of anyone else besides Abraham, and it would not be essential to Abraham's faith either if it were not that God had promised Abraham what He did. Thus, once again in *Fear and Trembling*, cognitive belief is necessary for faith. But in *Fear and Trembling*, as in the *Postscript*, that which is at the core of religious faith is not this derivatively necessary cognitive belief, but rather the passion and commitment of an individual's lived faith.

Wittgenstein also has a First-Perspective view on this subissue, or at least he is oriented toward the First Perspective, in both the 'Lecture on Ethics' and the *Lectures on Religious Belief*. In his earlier 'Lecture on Ethics' he directly addresses the issue of the cognitive status of religious belief. In this lecture he draws attention to religious feelings, or feelings that the religious, among others, occasionally have: wonder at the existence of the world, feeling absolutely safe, and feeling guilty.[46] The verbal expressions of these feelings, their religious expressions, Wittgenstein says, are 'nonsense', even 'mere nonsense'.[47] It is nonsense for one to say 'I wonder at the existence of the world', he argues, since this is wonder at the world whatever it is; thus there is no contrast. It is not like saying 'I wonder at the size of the Pacific Ocean', where there is a contrast. Similarly, he says, it is nonsense for one to say

'I feel absolutely safe' whatever happens. He also has a second argument to show that specifically religious terms are nonsensical. All religious terms, he says, are 'similes'. Religious people use 'God created the world' as a simile to 'refer' to the experience of wonder at the existence of the world. And they use 'We feel safe in the hands of God' to refer to the feeling of absolute safety, and 'God disapproves of our conduct' to refer to a sense of guilt. Now by the logic of simile one should be able to drop the figurative language and refer directly to the 'fact'. But this cannot be done with these religious expressions: there are no facts to refer to (apart from the feelings). Accordingly, for this second reason, these religious terms and phrases are 'mere nonsense'.

This is not to say that he dismisses religion – despite his terms 'nonsense' and 'mere nonsense'. At the end of the lecture he asserts that he has deep respect for 'ethics' (which here includes religion) and, he says, 'I would not for my life ridicule it'. As Rudolf Carnap noted, while Wittgenstein agreed with the Vienna Circle that the doctrines of religion lack 'theoretical content', he disagreed with them in his emotional reaction to religion.[48] Wittgenstein's positive attitude toward religion is evident throughout his written and dictated reflections on religion. In this respect there is no difference between the earlier lecture on ethics and the later lectures on religious belief. In other respects, however, there are noteworthy changes in his thinking about religion. For one thing, as we saw in the last section, Wittgenstein's thinking about the basis of religion's unreasonableness, or rather, why reason is inapplicable to religion, seems to undergo a change. For another thing, in the earlier lecture there is an apparent reliance upon linguistic standards of intelligibility that are applied universally, regardless of the form of life. In the later lectures, where Wittgenstein saw religious believers as holding before themselves, and being guided by, a religious 'picture', he was prepared to look for the meaning of religious discourse in accordance with standards embedded in the religious form of life.[49] It is this later Wittgenstein, who in effect appeals to criteria of meaning *internal* to religion, that Neo-Wittgensteinians such as Phillips draw upon in their own religious enquiries. However Wittgenstein, unlike Phillips, does not suggest that there are senses of 'truth' or 'reason' internal to religion. In his lectures on religious belief he recognizes that 'God' and other key religious terms have great significance for the religious, and that that significance relates to the way they live their lives (how they are guided by religious pictures), but beyond this he frankly says he can make little of religious talk. He offers neither a cognitive nor a non-cognitive construction of religious language.[50]

In short Wittgenstein's view on the cognitive status of religious belief seems to be this: Earlier, in the period when he wrote 'A Lecture on Ethics' and 'Remarks on Frazer's "Golden Bough" ', while he was closer to the *Tractatus* in his thinking, he pretty clearly thought of religious 'terms' and belief as lacking cognitive import. Those religious utterances he discusses he regards as expressions of religious feelings with the form of similes but without the logic of similes. Later, in the period of his *Lectures on Religious Belief*, when he is closer to writing *Philosophical Investigations*, he no longer regards the things religious people say as mere nonsense. But he regards their sense as closely connected to religious behaviour and practice: religious beliefs express, or are, pictures and the religious use of pictures is to guide behaviour and feelings, to 'regulate' in life. He does not deny a cognitive status to religious belief, but he does not affirm it either.

Wittgenstein's thinking on the cognitive status of religion, like other aspects of his thought on religious belief, has provided inspiration and direction for Neo-Wittgensteinians. Here again various Neo-Wittgensteinians have developed Wittgenstein's thinking in their own way. For Phillips, as for Wittgenstein, religious belief is belief in a religious picture and as such expresses itself in the behaviour of the religious. To have a religious belief is to use a picture to regulate in one's life. For both Phillips and Wittgenstein there are several religious pictures. Sometimes, though, Phillips refers to the religious 'story' (which, perhaps, is not too surprising), and when he does he seems to mean belief in God as a whole.[51]

Whichever we speak of – a religious picture or the religious story – Phillips agrees with Wittgenstein that it is not taken up on the basis of reason and enquiry. The religious story, Phillips says, either 'captivates' us or it does not. It appeals to us or it does not, it holds us or it does not. There is no justification of a picture or the religious story. For to ask for such a justification is to ask for a justification of the religious way of life, and Phillips regards such a request as illegitimate and confused (just as it is illegitimate and confused to ask for an external justification for the religious criteria for rationality).

At this point we can see that for Phillips, as for Wittgenstein, religious belief – using a picture or being guided by a story – cannot be made easier by looking for external support. However, Phillips, more than Wittgenstein, fills in the alternative to *religiously* taking up belief. For Phillips, if we relate religious belief to 'non-religious facts' in the way that what-is-justified is related to its justification, then what we end up with is *superstition* and not religious belief at all.[52] Belief in the Virgin Mary, for Phillips, may be a religious belief or it may be a superstition. If it is a religious belief, then when a mother calls upon the Virgin to protect her child she will understand protection in terms of her religious belief. Her belief will determine what is protection, and not the other way around. If her belief is superstitious, however, this is not so. Phillips proposes two marks of such a superstitious belief in the Virgin: (i) 'trust in non-existent quasi-causal connections' and (ii) seeing the Virgin Mary 'as a means to ends which are intelligible without reference to her'. Thus a mother who has a superstitious belief in the Virgin Mary might pray for the Virgin Mary to bring back her son from a war, trusting in a 'miraculous' intercession and construing 'protection' in concrete terms which are independent of religious belief. Elsewhere Phillips gives as another example of superstition a mother's hope that her mentally handicapped child will be compensated with future happiness in heaven.[53] Such a hope is superstitious because it is a hope 'in certain facts being realized', although here it seems that what is hoped for is partially characterised in religious terms. In any case we can see that what Phillips calls 'superstition' in these contexts involves a belief in either a kind of magical efficacy or certain future events or both, and thus there is room for a connection between what is believed and contingent facts. Consequently there is room for construing facts as either support for belief (the son of the first mother returns from the war unhurt) or as telling against the belief (he does not return). Moreover, it would be inviting and perhaps good sense to examine the support for such a belief before taking up the belief oneself. With a religious belief in God or in the Virgin Mary – which would show itself in regulating the mother's activity, in guiding her life – none of this is so or could be so.

For Phillips, if we treat religious belief as essentially a view of the world, we make it theoretical; and we make religious belief 'superstitious' if we connect it to 'facts'. Clearly, Phillips like

Wittgenstein is not eager to assign a place in religion to cognitive belief. But does he give any place at all to belief that religious propositions are true? Is he more like Kierkegaard (who allows a derivatively necessary place for cognitive belief) or the early Wittgenstein (who disallows cognitive belief)? In order to answer this question, let us look more closely at Phillips' position, bearing in mind what we have seen of it so far in this chapter. Initially, two elements in his thinking deserve our attention.

The first element is Phillips' suspicion of the idea that God exists or can be said to exist. 'Existence', Phillips is inclined to think, does not apply to God. Several interlocking reasons apparently lead him to this conclusion. (i) He agrees with Norman Malcolm[54] that it is not a religious belief *that* God exists; rather the religious belief is *in* God. (Malcolm's distinction between *belief in God* and *belief that God exists* is not unrelated to the distinction between two kinds of faith drawn by John Calvin in the *Institutes*, cited in the introduction. Later in this section when we turn to the Second Perspective, I shall have more to say about these two kinds of belief and the issue of their relationship to one another. And in section (4) I shall have more to say about Malcolm's views.) (ii) Phillips perceives a connection between thinking of God as existing and thinking of God as 'an object among objects'.[55] (iii) Phillips understands existence in the way that has been traditional since Hume and Kant: existence is 'contingent'. This means for Phillips that if God exists, then He might not exist; and this is not the way God is understood religiously.[56] To be sure, Phillips, like Rhees, allows that there is a place in religion for *confessing God's necessary existence*.[57] But for Phillips and Rhees it does not follow from this that the religious assert God's existence. Importantly, Phillips gives a place not to *affirming the truth* of God's necessary existence but to *confessing* God's necessary existence (or, as Rhees says, expressing one's faith). For Phillips belief in God is confessing, that is, the practice of confessing. Phillips, then, is content to disallow what to some seems a logical connection between believing *in* God and believing *that* God exists.

In sum, regarding God and existence, for Phillips it seems to be a mistake to think of belief in God's existence as a cognitive religious belief. At least as far as this belief goes, Phillips eschews a cognitivist position.

The second element that deserves our attention is Phillips' often repeated claim that religious belief is not factual belief. Such a claim can come to many things, of course. What it comes to for Phillips emerges especially in his article on John Wisdom's essay 'Gods'.[58] In this article Phillips discusses two distinguishable aspects of Wisdom's essay: (i) Wisdom's construction of the meaning of statements about God and (ii) Wisdom's views on the epistemological status of statements about God. The first need not concern us. Phillips rightly indicates that Wisdom's reduction of God, and the gods, to patterns in human reactions hardly captures Judaeo-Christian belief in God whatever justice it may do to belief in Dionysos and Cyprus. Phillips' discussion of Wisdom's view on religious epistemology, however, is germane, for it tells us as much about Phillips' view on the cognitive status of religion as it does about Wisdom's.

Phillips agrees with Wisdom that religious beliefs are not experimental hypotheses, and, he says, no one has done more than Wisdom to show us that this is so. However, Wisdom still allows that religious beliefs are hypotheses of a kind, even though no experiment is relevant to their investigation. For Wisdom religious belief in God presents an issue that can be settled, not by experimentally gathering new facts, but by enquiry into the patterns formed by facts already known. Against Wisdom Phillips argues that religious belief is not a hypothesis of any kind. It is the basis of his argument that helps to reveal Phillips' own view on the cognitive status of belief. Hypotheses, as Phillips understands them, have two characteristics that religious belief does not, and cannot, have. First, hypotheses involve inquiry into what is so, and the religious attitude is not one of inquiry. Second, hypotheses are true, or correct, by virtue of what happens to be the case; and religious beliefs are held as 'absolutes'. Phillips' objection to Wisdom's analysis is not merely that if religious beliefs were hypotheses, then they would not be held with conviction. His deeper objection is that it falsifies the character of religious beliefs to present them as having a truth which is dependent on what is so. But if this is Phillips' objection, then he surely seems to be denying what the truth of religious propositions requires: namely some correspondence between those propositions and what is so about the universe.

What seems to be emerging about Phillips' thought is, perhaps, not that surprising. Now let me go back and connect up Phillips' thinking about religious pictures and why, for him, no *new* religious picture can be created by theologians. For Phillips, as we have seen, there is no way to stand outside religion and weigh evidence for the religious picture. However, for Phillips, this is not to say that religious pictures cannot in certain circumstances lose their hold. To use one of Phillips' examples: 'the untimely death of one's child [may render] talk of God's love meaningless for one. One might want to believe, but one simply cannot'.[59] Could a new, more relevant religious picture be offered to such a person, or to people generally in a time of failing faith? Phillips thinks not. In fact it is 'nonsensical', he says, to imagine theologians creating new pictures.[60] They cannot because doing so presupposes measuring a religious picture and finding it to be all right or not all right. And believers do not measure pictures, Phillips says, pictures measure believers. That is, for Phillips, *not even believers* can measure their pictures. If they begin to, this is the first step in the picture's losing its hold. Thus, for Phillips, there are not even internal criteria for measuring pictures that believers with those pictures could use. This of course is just what one would expect if in Phillips' view pictures do not in any way correspond to what is so, for then all evaluation – internal or external – of the truth of a picture would be impossible.

So, what should we say about Phillips' intuitions about the cognitive status of religion? For Phillips, religious belief must have a connection to the world, especially to 'birth, death, joy, misery, despair, hope, fortune and misfortune'.[61] Peter Winch, as we saw in the last section, says something similar. For both Philips and Winch religion, as a way of life, has a noncontingent connection to the turning points of life. But this is not to say that these turning points provide a test for the truth of belief in God. Phillips, I think, must be considered a non-cognitivist if a non-cognitivist is one who either (i) denies the application of truth (or falsity) to the content of propositions relating to God, or (ii) denies any coherent question or assertion about the truth, correctness, or corre-spondence to reality of belief in God where the existence of God is understood as independent of the existence of people and ways of life. Phillips does both, and Winch at least the second.[62]

Phillips and Winch will allow that 'truth' applies to religious belief, but for Phillips and Winch it is an internal sense of 'truth', and for Phillips the religious sense of 'truth' does not apply to propositions but instead to persons (as in Jesus' being the truth). Phillips often repeats the claim that regarding the reality of God there is no *finding out*.[63] True, for Phillips there is a 'discovery' of God, but such a discovery is of a meaning to life: that is, it comes to taking up a way of life, of coming to be held by a picture. Only regarding a belief in relics does Phillips allow a propositional truth to religious belief, and then only because such a belief is historical and not essentially tied to belief in God.[64] For Phillips and Winch (and Rhees too, I believe) religious belief is practice, and in religious *practice* the question of God's existence does not, and cannot, meaningfully arise – there is only the use of the question to reject the religious way of life.

For Phillips, being religious is having a way of life, and a way of life is just that. It is not merely ethics, not even an ethics of love, but fashions our responses in moments of pain, despair, hope, and love. Still, Phillips is a non-cognitivist in the sense I have identified. He is more like the early Wittgenstein (who denied any role to cognitivist belief in religion) than like Kierkegaard (who allowed a derivatively necessary place to the WHAT of belief). Phillips' effort is to show us how the vitality of religious practice remains intact, and connected to the human events of birth, death, joy, and despair, even if there is no place inside or outside religion for the question, 'But is there this God believed in by our fathers?'

The Second Perspective

Many with a Second-Perspective position on the first issue, that regarding rationality, would also hold a Second-Perspective position on the cognitive status of religious belief, even though a Second-Perspective position on the first issue, strictly, may not entail a Second-Perspective position on this issue. On this issue once again thinkers of very different stripes tend to have a view that is Second Perspective.

Plantiga, rather clearly I believe, in *Gods and Other Minds* and *The Nature of Necessity*, gives a deep place in religion to cognitive belief. His whole effort (trying to prove the rationality of belief in the existence of God) presupposes the cognitive status of belief in God. For Plantinga, as for Kierkegaard, religion requires cognitive belief or, in Kierkegaard's language, an objective WHAT to be believed. However, there are very great differences between the two on the way that cognitive or objective belief is presupposed. Both, we may assume, are aware that religious belief has a passional or subjective side, and both would agree that the subjectivity of a believer can be distinguished from the articulated proposition believed. But for Plantinga, given his effort, it makes sense to convince a non-believer of the truth, or rationality, of religious propositions, especially that God exists, before the believer's subjectivity has developed: for Plantinga, as for others who have tried to prove God's existence, a proper subjective response can follow, and it is hoped will follow, once a person is convinced that there is a God. Whether it will follow or not, though, it makes religious and logical sense to try to demonstrate the truth of religious propositions to those at present lacking religious subjectivity. For Kierkegaard, on the other hand, while subjectivity requires objective belief, objective belief without subjectivity is 'habitual belief' and more the antithesis of religion that the first step in faith. It is in this sense that Plantinga and others who concentrate on proving religious propositions give a deep place in religion to cognitive belief, in contrast with Kierkegaard, who does not.

Others besides those who try to demonstrate the truth or rationality of religious belief hold a Second-Perspective view on this issue. At the furthest remove from religious apologists (in at least one sense) are those Plantinga calls 'natural atheologians', those who seek to prove that the central tenets of Judaeo-Christian belief are false. Included here, among contemporary philosophers, are J. L. Mackie and H. J. McCloskey.[65] But, returning to reflection sympathetic to religion, others as well would say and even insist that religious belief internally requires a deep place for cognitive belief. Some of these thinkers, like Basil Mitchell and John Hick, undertake to answer challenges to the cognitive status of religious language and belief. Since they themselves have no question that religious belief, to be religious belief in God, must be cognitive, their effort is not so much to give reasons why belief must be cognitive as to show how it can be in the face of these challenges.[66]

Others with the Second Perspective, addressing a different concern, do try to give reasons why religious belief internally requires a deep place for cognitive belief. Some who do this would draw attention to the existence and function of religious creeds. Early Christian creeds, though they may have been as simple as 'Jesus is Lord' (1 Corinthians 12.3), were a confession or affirmation of what is believed. In the first centuries of the

Common Era the Apostles' and Nicene Creeds provided for a more detailed confession and were as well a statement of orthodox belief, orthodoxy being no small concern of the early church. A concern with orthodoxy, of course, implies a concern with heresy, that is to say with false belief. And, as Renford Bambrough has put it,

> there cannot be any application of the notions of orthodoxy or heresy to any field in which there is no application for the closely related and fundamentally important concepts of assertion, proposition, reason, justification, knowledge and ignorance, truth and falsehood, consistency and contradiction.[67]

In other words to the extent that one is concerned with right belief one must assume a Second-Perspective view on a number of the five subissues, but certainly one must on this subissue. Creeds then serve at least two functions that are strongly Second Perspective: they provide a confession of *what* is believed, and they provide a statement of *right* belief. The Apostles' and Nicene Creeds, of course, are still used in Christian Churches and some would say that these two functions are as relevant in our contemporary secular world as they were in the Hellenistic world of early Christianity.

Moreover, others with the Second Perspective would maintain, quite independently of the use of a creed to confess one's faith or to adhere to orthodoxy, simply giving thanks to God has a more than contingent connection to cognitive belief. Terrence Tilley, who believes that Phillips mistakenly equates statements of fact with statements that we conclude to be true, draws our attention to the logic of giving thanks to God, which in itself, he believes, is sufficient to show us, not that God exists, but that for the believer it is a fact, a cognitive belief, that God exists:

> Just as the thanking [of] an unfaithful wife for being faithful is flawed, so the thanking of an absent God for his presence is flawed. If the delusion is even worse – thanking a non-existent wife for being faithful or thanking a non-existent God for his loving kindness – it is worse in both cases, sadder in both, crazier in both.[68]

As Tilley's point might be put, there is a grammatical connection between thanking God and believing that God exists (the God who is being thanked); if this connection is broken the 'thanking' loses its sense and becomes 'crazy'.

Again, belief *in* God, the sine qua non of Judaeo-Christian religion, seems to many to have a similar grammatical, or logical, connection to a belief *that* God exists. If one confesses a belief in God, there is at least the prima facie implication that one believes that the God believed in exists. Indeed, what sense would it make, it has been asked, for someone to affirm a belief in God while not affirming God's existence? Believing in God is not like believing in a principle, such as obeying the law or justice. It is more like believing in a person to whom one speaks and whom one trusts. As Kai Nielsen says, 'when we believe, we must believe something', and believing in God is not '*simply* to subscribe to a set of moral principles and to hope these principles will prevail'.[69] Many, I think, would agree with Nielsen that in traditional Christian and Jewish religion belief in God, as well as loving, confession, or praying to God, is logically connected to belief that God exists. John Calvin, for one, seems to agree with Nielsen on this. Calvin in the *Institutes*, as we have seen, distinguishes between mere belief that God exists and belief in God. The former is of no importance. The latter is more truly faith. However Calvin says that when we have the latter kind of faith 'we believe not only that God and Christ exist, but also believe in God and Christ . . .'.[70] That is, for Calvin, belief that God exists is a part of, or is presupposed by, belief in God – even though mere belief that God exists is of no religious importance.

It should be noted that both those with a First-Perspective view on this subissue and those with a Second-Perspective view on it appeal to religious practice and to belief in God. On the one hand there are Malcolm, Phillips, Winch, and Rhees. On the other hand there are, among others,[71] Tilley, Bambrough, Nielsen, and Calvin (although Nielsen assumes a Second-Perspective stance only for the sake of argument, and Calvin was not addressing the issue before us). Questions that are unavoidable at this point, then, are: What is the connection between specific religious practices and cognitive belief? And what is the connection between belief in God and cognitive belief? The first question relates to more than creed-saying: it relates as well to prayer, thanking God, loving God, and much more. Both questions raise grammatical issues. In succeeding sections we shall have occasion to reflect further on these questions and the issues they raise, especially the grammar of belief in God. However, I shall reserve my own final comments on that grammar, and on the above questions, until Chapter 3.

Strengths of the First Perspective. The First Perspective sees that holding beliefs to be true, that is, holding to be true propositions that are true independently of believers' attitudes, is not sufficient for, and may not be necessary for, true faith or a significant religious life.

Strengths of the Second Perspective. The Second Perspective does not lose sight of either the prima facie logical connection between religious practice and cognitive belief or the prima facie logical connection between belief in God and the cognitive belief that God exists.

(3) The Understanding Subissue: Is It Possible to Understand Without Believing?

The question here is whether it is possible for a person to stand outside religious belief, come to understand it, and then decide whether to accept it, to reject it, or to reserve judgement.

At issue here from one perspective is the coherence of religious scepticism. From the other perspective at issue is the coherence of religion conceived as a belief system, or as a form of life, open only to internal understanding.

The First Perspective

Those with the First Perspective on this subissue deny, or initially are inclined to deny, that one can understand religious belief without believing. Religious belief and understanding religious belief go hand-in-hand, or understanding is part of belief, or, in one First-Perspective view, they are identical. In fact, so far as this issue is concerned, the First Perspective is shared by religious thinkers as diverse as Protestants who emphasise the role of grace in a certain way, and Wittgenstein and his followers. (Kierkegaard's absence should be noted. Here, for the first time, Kierkegaard does not hold a clear First-Perspective view, which is not to say that his view is Second Perspective. In Chapter 3 I shall discuss Kierkegaard on this issue.)

Perhaps the home of the First-Perspective view on this issue, in contemporary philosophy, is the thought of Wittgenstein and Neo-Wittgensteinianism. Wittgenstein indirectly addresses the issue before us in *Lectures on Religious Belief*. There Wittgenstein (who, we will remember, did not count himself a believer) says that he cannot 'contradict' the religious believer:

> In one sense, I understand all he says – the English words. 'God', 'separate', etc. I understand. I could say: 'I don't believe in this,' and this would be true, meaning I haven't got these thoughts or anything that hangs together with them. But not that I could contradict the thing.[72]

The specific belief Wittgenstein is referring to is not clear: it may or may not be a belief in a Judgement Day. But the specific belief is not important. In one sense Wittgenstein understands what the religious believer says, whatever the belief, but in another sense he cannot understand. He understands the believer's words, for they are English words. In addition, since he appreciates at least some of the grammar of God, he can understand and answer some questions about God: Yes, God sees and rewards. No, God is not spoken of as having eyebrows.[73] But in another sense he cannot understand. He does not truly have the religious concepts: he does not have religious thoughts and he does not regulate his life by the religious picture (or pictures). He cannot fathom how religious people understand one another. They seem to depart from the 'normal technique of language' – regarding, for instance, the connections between belief and evidence and belief and normal expectations.[74] In this way, at the deeper level, Wittgenstein cannot understand religious belief as the religious do. It is not, then, that he understands but believes the opposite. Lacking belief himself he cannot make the deeper connections; he as it were speaks a different language and so cannot contradict the religious believer.

Once again Wittgenstein's thought on this issue has been heeded and amplified by philosophers who have followed him. Phillips agrees with Wittgenstein that those outside religion cannot contradict religious believers.[75] But he goes beyond Wittgenstein in his exploration of the relationship between understanding and belief. In fact he seems to develop two distinct First-Perspective views on this issue, one explicit and one implicit. For the moment let us concentrate on his first view, the explicit one, which he presents in his essay 'Faith, Scepticism, and Religious Understanding'. According to this view, the relationship between understanding and belief in the religious context, is precisely that of identity. Indeed belief, understanding, and love of God 'can all be equated with each other' he says when stating this first view most strongly.[76] Although, as we shall see, Phillips concedes that he has to modify this strong thesis, in this essay he continues to hold that belief and understanding are identical. For Phillips then, as far as his explicit view goes, to understand religious belief *is* to believe: one cannot know God and not believe, as it might be put. And, since to understand is to believe, of necessity one cannot understand without believing.

Stuart Brown is another philosopher who has a First-Perspective view on this issue. Brown heeds Wittgenstein, but he is not a Neo-Wittgensteinian, at least not in the sense Phillips is. Nevertheless Brown's view and Phillips' first view – that belief and understanding are identical – are very close, although some important differences do remain. Brown's view is one of sympathy for what he calls a 'B-thesis', that is, the thesis that, in one formulation, belief and understanding are inseparable.[77] Brown's B-thesis is not Phillips' thesis that belief and understanding are identical, but they are in fundamental agreement that understanding *requires* belief. Much of Brown's effort is to elucidate an apparent 'intelligibility gap' between believer and unbeliever, which prevents the unbeliever from attaching sense to the claims of religion. This gap, according to one form of the B-thesis, can be bridged by a species of insight. Involved in what Brown means by 'insight' is a grammatical shift or conceptual change. Brown does not insist that there are such insights, only that there are candidates and so a B-thesis is defensible. One candidate he discusses is seeing that 'the connection between being wicked and being "punished" ' is an internal one, not a contingent one.[78] This is the insight, or the seeming insight, that a believer would come to if he or she ceased to regard God as a super-human individual and came to regard wickedness as a part of its own Divine punishment.

It is worthwhile, I think, to compare Phillips' first, explicit view with Brown's view. Beyond Phillips' identifying belief and understanding while Brown finds them inseparable but distinct, Brown, unlike Phillips, gives an important place to insight. It is not accidental that Phillips omits a role for this category. *Insight* suggests *learning*, *discovery*, *finding out*. And Phillips is suspicious of these notions in a religious application. (He would rather talk about a picture *captivating* one or having a *hold* on one.) Again, for Phillips, since belief is understanding, failure to believe is failure to understand and sceptics, who do not believe and so do not understand, are not in a position to pronounce on religious belief. But for Brown, one can find religious assertions unintelligible (and so not understand them) and yet coherently judge them to be false. How, one might ask, can this be? Brown explains that one may find much of what an assertion says to be unintelligible and yet understand just enough of it to see that it entails what is false. Thus (to use his example) one may find talk about Fate unintelligible and yet judge a claim about the intervention of Fate to be false because, as those who believe in Fate allow, any such claim entails that the event in question was not brought about by human contrivance and one may know that it was. In the same way, even if belief and understanding are inseparable, someone could be both an atheist and find the claims of the believer to be unintelligible.[79] Although Brown does not say so, he may have the problem of evil in mind here. For regarding God and evil sceptics sometimes do hold both that talk about God is generally unintelligible (or unverifiable or involves logical paradoxes) and that the existence of evil is logically incompatible with God's existence. The nub of the difference between Phillips' first view and Brown's on this point seems to be this: for Phillips even a scintilla of understanding requires belief (since belief and understanding are the same thing), while for Brown substantive understanding requires belief but the limited understanding necessary to trace and to judge an implication to be false does not.[80] Clearly Brown's view is more tolerant of religious scepticism than is Phillips' first, explicit view.

Phillips also has a second, implicit view on this issue. But it too does not favour scepticism as much as Brown's view (which is not to say that Brown's view is as sympathetic to scepticism as a Second-Perspective view would be). Phillips' second view is implicit in his book *Death and Immortality*. In that work, at one point, he replies to Kai Nielsen.[81] For Nielsen it is a plain fact that at all times and all places, even mong the most primitive tribes, there have been sceptics and scoffers, people who though perfectly familiar with the religious language game played in their culture would not play the religious language game, not because they could not, but because, even though they were perfectly familiar with it even though they had an insiders' understanding of it, they found it incoherent.[82]

Phillips wants to deny that such 'sceptics and scoffers' understand what believers understand. He finds that Nielsen has made an assumption, namely, that 'the overthrow of a religious belief must consist in finding out that the evidence counts against it or that it is internally incoherent'. And this assumption, he believes, is wrong. For Phillips it is not that believers and sceptics understand equally well *what* is believed and together face the issue of whether belief is coherent and evidence supports it. For Phillips belief can be overthrown, or lost, but not because evidence against belief has been brought to bear. In *Death and Immortality* the correct account of the loss of faith is quite otherwise. Faith is lost when religious pictures lose their hold. And this happens, not when evidence shows them to be false, but when the individual's life changes so that a rival secular picture displaces the religious picture, or a tragic event makes it impossible to respond religiously, or there are cultural changes that make the religious picture decline generally.

Phillips, in arguing this case, usefully discusses these several distinct ways in which religious pictures can lose their hold or begin to. But in doing so he concedes that a religious picture may be understood and yet lose its hold on a person's life. This happens when, say, the loss of a child makes it impossible to respond in the way religious belief demands. Again, Phillips allows that 'a person may understand the force of a religious picture and yet feel that he could not live by it'. Wittgenstein was in this position, Phillips believes (although, as we have seen, Wittgenstein protested that he could not understand religious belief).

So Phillips in his second, implicit view retreats a little from the stronger thesis that understanding and belief are identical. Rather, he seems to be saying in his second view, the two elements that are identical are understanding and feeling the attraction or force of religion, even though, finally, one who understands may be unable to respond positively or indeed may be repelled emotionally.[83]

However there is a problem that faces First-Perspective views on this third subissue, and I would like to clarify further what Phillips and Brown say about this issue by looking at how each deals with it. The problem has to do with loss of faith and the rejection of belief. The later Alasdair MacIntyre gets at the problem by posing a dilemma.[84] Paraphrasing MacIntyre, we may cast the dilemma as follows:

> According to some Protestants, saving grace is necessary to understand the concepts of the Scriptures. But if so nobody has ever rejected Christianity, as these same Protestants claim, for all who have rejected what they called 'Christianity' must have lacked grace and so not understood and consequently rejected something else.

MacIntyre applies his dilemma not only to Protestants but also to those sceptics who believe that religious utterances are 'flatly senseless'; however we can set aside that portion of his concern (since such sceptics do not have the problem MacIntyre raises because they hold a First-Perspective view on belief and understanding, but for another reason). Also there is a reference to saving grace in MacIntyre's dilemma as it applies to Protestants. But this reference can be deleted. The heart of the dilemma, as it applies to certain Protestants and others who hold a First-Perspective view on belief and understanding, including Phillips and Brown, is this: Either understanding does not require religious belief or no one has ever rejected religious belief.

This dilemma, we should notice, relates to both (i) those who reject belief from the start and have never believed, and (ii) those who at some point in their lives are believers but later reject belief. The first rejection presents the lesser difficulty, for it can be said that, contrary to MacIntyre, non-believers reject belief without understanding what they reject. The second rejection is loss of faith and is the harder case for those with First-Perspective intuitions on this issue.[85]

How do Phillips and Brown resolve the problem this dilemma raises, especially as it relates to loss of faith? They do so differently. Let us take Brown first. Brown maintains that the question whether 'loss of faith' is possible is ambiguous, for it may be asked outside religion or inside religion. What counts as a loss of faith from the standpoint of someone outside religion need not be the same as loss of faith from an internal religious standpoint. A person's quitting church, for instance, might be referred to as a loss of faith by someone outside religion. Loss of faith in this sense is allowed by a B-thesis. But, Brown says, loss of faith in the internal sense – loss of faith *itself*, as opposed to what outsiders may refer to as 'loss of faith' – is not possible given the truth of a B-thesis. However, this is all right for Brown, for in his view it seems to be a part of the grammar of faith that it can be tested but not lost. He quotes Karl Barth (one of the Protestants MacIntyre may have had in mind): 'A man who believes once believes once for all.'[86] Barth's pronouncement Brown reasonably takes to be intended, not as an empirical generalization, but as a grammatical comment. And he accepts it as such.

Brown's resolution of the problem, then, is this: On the one hand what outsiders to religion refer to as 'loss of faith' can occur, but in such cases there is no real faith to lose; these are cases of rejection of belief by those who have never believed. On the other hand real loss of faith cannot occur: grammatically faith cannot be lost. Regarding real loss of faith Brown chooses one horn of the dilemma and accepts it, or insists, that once one has faith it can never be lost.

Phillips' resolution of the problem is a bit more elaborate. It is because Phillips has, not one view, but the two we have noted. Since they are rather different we shall consider them in order. Phillips is aware of MacIntyre's challenge to his first position and in 'Faith, Scepticism, and Religious Understanding' he explicitly addresses it.[87] In the first place, he points out, some forms of rejection do not require understanding: those who reject belief in God as confusion or mumbo-jumbo, as Oscar Wilde did Phillips suggests, reject belief to be sure, but without its meaning anything to them, without their understanding it. This form of rejection, of course, is only one form. There is a more troubling form, Phillips acknowledges: the case of rebellion against God by one who believes that there is a God, such as Ivan Karamazov. Ivan believes in God, but he does not love God; and so, Phillips allows, a modification of his thesis is called for. He means his strong thesis that belief, understanding, and love of God are one. The modification he admits is that while belief always requires *some* affective response, it need not be love. Rebellion against God and fear of God are also forms of belief. Still the primary form of belief is love of God, for rebellion and other attitudes are 'logically dependent' on it in that the rebel and those with other attitudes are reacting against love of God. This modification, though, Phillips believes, leaves intact his root-thesis that belief and understanding are identical. Ivan does not love God, but he believes in God – for, Phillips asks, whom does he hate if not God?

Thus far Phillips has not addressed the case of loss of faith. He does indirectly, however, in connection with his second, implicit view. For his second view loss of faith is possible – if loss of faith is understood as a religious picture losing its hold on a believer. And so it should be understood for Phillips. Such a loss of faith would occur when a person who has been held by a religious picture no longer can respond religiously. But it remains for Phillips that there is no such thing as one's ceasing to believe *because* one has sceptically examined one's religious picture and come to the judgement that it is false: such an abandonment of religious belief demonstrates that the 'believer' failed to understand in the first place.

We find then a certain latitude in First-Perspective views on the third subissue, and, we might feel, Phillips has gone so far in his second view that he no longer holds a First-Perspective view at all. In neither of his views, though, does he go so far as to allow that 'sceptics and scoffers' understand without believing. As I see it, a deep concern for those with the First Perspective is to keep in sight the closeness of understanding and religious belief–attitudes, if not belief itself. Both Phillips and Brown insist upon this connection.

Also the apologetic thrust of this view has struck many: if sceptics cannot understand religious belief, then their criticisms and challenges can be set aside as based on misunderstanding. However, typically an apologetic thrust is not part of the intent of those with a First-Perspective view on this issue. Certainly it is not Wittgenstein's or Phillips' concern. Both, as we have seen, reject apologetics. While the First-Perspective view on this issue could be put in the harness of apologetics, it itself remains a purely epistemological position. This is not to say that it is not anti-scepticism. It is, and thoroughly so. But those with a First-Perspective view on this issue see themselves as getting at what is wrong with an epistomological presupposition of scepticism, namely, that sceptics and believers understand religion equally well and the task at hand is to test the truth, or cognitive sense, of religious belief. There is more to the First-Perspective view than a rejection of scepticism, but this element is near the heart of the First-Perspective view and is a chief locus of disagreement between the First and Second Perspectives.

The Second Perspective

Those with the Second Perspective on this subissue are as strongly inclined to affirm that one can understand without believing as those with the First Perspective are inclined to deny it. Sharing the Second Perspective here are thinkers on religion of various allegiances, including – not surprisingly – religious sceptics. Scepticism is perhaps logically constrained to take a Second-Perspective view here, for if understanding requires belief, the doubts and animadversions of sceptics would be pointless. Kai Nielsen is a good example of a sceptic who holds a Second-Perspective view on this issue. For Nielsen, though the intelligibility of religion has never been made out, to the extent that it can be understood, it can be understood by sceptics as well as it can by the religious. In *Scepticism* he makes the point that many who have grown up in a Jewish or Christian culture can play the 'religious language-games', that is, 'know how to pray and confess to God'.[88] Yet, though they have a mastery of religious language and the use of religious 'pictures', even with this understanding, they can remain 'utterly agnostic about whether these practices make sense or whether such talk is intelligible'. The point that Nielsen is making here is very close to that which he made in the passage quoted above (the passage Phillips cites and criticises). However here Nielsen avoids making the strong claim that one can understand religious belief while rejecting it as false or incoherent. Instead he makes the lesser claim that one can understand religious belief and at the same time be agnostic about its truth or coherence – a weaker claim, but all he needs to affirm that one can understand religious belief without believing. (It should be noticed that Nielsen couches his point in Neo-Wittgensteinian language – 'pictures', 'language-games', 'forms of discourse' – for he believes that he can make his point without denying the Neo-Wittgensteinian thesis that religious belief is a form of life involving the religious use of a picture or religious practice.)

The Second Perspective on this subissue of course is not held by sceptics alone. Those like Plantinga and Aquinas, who devise proofs for the existence of God which are addressed to non-believers as well as to believers, allow that in some sense non-believers can grasp what they do not believe. Again a religious thinker like H. H. Price, who allows that religious belief may be investigated and entertained by non-believers, holds some form of a Second-Perspective view on this issue. The same can be said of John King-Farlow and William Christensen, who develop the notion of 'hypothetical faith' and suggest that faith may appropriately be held tentatively in the spirit of a hypothesis.

It is a corollary of this view of religious faith that dialogue between sceptics and believers is possible and desirable, in the spirit of honest investigation. But for such a dialogue to take place two 'fundamental requirements must be met'. As King-Farlow expresses them, they are, first, that 'the theist must try harder, and with real sympathy for the sceptic in his bafflement, to clarify what he means by his religious assertions'. Second, 'the sceptic must become more chary of shouting either "False!" or "Sense-less!" before he too has made a hard and sympathetic effort to understand'.[89] Each of these requirements presupposes that the sceptic, while still a sceptic, *can* understand the beliefs held by the religious.

However a religious thinker may neither be involved in proving the existence of God nor construe faith hypothetically and still embrace a Second-Perspective view on this issue. Roger Trigg in *Reason and Commitment* gives us reasons in support of a Second-Perspective view that derive from what many would regard as a straightforward, traditional understanding of religious belief.[90] For Trigg it may well be that many non-believers do not understand the claims of religion, but it is rash to say that they 'logically cannot understand' religious claims (that it is a matter of the grammar of belief that they cannot). Rather it is that the non-believer cannot understand 'without some explanation of what is being presupposed and without some elucidation of technical terms [like "grace"]'. But such an elucidation can be provided by believers, or, alternatively, believers can avoid the use of technical terms altogether. As far as this point is concerned, religious language, with its theological terminology, is analogous to any other technical or quasi-technical language.

Also for Trigg it is not only a plain fact but an important one that atheism and Christianity clash, and they do, for Trigg, precisely because atheists and Christians disagree about the truth of Christianity.[91] Granted, atheists and Christians disagree in their commitment (as First-Perspective proponents emphasise), but finally commitment is based on belief. Thus the fundamental difference between Christians and atheists is one of belief. Many, I suspect, would agree with Trigg and the Second Perspective here. Drawing upon Trigg and Second-Perspective intuitions generally, it *seems* that we can straightforwardly reason as follows: Christians believe that there is a God, atheists deny it. But if one affirms what the other denies, each understands what the other says. So, contrary to Wittgenstein and Neo-Wittgensteinians, atheists and Christians do contradict one another and atheists do understand the religious belief that they reject as false.

So much for some basic Second Perspective views on this issue. Now let me briefly compare the stance of the Second Perspective with that of the First Perspective on a number of related secondary and tertiary issues. First, the matter of loss of faith. As we have seen, Brown's First-Perspective view disallows loss of faith, while Phillips' implicit view allows it under certain circumstances; but neither allows that a believer can have faith, become a sceptic, and thereby lose faith. The Second Perspective, especially for Nielsen, allows such an evolution. Similarly, the two perspectives differ on conversion. For the First Perspective conversion of a non-believer is odd, for how could one come to believe something without first understanding it? Phillips' implicit view, it is true, does allow that a sympathetic non-believer can understand the 'force' of religious belief. But in addition, those with the Second Perspective would say, even atheists and sceptics can (at times) be converted to religious belief after reflecting on the claims of religion.[92] At least there is no logical or grammatical reason why atheists and sceptics cannot reflect on the claims of religion and thereupon be converted. Third, there is a difference between the two perspectives on comparative religion. For the First Perspective the whole idea of comparing religions is suspect, since typically one is committed to, at most, only one religion.[93] For the Second Perspective, on the other hand, the existence of the study of comparative religion comprises an argument against thinking that one must believe in order to understand. Fourth, the two perspectives must view the doubts of believers themselves differently. Barth (as quoted by Brown) allows that believers can doubt, but if believers have faith their doubts cannot win out, logically cannot. For the Second Perspective, since faith can be lost, religious doubts – rightly or wrongly – can win out.

To a great extent whether we see these implications as strengths of the Second Perspective will depend on whether our own intuitions on this subissue are First or Second Perspective. However, just as a problem regarding rejection of belief faces the First Perspective it seems to me that a problem faces the Second Perspective, and the force of that problem must be conceded, I believe, even by those whose intuitions tend toward the Second Perspective. The problem, put one way, is this: What is the difference between religious belief and a theoretical belief if atheists show understanding of religious belief by proclaiming 'I do not believe in God'? A theoretical belief is a belief that we can accept or reject without attaching any importance to it. That Jupiter has (or has not) several moons is, for most of us, such a belief: we may accept it as true that Jupiter has several moons and yet quite understandably be indifferent to it. Religious belief it seems, is quintessentially not a theoretical belief. However, atheists may well accept God's non-existence as insouciantly as many of us accept Jupiter's moons and so have a theoretical belief about God's non-existence. What such atheists understand, and what they deny, then, is a theoretical assertion of the existence of God. Accordingly, it seems, if such atheists understand religious belief, religious belief is, or at least can be, merely theoretical.

There are several ways that those with a Second-Perspective view on this third subissue could respond to this problem. They could of course simply allow that religious belief can sometimes be theoretical. But I suspect that typically they would not allow this. Certainly they need not. One response would recognise the kind of distinction that Roger Trigg has drawn between 'what prayer means' and 'what prayer means to someone'.[94] If Trigg's distinction is extended, it becomes a distinction between (i) what belief in God means and (ii) what it means to someone to believe in God. What the atheist can understand, Second-Perspective thinkers may say, is the first. At the same time, they can say, the atheist is debarred from understanding the second. For, it is open to them to hold, in order to understand what it means to believe in God, to understand the psychological meaning of belief for an individual, it is necessary to believe oneself. And so, by virtue of this psychological meaning, which is beyond the grasp of the atheist, religious belief is not theoretical. However, they can still say, even though this psychological meaning is significant for the belief of a religious person, it is not necessary to understand it in order to understand *what* a religious person believes or accepts.

A second reply would draw upon a distinction made by W. D. Hudson between (i) making an assertion that there is a God and (ii) sharing in the believer's explanatory, commissive, and affective use of religious pictures.[95] Using this distinction those with a Second-Perspective view can say that all an atheist needs in order to deny what the religious believe is an understanding of the first, what it is to make an assertion that there is a God, for it is merely this assertion that an atheist denies. At the same time, they can observe, the atheist does not share in the use of religious pictures. Atheists may or may not appreciate how religious belief is used (Nielsen, and Hudson too, would allow that they can understand the uses of religious belief), but atheists clearly do not *share* in that use. For each of these two replies, even though the atheist understands and is indifferent to *what* the religious person believes or accepts, religious belief is saved from being theoretical by an element not available to the atheist. For the first reply that element is understanding what it means to believe, for the second it is sharing in the use of religious belief.

Each of these replies provides a place in religious belief for what we may call the life-involving aspect of religion. The Second Perspective as well as the First can recognise that religious belief is life-involving for the religious in a way that proposition-asserting per se is not. Even Nielsen, who is himself a sceptic, allows that there is a place for the use of religious pictures in religion. What these Second-Perspective replies vividly bring out is that the Second Perspective is not denying that religious belief has an affective, life-involving aspect; rather, the Second Perspective is insisting that *what* is believed by the religious can be understood without one's being religious, without one's sharing in that life-involving aspect, and it is *what* the religious believe that atheists deny and sceptics question. The root-issue between the First and Second Perspective here is not whether there is a life-involving element in religion, it is whether we can distinguish a propositional element of belief that can be understood, and denied or questioned, without participation in the religious life.

First-Perspective Strengths. The First Perspective brings to our attention the possibility that there is in *some* sense a logical connection between religious understanding and religious belief, so that we need not think that the only difference between the believer, who believes in God, and the non-believer, who denies or questions God's existence, beyond what they say, is an emotive or behavioural difference.

Second-Perspective Strengths. The Second Perspective can more easily account for loss of faith and the variety of conversion cases, and it can consistently hope for a dialogue between sceptics and believers.

(4) The Evidence Subissue: Is There a Place for Evidence, for Grounds, in Religion?

The issue that is presented here is not whether in fact anyone has evidence that can be adduced for or against religion. Still less is it whether thinkers have understood themselves as presenting evidence for or against religion. The evidence subissue comprises a logically prior question. It comprises the grammatical issue: Is religious belief such that there *can* be grounds for it? Is it possible to accept religious belief on the basis of evidence? If we try to provide grounds for religious belief, do we thereby make it into something else, into superstition, say? This subissue connects in an obvious way to the first two, the rationality and cognitivity-of-belief subissues.

The First Perspective

Those with the First Perspective on this issue are inclined to deny that evidence has a place in religious belief. However this basic denial, though it characterises the First Perspective on this issue, can be developed, and qualified, in various ways. Kierkegaard of course has a strong First-Perspective view on this issue. Wittgenstein also has a First-Perspective view, nearly as strong, and in many ways like Kierkegaard's. Neo-Wittgensteinians like Phillips and Malcolm follow Wittgenstein here and in doing so extend and develop Wittgenstein's thought. At the same time they qualify their own First-Perspective stands somewhat. In addition other modern religious thinkers, who may be aware of Wittgenstein's thought but have been less influenced by it, have developed First-Perspective views on this fourth subissue that

owe more to theological concerns. Let us begin with a consideration of Kierkegaard's view.

Earlier when I discussed Kierkegaard's view on religion and
rationality I showed that for Kierkegaard faith cannot, grammatically cannot, have reasons in its support. It cannot because, first,
to seek reasons is to renounce faith's subjectivity. Second, the
object of faith proper, the absolute paradox that the eternal
became temporal, is a 'contradiction' and, logically, no reason
can support a contradiction. Third, to seek reasons in support of
faith is ipso facto to vitiate faith by seeking to avoid the possibility
of offence. Kierkegaard's three reasons why faith cannot be
supported are of two basic kinds. The first and third focus on the
subjective attitude of faith. The second focuses on the object of
faith. Reasons in support of faith are essentially evidence in
support of faith, and, consequently, Kierkegaard's objections to
reasons for faith serve equally as objections to evidence for faith.

Still there may be a bit more to add. Evidence, as many think of
it, can be offered in support of a belief to make what is believed
more probable. The more evidence gathered and applied the more
probable the belief, other things being equal. Kierkegaard in the
Postscript addresses the effort to make faith probable by such an
'approximation-process' and objects to it on the specific grounds
that religious faith (or belief)[96] by its nature cannot be made
probable:

> Suppose a man who wishes to acquire faith; let the comedy
> begin. He wishes to have faith, but he wishes also to safeguard
> himself by means of an objective inquiry and its
> approximation-process. What happens? With the help of the
> approximation-process the absurd becomes something dif-
> ferent; it becomes probable, it becomes increasingly probable,
> it becomes extremely and emphatically probable. . . . Now he is
> ready to believe it; and lo, now it has become precisely
> impossible to believe it.[97]

Just as there are, for Kierkegaard, two basic kinds of reasons why
faith cannot be supported, one having to do with the object of faith
and one having to do with the subjective attitude of faith, so in a
similar way there are two fundamental reasons why faith cannot
be made probable. First, for Kierkegaard, while an ordinary
historical belief can be made probable, the object of faith, that is,

the absurd, the absolute paradox that the eternal became temporal, cannot be; and so if what one would believe is made probable it necessarily is not the absolute paradox, but something 'different', a historical belief.[98] Second, gathering evidence, or even only seeking to make what is believed probable, runs counter to the attitude of faith. Faith requires uncertainty and risk, and the greater the risk the greater the faith. Thus even if the object of faith could be made probable, if it were it would no longer be an object of *faith*, at least not the object of the greatest, or even great, faith.

True, Kierkegaard at points in the *Postscript* seems to allow that there can be evidence for and against the object of faith. For instance he says that when he contemplates the order of nature he sees 'omnipotence and wisdom' but much else that 'disturbs [his] mind and excites anxiety'.[99] Presumably, though, if he is allowing positive and negative evidence here, it is for and against God's omnipotence and wisdom, not for and against the absolute paradox, which is the ultimate object of faith.

It is also true that at one point in the *Postscript* Kierkegaard suggests that subjectivity can provide a 'proof' where objectivity cannot. Immortality, he says, cannot be proved. But, he says, 'immortality is the most passionate interest of subjectivity; precisely in the interest lies the proof'.[100] Once again what is 'proved' here is not the ultimate object of faith, and, in any case, what Kierkegaard seems to mean by 'proof' is conviction, or 'consciousness', as he says.

For Kierkegaard, then, as far as faith proper is concerned, it is not merely the less evidence the better, but, moreover, faith and the object of faith proper (the absolute paradox) by their natures rule out making faith probable. The faith-attitude is even at odds with seeking evidence. For such a seeking to make belief probable by an 'approximation-process' amounts to an effort to subvert the risk of faith.

Wittgenstein, especially the Wittgenstein who wrote *Lectures on Religious Belief*, substantially agrees with Kierkegaard that there is no place in religion for evidence. However Wittgenstein comes to this view, not by reflecting on the demands of faith's subjectivity or the 'contradiction' of the absolute paradox, but through a consideration of religious language. In religious discourse, Wittgenstein says, there is no talk about 'hypotheses' or 'high probability'.[101] Religious belief is not a matter of first investigating a hypothesis and then holding a 'view' on the basis of gathered evidence. In religion there is no room for the gathering of evidence, for this would require belief in God to be tentatively held. Such a belief-attitude is appropriate toward a hypothesis but is incompatible with the religious use of 'believe'.[102] On the other hand, if evidence applied to religious belief and if much evidence were brought to bear, religious belief would be made only 'highly probable'. But just as religious belief is not spoken of as probable, so too it is not spoken of as highly probable. Wittgenstein's point is the linguistic counterpoint of Kierkegaard's point that just when religious belief becomes 'probable [or] increasingly probably [or even] extremely and emphatically probable', it ceases to be religious belief. Each is making the same grammatical point in his own way.

Yet, Wittgenstein is aware, Christianity has been said to 'rest on an historic basis'.[103] While in a sense Christianity has an historic basis, still, for Wittgenstein, Christianity could not have 'ordinary belief in historic facts' as a foundation. In Christianity belief in historic facts is not a belief in *ordinary* historic facts. (Presumably Wittgenstein has in mind beliefs about events in the life of Christ and the central Christian belief that God became man in Christ.) These beliefs are not treated as empirical propositions, Wittgenstein says, and the doubt which would ordinarily apply to any historical proposition does not apply to them. Again Wittgenstein seems very close to Kierkegaard: while ordinary historical beliefs, as empirical propositions, can be made probable, the Christian belief that God became man, or a man (the absolute paradox), is not an empirical proposition and cannot be made probable.

But, Wittgenstein imagines someone saying, surely religious people do say that they believe on the evidence of religious experiences. They do say this, Wittgenstein concedes, but this is not enough for their belief to be based on evidence. Why not? Because, as Wittgenstein might have put it, the grammar of evidence is not in place. First, there is no clear idea of what would be unsatisfactory or insufficient evidence and, second, what is appealed to – dreams, for instance – does not relate to religious belief as evidence would.[104]

Moreover, Wittgenstein says, 'if there were evidence [for religious belief], this would destroy the whole business'.[105] Here too Wittgenstein echoes Kierkegaard. (Although Wittgenstein does not appeal to the 'subjectivity' of faith. Wittgenstein would instead appeal to religious belief's status as a 'regulating picture'.) He goes on to say in the next sentence, 'Anything that I normally call evidence wouldn't in the slightest influence me [that is, a religious believer]'. I think that it is interesting and significant that Wittgenstein rules out what he *normally* calls evidence. A few pages further on it becomes clear that he has in mind what is called evidence 'in science'.[106] Later (in Chapter 2) I shall want to examine the dimensions of the grammatical gap that Wittgenstein leaves open here.

Now, however, let us look at D. Z. Phillips' Neo-Wittgensteinian thinking on the place of evidence in religion. On this issue, as on others involved in the general issue of cognitivity, Phillips has developed Wittgenstein's intuitions and evolved a view that carries the stamp of his originality while being a logical extension of Wittgenstein's reflections. Earlier we saw that, for Phillips, if 'facts' characterised independently of religious belief are taken as support for one's belief, then one's belief is 'superstition' and not religious belief. Phillips then of course agrees with Wittgenstein that there are no hypotheses in religion. For Phillips this means that there are in religion no *experimental* hypotheses (as there are in science), but also it means that there are in religion no *non-experimental* hypotheses (as there are in the law and aesthetics, where, after 'the facts' are known, meaningful questions about further facts can arise, as John Wisdom helps us see). For Wittgenstein a part of the reason that religious beliefs are not hypotheses is that they are not held tentatively, more or less proportionately to applied evidence. For Phillips part of the reason that religious beliefs are not hypotheses of any sort is that religious belief is not the result of any sort of intellectual enquiry, whether experimental or non-experimental. Another part of the reason that, for Phillips, religious beliefs are not hypotheses is that, for him, in accord with his non-cognitivism, they in no sense have a truth that is dependent on what is so.

Nevertheless, while for Phillips religious beliefs cannot be hypotheses, he moderates his First-Perspective position on the place of evidence in religion. First, he allows that there are 'grounds for doubt and denial where religious beliefs are concerned' provided the issue is whether a person's belief is 'genuine' or 'false'.[107] Phillips of course wants to allow that religious belief can be false in the sense of insincere, but, he wants it to be understood, allowing this does not mean that we can 'ask in general whether religious beliefs are true or false, appropriate or inappropriate'. For Philips such 'grounds' relate to individual beliefs and to the way belief is held, not to the truth of what is believed.

Second, and more significantly, Phillips allows that religion may have a 'basis' of a kind. In *Religion without Explanation* he sketches in a reaction 'to the question whether religious beliefs have a rational basis' which, it emerges, is essentially his own. As he describes it, it is this:

> so far from bewailing the fact that no such [rational] basis can be found, the independence of religion from reason is celebrated as a sign that such activities have a higher basis than reason. We may come to see that religion does lack what has already been defined as a rational basis. This is not to say that it has no basis, but simply that it lacks the kind of basis that is called rational.[108]

For Phillips it is not an implication of this reaction that religious belief or activity is irrational (religious belief for Phillips, we should bear in mind, *is* practice or activity). Rather the implication is that it does not conform to the paradigm of rationality that others lay down as the single norm. In this sense, Phillips is saying, religious belief has a *higher* basis than reason. What is this 'higher basis' for religious belief? In 'Faith, Scepticism, and Religious Understanding' he seems to answer this question. There he denies the appropriateness of seeking *external evidence* for religious belief but allows that within religion there are *internal reasons* for belief. Thus, just as Phillips allows a rationality internal to religion, so he allows a kind of evidence for religious belief internal to religion. In fact he provides several specific examples.

> Religious believers, when asked why they believe in God, may reply in a variety of ways. They may say, 'I have had an experience of the living God', 'I believe on the Lord Jesus Christ', 'God saved me while I was a sinner', or, 'I just can't help believing'.[109]

While it is not altogether clear exactly how Phillips understands the category of internal reasons, it seems that, for Phillips, such internal reasons as these carry evidential weight for those who accept the framework of faith, even if they do not for those who stand outside faith.

In any case Phillips accepts it that the opposition between belief and unbelief is not amenable to evidence, that finally belief has nothing to show unbelief and unbelief has nothing to show belief. He explicitly rejects John Wisdom's idea that there is a meaningful issue over the existence of God which in principle is settleable though it is neither experimental nor mathematical. For Phillips Wisdom was on the right path when he showed us that religious beliefs should not be seen as experimental hypotheses, but he did not go far enough.[110] Religious belief is in no sense hypothetical, and this means for Phillips that while one person may accept religious belief and another may reject it, there is no settleable issue between them and no evidence of any kind that supports one side against the other.

Another philosopher who follows Wittgenstein and extends his thought as it relates to this fourth subissue is Norman Malcolm. He too denies that grounds have a place in religious belief. He denies, that is, that belief in God can have external evidence for it pertinent to conversion. Internal evidence, of a kind, he allows. Within a 'language-game', like belief in God, there is 'justification and lack of justification, evidence and proof'.[111] Thus within Christian belief there can be evidence offered for or against, for instance, 'doctrinal beliefs about Jesus and the Holy Spirit'.[112] But he agrees with Phillips, and Wittgenstein, that evidence and justification do not externally apply to religious belief as a whole.[113] Religious belief is in a sense 'groundless', he says. He of course does not mean that religious belief lacks grounds it should have in order to be accepted. He means that grammatically religious belief is without grounds. In this respect it is like other 'language-games', such as chemistry and our basic beliefs about material objects. Our belief that material objects – watches, wallets, lawn chairs – do not by themselves just cease to exist is in the same way groundless, Malcolm argues. We do not for a moment question this belief, but at the same time we do not support it or hold it on the basis of support: it is a part of '"the framework" of our thinking about material things'.[114]

A main point that Malcolm wants to make in 'The Groundlessness of Belief' is that religious belief is not taken up on the basis of grounds. (By 'religious belief' he means not only belief in God – he also includes Buddhism. But he means particularly belief in God.) It may be, he allows, that one person's conviction, passion, or love will move another 'in the direction of religious belief', provided that he already to some degree, sees the world as 'throbbing with love', provided, that is, that he has begun to share the religious vision of the world.[115] But Malcolm, who goes beyond Phillips in explicitly heeding the epistemological distinction between causes of belief and grounds for belief, says that he is here speaking of causes of belief, not grounds. In an earlier essay 'Is it a Religious Belief that "God Exists"?' Malcolm had questioned the distinction between *causes of belief* and *grounds for the truth of belief* in its application to religious belief.[116] Here in this essay he is clear that the distinction does apply and that causes, as opposed to grounds, can play an important role in creating or deepening religious belief. For Malcolm many things can act as the cause of religious belief in a person, provided there is some inclination toward belief: 'the wonders and horrors of nature, the history of nations, great events in personal experience, music, art, [and] the Ontological Proof'.[117] However, Malcolm insists, we should be clear that these do not act as grounds for belief. They do not because they 'can be responded to either religiously or nonreligiously'.

It is not accidental that Malcolm mentions the ontological argument, for Malcolm holds the ontological argument to be valid, or rather sound, in one version.[118] But, given that he holds this, how can he say that the ontological argument, as a valid proof, is *not* evidence for religious belief? It would seem that an atheist working through the argument would come to have evidence – very good evidence, if the argument is sound – that God exists. In fact Malcolm considers just such an 'atheist'.[119] Malcolm's atheist has come to see that the ontological argument is sound and so realises that he cannot say consistently that there is no God. Yet religiously he remains an atheist. For he has not gained a living faith; he has not begun to turn toward God in his heart. For Malcolm, if I have him right, the logic of the ontological argument can bring an atheist to accept it that there is a God; however such an atheist's belief would be a non-religious belief that God exists (even though it would be in the Judeao-Christian concept of God, which arguably is the concept that Anselm used). Thus it seems to me that Malcolm would say, or could say, that the ontological argument is conclusive evidence for his atheists's belief, but his atheists's belief is *not* a religious belief. It is only a theoretical belief that comes to little more than a propensity to defend the ontological argument. On the other hand, for Malcolm, if one is brought to a religious belief *in* God it cannot be by the ontological argument acting as evidence, or by anything else acting as evidence; it must be by a cause acting psychologically on one's inclination. Such a cause might be another's passion or indeed almost anything, including the ontological argument acting as a cause. Conceivably then Malcolm's atheist, after he has begun to have religious stirrings, could return to the ontological argument and view it in a completely different light – not as a formal piece of logic, but as something closer to a hymn or psalm which moves him in the direction of religious belief.

Not all First-Perspective views on the evidence subissue are Kierkegaardian or Wittgensteinian. Some religious thinkers object to the concept of religious evidence because evidence coerces belief and religious belief by its nature cannot be coerced. The early Alasdair MacIntyre is one such religious thinker.

MacIntyre in his essay 'Visions'[120] argues that religious visions do not provide evidence for religious belief. His argument in 'Visions' leaves it open that miracles, say, or scripture, might provide such evidence. But in his long essay 'The Logical Status of Religious Belief' he argues that evidence, whatever its source, has no place in religion. Religious belief, he argues, is not accepted on the basis of evidence: accepting belief is a matter of accepting an ultimate authority, and there can be no justification for accepting an *ultimate* authority. What we say about God, he says, we do not derive from evidence. Rather in the Christian religion, our

> ground for saying [what we say about God] is that we have the authority of Jesus Christ for saying it: our ground for accepting what he says is what the apostles say about him; our ground for accepting the apostles? Here the argument ends or becomes circular . . . .[121]

Finally, accepting religion is a matter of accepting, without further justification, an authority: the authority of the Bible for a Protestant, the authority of the Pope and the Church for a Catholic. A decision must be made of course, but what is essential for that decision is the content of faith, not justification. 'The only apologia for a religion', MacIntyre says, 'is to describe its content in detail: and then either a man will find himself brought to say "My Lord and my God" or he will not.'[122]

For MacIntyre, as for Malcolm, once a person accepts a religious authority then that person can appeal to it to resolve issues about doctrine and practice. This is what MacIntyre sees theologians doing. But to cite authority in order to decide doctrine is not to offer evidence for doctrine. Doctrines like original sin can be *illustrated* by an appeal to the state of the world, but illustrations should not be confused with evidence.[123] MacIntyre is more chary of the concept of internal evidence than is Malcolm. However he is in accord with Malcolm, Phillips, and Wittgenstein (to whom he refers, but sparingly) in his insistence that religious belief as a whole is not based on, cannot be based on, evidence.

What is noteworthy in MacIntyre's case against religious evidence, though, is the connection he sees between evidence and coercion. That connection comes out very clearly in the following quotation:

> Suppose . . . that the divine omnipotence was so manifest that whenever anyone denied a Christian doctrine he was at once struck dead by a thunder-bolt. No doubt the conversion of England would ensue with a rapidity undreamt of by the Anglican bishops. But since the Christian faith sees true religion only in a free decision made in faith and love, the religion would by this vindication be destroyed. For all possibility of free choice would have been done away. Any objective justification of belief would have the same effect. Less impressive than thunder-bolts, it would equally eliminate all possibility of a decision of faith. And with that, faith too would have been eliminated.[124]

As we have seen, MacIntyre is clear that religious belief is not based on evidence. And, as we see in this quotation, he is clear that if religious belief *per impossibile* were given objective evidence in its support, then it would cease to be religious belief. That is, religious belief grammatically cannot be supported. On these points MacIntyre agrees with Kirkegaard, Wittgenstein, Phillips and Malcolm. But about how and why evidence destroys religious belief MacIntyre has something new and noteworthy to say. Objective evidence destroys religion because it, at least when it is conclusive, *compels* belief, and religious belief must be given a free choice. This is not Wittgenstein's reason why evidence would destroy religion. Nor is it Kierkegaard's, although it is more closely related to Kierkegaard's thinking. For Kierkegaard faith is indeed the result of a decision, a 'leap', but in the *Postscript* his implicit argument against evidence is not that it would compel belief. Kierkegaard's argument, rather, at the point of comparison, is that evidence or seeking evidence would vitiate the subjective response of faith.

MacIntyre is not alone in finding evidence to have a coercive quality at odds with the free choice required by faith. Nor is MacIntyre the first to have this perception. Those familiar with *The Brothers Karamazov* may recall that the conflict between the freedom to choose faith and the coercive power of revelatory miracles is more than peripheral to Ivan's poem 'The Grand Inquisitor'.[125] Among contemporary philosophers of religion John Hick also seems to have this perception, with qualifications, although he does not address the issue of evidence directly.

In more than one place Hick has discussed and developed a distinction between experience of our physical environment, which 'everyone is compelled to have', and religious experience of God, which 'no one is compelled to have'.[126] The first is sense perception of our material surroundings and is 'coercive' in the sense that it 'impresses itself upon our consciousness whether we like it or not'. As a matter of undeniable psychological fact, 'when we open our eyes in daylight we cannot help seeing what is before us'. The second is religious perception of God and is not coercive in this sense. 'God does not force himself upon our attention as does our physical environment.' Rather 'the individual's own free receptivity or responsiveness plays a part in his dawning consciousness of God'. In this way the individual is free to accept or to reject religious experience.

In the case of religious experience, then, there is a 'cognitive freedom' that allows us to have a 'voluntary awareness' of God. For Hick this cognitive freedom is essential to religion, for a personal relationship between God and man requires an uncompelled response on the part of the religious individual.[127] He accepts it as a 'commonplace of contemporary theology' that God leaves individuals 'free to become conscious of him by an uncompelled response of faith'.[128]

Faith for Hick is this free response. In its cognitive aspect faith is the interpretive element in the believer's cognition of the world.

It is, Hick says, comparable to what Wittgenstein called 'seeing as', although in the case of religious interpretation is 'experiencing as'. The religious act of interpreting the world as divine occurs when a person chooses or freely decides to experience the world as having religious significance.[129] And as the world can be interpreted religiously, so it can be interpreted non-religiously. God's presence is 'mediated in and through the world'; it is not evident or manifest. Indeed it cannot be. For if it were, our cognitive freedom to interpret the world religiously or not would be lost, and with it any chance for a personal relationship between God and ourselves.

In brief this is Hick's thinking about the uncompelled nature of religious experience and the role therein for freedom. The implications for the possibility of religious evidence seem clear (although they are for the most part left implicit by Hick). If God's presence cannot be manifest or evident, then, obviously, there cannot be manifest signs or indications of God's presence. True, in places Hick seems to countenance the possibility of evidence. For instance he allows that the 'fact of evil' tells against the existence of God while the 'fact of Christ' supports it. But as Hick says in one place such evidence is *prima-facie evidence* which, in the first case, is appealed to by non-believers and rejected by believers and, in the second case, is appealed to by believers and rejected by non-believers.[130] That is, if I have Hick right, what is counted as evidence depends on the individual's prior interpretation of the world, on whether it is religious or non-religious. Hick, however, allows that *after* one has freely interpreted the world religiously then one may have a consciousness of God that has a 'coercive and indubitable quality'.[131] For those with faith their religious experiences constitute 'adequate grounds' for certainty that God is real, and their religious consciousness may be as compelling as their consciousness of the natural world.[132] On this point Hick's view is rather different from MacIntyre's.

Hick's view on religion and evidence, summed up, seems to be this: a fruitful ambiguity in the 'given' allows us to experience the world as having religious significance, but we are not forced to; we must freely turn toward God, which we do by choosing to interpret the world religiously; this is the response of faith, and once we have faith then – but only then – there may be evidence, even coercive, undeniable evidence in support of religious belief. Hick's thinking on evidence and related epistemic concepts, in my view, is a good example of an effort to retain an application of epistemic concepts in religion, but an application that will not do violence to religion, especially not to the requirements of faith.

Why, then, is Hick's implicit view on religious evidence First Perspective since it does allow a place for evidence, even compelling evidence? Granted, Hick's view does not fit all too well in the First Perspective, but still on this issue, though not on others, he seems to me to have a First-Perspective view. It is First-Perspective because it insists that decisive evidence cannot be recognised as such before one accepts religious faith. To be sure there is room for dispute over the nature of evidence, and we might legitimately wonder to what extent Hick's thinking clarifies the concept of religious evidence and to what extent it modifies it. But I believe that his analysis, in its insistence that decisive evidence cannot be recognised before belief, puts more than a little strain on the general concept of evidence. Normally the concept of evidence is thought to allow that persons can come to accept a belief that evidence supports precisely because – that is, after – they have come to see that evidence supports it. To deny this feature of evidence is to make evidence 'internal' to faith in something like the way it is for Phillips. And if this feature of evidence is necessary to the concept, as is normally assumed, to deny it is in effect to deny religious evidence in at least the ordinary concept of evidence.

Still, Hick's analysis highlights an area of tension in religion, or religious thought, between the requirements of evidence on the one hand and the role of choice, decision, and will on the other, to which I shall return in Chapter 4.

Now, however, finally in our consideration of the First Perspective on this fourth subissue, let us turn to the thought of one other contemporary philosopher of religion, Robert Herbert. Herbert, like Hick, would insist on the cognitive status of belief, and there they are both Second-Perspective; but, also like Hick – in fact more explicitly than Hick, he denies that evidence has any place in religion. However he does so for reasons that we have not yet encountered. Herbert in *Paradox and Identity in Theology* examines and rejects the view that a religious believer is one who chooses to believe what is paradoxical and against the evidence. To a great extent Herbert is questioning Kierkegaard's view of faith. In its broadest construction, though, Herbert's concern is with any view of faith according to which it is choosing to take up a conviction not justified by the available evidence. This is a wrong view of faith, Herbert argues. The believer is not one who irresponsibly ignores the insufficiency of the evidence nature affords. But this does not mean that there is sufficient evidence to justify religious conviction. Rather the mistake in the view is in thinking that religious believers take up belief on either sufficient or insufficient evidence, either responsibly or irresponsibly. As Herbert puts it:

> The believer does not come to the conviction that God exists by *concluding* to it – either responsibly or irresponsibly. The psalmist who declares the heavens to be the work of God's fingers is not 'announcing his findings'. He is not, then, irresponsibly ignoring contrary evidence in nature, for nature is not evidence in his enterprise. His conviction arises quite otherwise.[133]

If not by evidence, how does conviction arise in the religious believer? Herbert goes beyond Wittgenstein (with whom he thus far agrees) in giving an answer to this question. The answer he gives – the 'answer of Belief' – is essentially a theological answer. For Herbert, Hume in the *Enquiry Concerning Human Understanding* was right (in spite of himself) when he said that if one is moved by faith to assent to the Christian religion it is through a miracle.[134] As Herbert puts the point elsewhere in his book, coming to faith or conviction is not a matter of leaping across the chasm (to belief'), it is a matter of being 'yanked' across it.[135] Coming to conviction is not a matter of choosing (either arbitrarily or not, either with reliable evidence or without), it is a matter of being chosen – by God. That is, it is a matter of God's acting in one, a matter of miracle, of grace: it is God who gives the believer conviction.

Accordingly, for Herbert, as religious conviction is not a matter of evidence, so religious doubt is not either. As religious conviction is God's gift, so religious doubt is a rejection of God's gift. The doubts of a faltering faith, he says quoting Kierkegaard, 'spring from insubordination'; they are not the products of an intellect facing countervailing evidence.[136]

Interestingly, then, if we consider the early MacIntyre and Hick on one side and Herbert on the other we find that there are two distinct theological reasons for denying that evidence relates to religious belief as it has been supposed that it relates to other belief. For MacIntyre and Hick evidence – or at least *conclusive* evidence (for MacIntyre), at least *before* religious belief (for Hick) – would destroy the free choice faith requires. For Herbert, on the other hand, faith is not a matter of choosing, with or without adequate evidence; it is a matter of grace creating conviction, to which evidence is irrelevant. At least on the surface these two theological reasons are at odds. However, to call attention to this fact is not to deny that either provides a reason against saying that evidence has a place in religious belief. It perhaps is not accidental that those religious philosophers who draw upon the theological requirements of faith in arguing the First-Perspective case find in faith a moral dimension wherein the role of the will is paramount. (For Herbert, though faith is not chosen, religion is willful.) Two questions that Herbert raises and to which we shall return (in Chapter 3) are: If religious doubt is essentially a matter of will, is every role for evidence *vis-à-vis* doubt ruled out? And if grace is what brings one to faith, or conviction, is every role for evidence *vis-à-vis* faith ruled out?

The Second Perspective

As those with the First Perspective on this subissue are inclined to deny evidence a place in religion, so those with the Second Perspective are inclined to affirm a place for evidence in religion. That is, they are inclined in some way to give a grammatical place to evidence for belief in God, or at least to a belief that there is a God. They do not deny that evidence can 'objectively' support religious belief, just as other beliefs are supported by evidence appropriate to them; and they allow that converts can be brought to belief through seeing this evidence. They do not, then, restrict religious evidence to doctrinal matters that arise within a religion.

In contemporary religious reflection there is a range of Second-Perspective views on the evidence issue. All those contemporaries who address believers and non-believers with proofs that they maintain offer conclusive, or some, evidence for the existence of God, or the rationality of belief in God, share one kind of Second-Perspective approach. So too, of course, do those who offer evil as negative evidence against the existence of God, it should be noted. However our primary concern is with the Second Perspective as a perspective within religious reflection, and so we shall limit our focus to those who are in some way sympathetic to religion. Among these there are Second-Perspective philosophers who apply to religion what amounts to a scientific concept of evidence, there are others who argue for a less scientific mode of support, and there are still others who look more to uniquely religious experience. Let us begin with those who apply a scientific concept of evidence to religion. One such contemporary philosopher is George Schlesinger.

Schlesinger in his book *Religion and Scientific Method* maintains as his main thesis that 'the traditional theist need not recoil from examining his basic propositions by a method of inquiry which adopts the standards employed in science'. He continues: 'On a correct understanding of the essence of scientific method, Theism does not stand to lose from such an inquiry; in fact it gains, emerging from it with enhanced credibility.'[137] By 'Theism' Schlesinger means the 'theistic hypothesis' that there exists a God, a Perfect Being, omnipotent and omniscient, 'who is interested in creatures capable of responding to him'.[138] Clearly Schlesinger's thesis is a Second-Perspective thesis with a vengeance.

Schlesinger supports his thesis in two primary ways. First he deals with 'evidence which tends strongly to disconfirm Theism', that is, the apparently strong negative evidence comprised by evil. In doing this he proposes his own solution to the problem of evil. However the second way in which Schlesinger defends his thesis is more important for our concerns. In this second and major thrust, Schlesinger tries to show that 'Theism is in principle confirmable by all sorts of possible observations and is in fact confirmed by some actual observations.'[139]

The evidence that Schlesinger would draw to our attention is just this: the existence of 'laws of nature governing the universe and . . . initial conditions in it . . . such that creatures capable of responding to the Divine are permitted to exist'.[140] It is not necessary for Schlesinger's purposes that the laws of nature be stated or even well understood; it is only necessary to see that, whatever these laws are, they allow the existence of creatures – human beings – who are capable of responding to God and leading God-oriented lives. Schlesinger is not arguing that since human beings respond to God, there must be a God to whom they respond. His evidence requires only the capability – exercised by some – that human beings have to lead religious, and in this sense, God-centred lives.

But this evidence is more probable on the theistic hypothesis than on the naturalistic hypothesis, Schlesinger argues. It is because it follows from Theism as Schlesinger has stated it that God, who is all-powerful and so able to realise all that he wishes, must create creatures who are capable of responding to him. On the other hand no such proposition follows from naturalism: Naturalism itself implies nothing about human nature. Given Theism, it must be true that the laws of nature allow there to be creatures capable of responding to the Divine; given Naturalism, it need not be true. Nothing more is required to see that this evidence is more probable on the theistic hypothesis than it is on the naturalistic hypothesis, Schlesinger argues. But if so, this evidence confirms Theism as compared to Naturalism.

So far, then, Schlesinger has argued that certain evidence confirms Theism over Naturalism. But a question remains: Why should we adopt Theism over other hypotheses that seem to be confirmed equally with Theism by the evidence that Schlesinger presents? Schlesinger answers this question by invoking the scientific principle of parsimony, or rather, 'adequacy'. On this principle, he argues, we should reject the hypothesis that there exists a powerful but malicious demon who wishes to deceive people into thinking there is a God, and similar rival hypotheses, for they lack the 'adequacy' of the theistic hypothesis.[141] At this point Schlesinger feels that he has made out his case and shown that an appreciation of the principles of science, very far from damaging Theism, enhance its credibility.

My purpose is to present Schlesinger's Second-Perspective view, not to criticise it. Still there is one point, pertinent to what I take to be Schlesinger's major thrust, that I perhaps ought to bring out. It is important for Schlesinger's reasoning that Theism should entail the existence of religiously inclined human beings while Naturalism should not. But is this right? Naturalism includes all the laws of nature, known and unknown. Some of these presumably could be psychological laws. Given something like a Freudian view of psychological laws, Naturalism would or could well, entail belief in God, although such belief would of course be a neurotic expression of repressed desires. If this is the way Naturalism is to be filled in, Schlesinger's evidence confirms Theism no more than Naturalism. Nevertheless, however successful Schlesinger is in establishing his thesis, he shows us that one can be a theist, a believer, and not hesitate to look for empirical evidence for religious belief and even insist upon evaluating that evidence in accordance with the very principles science uses to decide between rival hypotheses.

Another philosopher who applies to religion a scientific concept of evidence is Richard Swinburne. Swinburne, unlike Schlesinger, does not discuss scientific principles for determining the relative confirmation of hypotheses. However in his *The Concept of Miracle* he does consider what events would be evidence for miracles should they be discovered by empirical observation. His main argument is that certain events, should they occur, would be evidence for the existence of miracles. Swinburne follows the Humean tradition in his definition of 'miracle'. For him a miracle is a *violation of a natural law brought about by a god*.[142] Accordingly the issue breaks down into two parts: (i) What would be evidence that an event was a violation of a natural law? and (ii) what would be evidence that a violation was caused by a god?

Since Hume philosophers have generally conceded that there is a conceptual problem with the idea of a violation of a natural law. Swinburne recognises this and addresses the conceptual issue before he tries to say what would be evidence that a violation has occurred. He suggests, following Ninian Smart, that there would be a violation of a law of nature if there were a 'non-repeatable counter-instance to a law of nature'.[143] If natural laws are construed as statistical, as opposed to universal, then a counter-instance would be a non-repeatable event that is highly unlikely given the truth of the law in question. With this clarification in mind, Swinburne names several good candidates for violations, including levitation, water turning into wine without the use of apparatus or chemicals, and a person's getting better from polio in a minute.[144]

What, then, would be evidence that such a non-repeatable counter-instance has occurred in the past? Swinburne suggests that there are what amount to three kinds of historical evidence. First, 'our own apparent memories of our past experiences'; second, 'the testimony of others about their past experiences'; and third, 'physical traces'.[145] Swinburne discusses the interrelations among these kinds of evidence and deals with Humean animadversions of testimony. However, for our purpose it will suffice to observe that, for Swinburne, historical evidence for past violations is of the same kinds as evidence for other past events.

Once evidence has been presented in support of an event's

being a violation, the issue of the violation's cause arises. A miracle is caused by a god. What evidence can there be that a violation-event was wrought by a god? Swinburne suggests that all of the following would constitute such evidence: (i) the violation was requested, as in a prayer, (ii) the request was specifically addressed, say to Allah, (iii) the request is often followed by a voice, not that of an embodied agent, giving reasons for granting or refusing the request, and (iv) the voice praises some requests and rebukes petitioners for others.[146]

At this point, then, Swinburne has outlined for us what would be evidence, in a public and scientific sense, for the occurence of a miracle. So far he has considered *historical* evidence in isolation from other possible evidence for the existence of a god or gods. In the last chapter of his book he considers the possibility that there is *external* evidence for God's existence. 'Many Christian theologians', Swinburne says, count as evidence for God's existence, 'the existence of the world, the design of the world, the existence of moral codes, . . . religious experience', and more.[147] He does not assess the force of this evidence. But he does make two points. First, external evidence 'could join' with historical evidence concerning violations to support the claim that at least one god exists. Second, external evidence might also support the claim that at least one god *of a certain character* exists.

Swinburne throughout his book has what must strike many as a curious tendency to speak of evidence for 'a god's existence' or evidence for 'at least one god'. This tendency is a result of his Humean definition of 'miracle' and also a result of his scientific or quasi-scientific approach to the search for possible evidence for miracles. Scientific disinterestedness, especially after Hume, it could be argued, requires not closing off beforehand the possibility that there are many gods. In the language of the Second Perspective, or of those forms of it favoured by Swinburne and Schlesinger, the polytheistic hypothesis is as viable as the monotheistic hypothesis until evidence confirms or disconfirms one as compared to the other.

Another philosopher who applies scientific standards of evidence to religion is H. H. Price. In fact he goes so far as to provide a quasi-scientific experiment that will enable one to test the 'Theistic hypothesis'.[148] For Price, in order to test the theistic hypothesis it is not necessary for one to believe already and still less is it necessary to believe with conviction. Nor is it necessary to trust in God or in anything else. One need not have the conviction that the procedures to be undertaken will work. One need only think that they are worth trying. Granted, to test the Theistic hypothesis one must have an 'interest' in 'the basic propositions of theistic religion', which are 'that there is a God who created the world, and that he loves each one of us'. However, such an interest need only be sufficient for a certain effort in trying out the testing procedure. It need not amount to a prior acceptance of their truth. Price's model thoughout is the empirical testing of a scientific hypothesis.

The procedure to be followed in testing the Theistic hypothesis involves meditative and devotional practices. These include privately fixing one's thoughts on the theistic propositions and taking up the practice of prayer. Of course the 'praying' involved will be that of an agnostic and will have the character of a 'devotional experiment'. The tester of the Theistic hypothesis is to conduct the imaginative exercise of 'taking up the role' of a religious person: not in order to precipitate belief, but to test the religious hypothesis, so that belief may be justified. Price's intuitions on the issue of evidence, and on evidence gathering, could hardly be more opposed to the First-Perspective intuitions of, say, Malcolm. True, Price allows that there is no evidence that is conclusive and obvious to all, and in allowing this he sounds like MacIntyre and Hick, who have First-Perspective views. Nevertheless, I believe that Price's own intuitions here are resolutely Second Perspective. While for Price the 'uncompell- able' character of the love we are to give to God best explains the lack of conclusive evidence for the Theistic hypothesis,[149] Price does not appeal to the compulsive nature of evidence to *support* his view (as do MacIntyre and Hick), he cites it to explain what on his view is something of an oddity.

So far we have dealt with contemporary Second-Perspective views that explicitly or implicitly appeal to the standards of science. Philosophers with these views do not quarrel with the notion that all evidence is essentially scientific, gathered by observation or experimentation, and related to a hypothesis, which in the case of religious belief is the Theistic hypothesis. However, there is another class of Second-Perspective views on the role of evidence in religion, and philosophers with these views are less inclined to appeal to the model of science. Such philosophers may not use the word 'evidence' prominently, but they still hold that belief in God is, or may be, well grounded. Some among these philosophers argue that the existence of God is open to enquiry of a non-scientific sort and that grounds of some sort for religious belief can in principle be discovered, or if not discovered, developed from what we already know.

Two philosophers with Second-Perspective views of this latter kind are Renford Bambrough and John Wisdom. As we have seen, Bambrough in his book *Reason, Truth and God* makes the point that if there is religious orthodoxy, then there must be religious truth and falsity. In the passage we quoted earlier Bambrough maintains that other epistemic cognates are equally required by orthodoxy; among them is justification. For Bambrough it is not merely that religious orthodoxy internally requires some means of justifying one belief over another; rather, argument or evidence can be the means whereby one comes to religion (or to new morals or politics). It is a mistake, Bambrough argues, to observe that books, lectures, and conversations – and the reasoning they contain – rarely if ever bring about a dramatic conversion and then to conclude that they make no difference at all to religious issues.[150] It is a central thesis of Bambrough's book that no 'question that can be at issue between two thinkers or writers or speakers is ever beyond the scope of reason'.[151] Specifically the issue of God's existence is not beyond the scope of reason.

'Reason', however, is to be construed broadly, not narrowly: various modes of intellectual enquiry qualify. In construing reason broadly, and in thus countenancing modes of evidential support other than the scientific, Bambrough follows John Wisdom. Wisdom's contribution here is chiefly in his classic paper 'Gods'.[152] This of course is the paper that Phillips takes such strong exception to for making belief in God into a 'non-experimental hypothesis' (see section (2) above), but now we want to take a more sympathetic look at it from the Second Perspective. In 'Gods' Wisdom says that the issue of God's existence is no longer an 'experimental issue'. He means that it will not be settled by experimentation and data gathering, and in this precise sense is not an experimental hypothesis. But after saying this Wisdom goes on to show that it nevertheless could still be a meaningful issue. This he does by showing that meaningful issues in various areas of life can arise and be intellectually pursued after all the data are in, after all the particulars are known. Wisdom is in effect denying that what Bambrough calls 'Hume's fork' poses a dichotomy.[153] For many philosophers in the Humean tradition there were just two kinds of meaningful issues: standard inductive and deductive issues. In 'Gods' Wisdom pretty well demonstrates that there are meaningful issues that can arise and be settled after empirical observation is complete, even though the issue is not over strict entailments. He shows us that there are all of the following: (i) certain *legal issues* (Is such-and-such an act of negligence?) that arise after testimony is complete, which are settled by redescription, appeal to precedent and judicial judgement; (ii) certain *esthetic issues* (Is the composition of a certain painting powerful?) that arise when both parties to the dispute have before their eyes the same art object, which are settled by rediscription, emphasising features, comparison, and re-examination from different perspectives; and (iii) certain *issues regarding human emotions and relations* (Are John and Mary happy together?) that arise after the myriad facts of the relationship are familiar, which are settled by seeking and finding a pattern in those facts.

As Bambrough says, Wisdom 'widens our conception of fact, of reason, of assertion about what is so in the actual world'.[154] More importantly, for our present purposes, he makes us see that not everything that is a good reason, or evidence, is a matter of empirical observation. This is just the case regarding the religious issue of God's existence for Wisdom and Bambrough.

At the same time, however, it appears that Wisdom reduces or reinterprets 'God exists' so that it became an assertion about patterns in human reactions (a point that, as we have seen, Phillips makes). As Bambrough puts it, Wisdom 'has detranscendentalised statements about God's existence'.[155] Bambrough too may come close to reinterpretation. In the last chapter of his book he suggests that Christianity may embody insights relating to life and to ourselves that would survive if its 'transcendentalist propositions' were abandoned.

Nevertheless, while both Wisdom and Bambrough may reinterpret the existence of God, it is not clear that their Second-Perspective view on this fourth subissue requires them to do so. In fact I think that clearly it does not. Their Second-Perspective view combines two elements: an insistence on the cognitive status of 'God exists' (which is an element of all Second-Perspective views on this issue) and the thesis that there is a meaningful issue about God's existence which, though not experimental, not scientific, still is factual and amenable to a mode of evidential support. These two elements in themselves require no comment on how 'God exists' is to be understood, except that it should be understood as saying something that is either true or false and capable of being supported. That is, these two elements by themselves do not require a reinterpretation of 'God exists'. The core of Wisdom's philosophical contribution in 'Gods' – his widening the way we think of fact, reason and other epistemic concepts – would remain intact if the reinterpretive element were jettisoned.

Now let us turn to a Second-Perspective view on the evidence issue that is different from any we have seen so far. H. D. Lewis in his book *Our Experience of God* provides a sustained discussion of the import of religious experience for religious belief. Lewis' task as he sees it is not to try to prove that God exists; he does not see this as philosophy's role in religion.[156] Nor does he insist or even allow that religious experience can provide *scientific* evidence for God's existence. It is a mistake for us to 'look for God as [we] would look for some other peculiar entity, something . . . to be found, if at all, as we find other things in the world'.[157] 'There is a sense', Lewis says, 'in which God is not known by evidence, and in which the reply to those who ask us "What would need to be different for your belief not to be true?" must be "nothing" '.[158] That is, there is no falsification condition that can be stated and in principle be scientifically determined to obtain or not. Nor does Lewis suggest that evidence for God's existence will be found by intellectual enquiry of a non-scientific sort. However, for Lewis there is religious evidence. Indeed, he says, 'there is a sense . . . in which we have abundant evidence of what God is like and what He does'.[159] Religious evidence is found in religious experience, and by religious experience Lewis means experience of a transcendent God – a God beyond and other, absolute and complete.[160] There is in Lewis' book no hint of the reductionism or reinterpretation that we find in Wisdom's 'Gods' and is suggested by Bambrough. Also, we should be clear, the evidence provided by religious experience is not for Lewis 'internal evidence' in the sense allowed by such Neo-Wittgensteinians as Phillips and Malcolm. For Lewis the evidence of religious experience supports the objective truth of religious belief in God, and, for Lewis, to disregard truth and its support in favour of 'commitment' and to 'opt' for faith is to come close to nihilism.[161]

Lewis' approach in *Our Experience of God* is to look carefully at the interlocking points where religious experience and the rest of religion meet in the lives of individual believers. In doing this, in a way, he is more Wittgensteinian than Wittgenstein, although I suspect Lewis would never make this claim. In any case Lewis more than the followers of Wittgenstein focuses on the unique experiences of religion (as opposed to religious discourse), and it is here, in what Lewis regards as the core of religion, that he finds religious evidence for the objective truth of belief in a transcendent God.

One primary religious experience is that experience of wonder that 'comes with the realisation . . . that all existence . . . stands in a relation of dependence to some absolute or unconditioned being . . .'.[162] Also crises of various sorts 'will precipitate the leap which takes the mind beyond finite things'.[163] Again, within a developing religious life there will be moments of need, grief, or perplexity when the believer has the distinct 'impression of being helped or solaced or strengthened'. And in moments when believers deviate from their relationship to God they may experience God's presence as restoration and deliverance or alternatively as a righteous accuser who has searched their hearts.[164] In these last cases not only the existence of a transcendent God, but His character is presented.

While religious experience for Lewis is contact with God, it is not immediate contact with God. It is wrong, he says, to assume that the consciousness of God 'comes in the first place, or indeed at any time, in clear detachment from other experiences and the attitudes they engender'.[165] Lewis disassociates religious experience as he understands it from 'literal union with God' and direct awareness of God as these experiences are sometimes described in mystical traditions.[166] For Lewis a person's experience of God is mediated and even fashioned by what that person believes 'His character and activity to be or what he requires of [the person] in some situation."[167]

Lewis, it should be noted, recognises that those in different confessions, some not unmarked by enthusiasm, may appeal to and even have religious experience. In fact he allows that the 'religious crank', because of temperament and history, may have religious experience *more* intensely than others. He then may go on to make 'foolish and ill-founded claims' on the basis of that experience because he misunderstands it, relying on notions to which he is independently committed.[168] Just here, then, a problem arises for Lewis. What beliefs about God does religious experience support, and how do we tell which are supported? Some would point to another problem: If beliefs about God are needed beforehand to mediate our experience of God, how can religious experience be independent support of beliefs about the character of God? For, in this case, will not the beliefs determine the experience?

However, our concern here is to present Lewis' Second-Perspective view, not to criticise it unduly. And surely, it must be allowed, Lewis in his book draws to our attention a panoply of experiences that the religious and the incipiently religious have, which they, or some of them (and not Lewis alone), point to as evidence in their own lives for the existence and presence of God.

Finally in this section let us look briefly at Stephen Davis' Second-Perspective thinking on religious evidence. In his book *Faith, Skepticism, and Evidence* Davis treats the category of evidence at length and suggests a distinction between *public* and *private* evidence.[169] Public evidence is 'objective' in the sense that it 'is open to the awareness and inspection of anyone who is interested enough to consider [it],' and it is 'transpersonal' in the sense that, if adequate, it should convince anyone of the truth of the proposition in question.[170] Davis does not insist that there is public evidence for religion, but he allows that there could be. His example of what would be public evidence for the existence of God is a valid argument, with premises known to be true, which establishes the probability of God's existence.

But Davis is much more interested in *private evidence*. Private evidence in his sense is neither objective nor transpersonal. That is, it is not open to the inspection of all who are interested, and it should not convince anyone except the single person for whom it is evidence. Private evidence, though, is not 'logically private' in the sense Wittgenstein meant: one can state one's private evidence and be understood by others (although it will not be, or should not be, convincing to others). Davis' example of private evidence for God's existence is the word of parents, spoken to and convincing for only their son.[171]

In 'Is it a Religious Belief that "God Exists"?' Malcolm considers very nearly the same example. However, as we might expect, Malcolm's reaction is rather different from Davis'. Malcolm recounts a discussion in which one philosopher

repeatedly asked another, 'How do you know that God exists?'
Finally the second philosopher replied, 'Because my father told
me so!' Malcolm says:

> It was a long time before I saw what was impressive in this
> reply. My first reaction was to think it was absurd; it did not
> offer anything which could be considered a *good reason*. But do
> we know what a good reason would look like? I do not believe
> so.[172]

Malcolm goes on to say that in the New and Old Testaments
nothing is put forward as evidence, and that when the question of
evidence does misguidedly arise religious language – in Wittgenstein's phrase – 'is idling'. It is not insignificant that in the
setting of Malcolm's example a reason is asked for and given in a
philosophical discussion, while in the setting of Davis' example
parents speak to their child. For Malcolm no good reason is given
by the philosopher's reply; indeed no reason at all is given. For
Davis, the word of one's parents is evidence, private evidence, and
possibly good evidence. And for Davis such evidence can be a *basis*
for one's belief, not merely a reason to be cited after one believes
and after one has accepted new rules of evidence internal to belief,
as with 'internal evidence' for Phillips.

What Davis means by private evidence is perhaps not that
different from what Pascal meant by 'reasons of the heart'. In fact
Davis says as much. However, Davis may include more in the
category of private evidence than Pascal would countenance. For
Davis 'the consensus of rational persons' determines both what is
public evidence and what is adequate public evidence. On the
other hand, 'a person believes for a private reason,' Davis says,
'when he believes either on the basis of inadequate public
evidence or on the basis of some non-evidential reason (indoctri-
nation, desire, prejudice, hypnosis, etc.)'.[173] For Davis, then, the
category of private evidence is quite wide: it includes all those
reasons a person would give or could give that do not constitute
public evidence.

However, this is not to say that for Davis all beliefs held on the
basis of private evidence are justified. On his view a 'faith-
proposition' is justified when, but only when:

> it is an instance of a Jamesian case, i.e., I am forced either to

accept it or reject it and its truth cannot be settled on [public] evidential grounds alone,

and

it is a belief that for public or private reasons I find more illuminating, i.e., more helpful in explaining my experience than any alternative belief.[174]

Thus for Davis private evidence can justify belief only when adequate public evidence is not available. His view is very much like James's in this respect. James (see section (1) above) allows that a belief can be held rationally on the basis of our psychological or 'passional' needs if one must believe one way or the other and there are no 'intellectual grounds' – or, in Davis' terms, public evidence is lacking. The chief difference between James and Davis is that for the former, belief in such cases is rational in the absence of evidence, while for the latter it is justified by evidence of a sort, private evidence.[175]

An implication of Davis' view on evidence with which some might feel uneasy is that all beliefs turn out to have a basis in evidence, for anything that supports or only brings about a belief – including prejudice and hypnosis – will qualify as either public or private evidence. Nevertheless Davis draws attention to the narrowness of the concept of evidence as usually understood, the concept of public evidence. He make us ask whether there could be a species of evidence that, like public evidence, truly supports belief but is private in the sense that it cannot be seen by all who consider a matter disinterestedly in the spirit of enquiry. To this question we shall return when (in Chapters 2 and 3) we consider questions about the nature of evidence and, as well, the nature of rationality.

Let me end this section by drawing attention to Hebrews 11.1:

Now Faith is the assurance of things hoped for, the conviction of things not seen.

In this passage, it seems to me, there is a logical tension that parallels the dividing line between First and Second-Perspective intuitions on the issue of evidence. Those with Second-Perspective intuitions, looking at this passage, would see an implicit place for evidence: for whence assurance and conviction, if they are not to be irrational, except an evidential grounding? While those with the First-Perspective would reply that if faith is conviction *regarding the unseen*, then surely a place for evidence is implicitly denied.

Strengths of the First Perspective. The First Perspective raises an alarm about the concept of evidence applied to religious belief. It points to a prima facie incompatibility between evidence and the requirements of the faith-attitude and to the danger that faith will become theoretical if it is made contingent upon evidence. It points to the role of will in belief and dramatically reminds us of the moral dimension in the religious response of faith.

Strengths of the Second Perspective. The Second Perspective recognises the dangers run by regarding religion as unique or special in deserving strong belief in the absence of support: first, the danger of compartmentalisation, and as a result a morally questionable 'double think', and, second, the danger of basing one's life on what will turn out to be illusory.

(5) The Knowledge Subissue: Is There or Can There Be Religious Knowledge?

Though the knowledge subissue is not the single paramount issue in the general issue of cognitivity, it is central. It is in various ways connected to the other subissues, but especially to the rationality and evidence subissues. On the face of it, what can be cited as evidence in support of one's belief also supports one's rationality and, in another way, can be brought forward to say how one knows. The issue that comprises the knowledge subissue, however, is not whether any human being has gained religious knowledge. The issue here is the logically prior grammatical issue whether religious depth allows religious knowledge. It is on this issue that contemporary First-Perspective and Second-Perspective intuitions are sharply, almost aggressively, divided. It is as clear to the First Perspective that knowledge is incompatible with, and seeking it anathema to, religious depth as it is clear to the Second Perspective that knowledge is the fruition of the religious life and a state to be hoped for.

The First Perspective

While those with the First Perspective on this issue are in basic agreement that there is no place in religion for knowledge, their objections to religious knowledge vary somewhat in focus and tone. There is no doubt where Kierkegaard, the Kierkegaard of the *Postscript*, stands on this issue, and other religious existentialists share his basic intuitions. So do Wittgenstein and Neo-Wittgensteinian philosophers of religion. Once more we shall start with Kierkegaard.

For Kierkegaard, as we saw in the last section, when one tries to make belief safe by using the 'approximation-process' to render probable what is to be believed, one ends up by making faith impossible. One the same page from which I quoted earlier he emphasises the opposition between faith (or belief) and knowledge: as he says, the approximation-process can bring one to a point where one 'can almost know, or as good as know, or extremely and emphatically almost *know* – but it is impossible to *believe*'.[176] Really all Kierkegaard is doing here is tracing a prima facie implication of his *Postscript* definition of faith, according to which faith is the passionate embracing of an 'objective uncertainty'. If what is believed by faith is uncertain, and thus doubtful, it follows, most would agree, that it is not known to be true. And, for Kierkegaard, if one merely seeks to know the WHAT of religion through a demonstration or by gathering reasons or evidence one ipso facto alienates faith.

But it is not only to demonstrations, reasons, and evidence, and to seeking them, that Kierkegaard objects. His root objection is deeper. It relates to what might be called the 'attitude of knowledge', the attitude intimately associated with knowledge however it is gained. For Kierkegaard, it is this attitude, at bottom, that is antithetical to faith. What, then, does Kierkegaard say about this attitude? In fact he does not in any one place characterise it. But nevertheless we can piece together a characterisation, drawing upon different works but especially the *Postscript*.

For Kierkegaard, knowledge is essentially an objective attitude: it is concerned with the WHAT of belief. For him when 'the objectivity is given' and we know a truth, as we may know a mathematical proposition, the proposition becomes an *indifferent* truth.[177] Those who are concerned 'to know objectively what

Christianity properly is' become *investigators*.[178] They take up the attitude of speculative philosophy, becoming 'objective and abstract'.[179] And 'abstract thought requires [one] to become *disinterested* in order to acquire knowledge'.[180] For Kierkegaard, then, religious knowledge, or one's trying to attain religious knowledge, of WHAT one is to believe, and especially *that* WHAT one is to believe is true, is in various ways at odds with the passion of faith, which for Kierkegaard in the *Postscript* arises precisely from a decision to embrace an uncertainty.

While the *Postscript* is the main work in which Kierkegaard saw faith and knowledge as deeply antithetical,[181] he similarly regards them in other works. In fact perhaps a passage in *Philosophical Fragments* best brings out the Kierkegaardian perception of the antithesis between faith (or belief) and knowledge that informs the *Postscript*. 'Belief', he says in the *Fragments*, 'is not a form of knowledge, but a free act, an expression of will.'[182] It is this act of will that overcomes uncertainty: with faith doubt is 'overcome' by will, as opposed to being resolved by knowledge.[183]

In *Training in Christianity*, published some years after the *Postscript*, Kierkegaard once again is clear that knowledge and faith are deeply antithetical. In *Training* Kierkegaard develops a conception of contemporaneousness with Christ in His humility, and he presents knowledge as at odds with faith because, at bottom, it is at odds with this contemporaneousness. 'About Him [Christ] nothing can be known', Kierkegaard says, 'He can only be believed'.[184] And Kierkegaard says: 'Jesus Christ is the object of faith; one must either believe on Him or be offended. For to "know" signifies exactly that the reference is not to Him.'[185] Again in reference to contemporaneousness, Kierkegaard says that we must not 'fancy presumptuously that we know as a matter of course who He was. For no one *knows* that, and he who *believes* it must be contemporary with Him in His humiliation'.[186] Kierkegaard focus in *Training* is not on the *Postcript* definition of faith, but in *Training* he remains clear that there is an essential opposition between faith (or belief) and knowledge. There is more to be said about Kierkegaard's thinking on faith and knowledge. In the last chapter I shall want to return to Kierkegaard's perception of their essential antipathy and to examine more carefully the germ of that perception. For the present it is sufficient to note the extremity of Kierkegaard's recurring perception that faith and knowledge are antithetical.

This perception is not idiosyncratically Kierkegaardian. It is found in the thinking of more than one religious existentialist.[187] Miguel de Unamuno is one. Unamuno shares Kierkegaard's concern with what it is to be a Christian, and he follows Kierkegaard in his own reflections on faith. For Unamuno faith is 'agonic', and the 'gimlet of doubt' is the 'mother of faith'.[188] Unamuno, following Kierkegaard, makes uncertainty and doubt a condition of belief in God. Obviously, then, Unamuno, like Kierkegaard, must regard knowledge as faith's enemy. For both Kierkegaard in the *Postscript* and Unamuno knowledge is a comforting state that would destroy the passionate uncertainty of faith.

Martin Buber also shares with Kierkegaard strong First-Perspective intuitions about religious knowledge. For Buber making God an object of knowledge renders God an It, or rather, makes that-to-which-we-are-related an It. The God who is a Thou and to whom we may religiously say 'Thou' disappears. To the extent we try to know about God we treat God as a thing to be discussed and used in various ways. God may be religiously encountered as a Thou or described and objectively analysed as an It which is 'absorbed into [our] store of knowledge'.[189] But these two modes are antipodean modes of existence or relationship to what we confront. To the extent we encounter God religiously, of necessity we have renounced knowledge of God. Buber's First-Perspective intuitions, then, are just as strong as Kierkegaard's. However there is a difference between the two. For Kierkegaard knowledge is antithetic to faith. For Buber it is antithetic to an I–Thou encounter. Faith for Buber in *I and Thou* almost assumes a secondary role: it originally 'fills the temporal gaps between the acts of relation' to God, but then it becomes a 'substitute for these acts'.[190] Nevertheless Kierkegaard and Buber agree on the primary First-Perspective point, which, put generally, is that knowledge is deeply opposed to what gives depth to the religious life. There is more that could be said about Buber's thinking here, especially about an important distinction between knowing and 'beholding' that he draws (to which I shall return in Chapter 3). For the present, though, it remains that Buber's intuitions about religious knowledge of God are as negative as Kierkegaard's, if differently based.

Wittgenstein too has First-Perspective intuitions on the place of knowledge in religion, although Wittgenstein's view is not simple or unified. For one thing, as we have seen, there are differences between his early 'Lecture on Ethics' and his later *Lectures on Religious Belief*. In his lecture on ethics, we should recall, his view is that religious expressions are 'mere nonsense' and that ethics (which for Wittgenstein in this lecture includes religion) 'does not add to our knowledge in any sense'. In Wittgenstein's early view, then, of necessity knowledge has no place in religion, for religious expressions are not cognitively meaningful.

Wittgenstein in his later lectures on religious belief is not so clearly non-cognitivist. He seems to leave that issue open. Still, in this work too he clearly has First-Perspective intuitions about religious knowledge. In these lectures he says of religious belief that it is 'unshakeable'. Wittgenstein's saying this may suggest that, for him, religious believers are certain about their belief, and this in turn sounds like the cognitive attitude associated with knowledge. However Wittgenstein carefully cuts off this inference. The unshakeable character of belief shows itself in the 'regulating' function of belief, not in the making of knowledge claims. He grants, or argues, that in religion 'believe' has an extraordinary use – for it is not used to express tentative belief. But, he is clear, 'believe' is not used in religion 'as we generally use the word "know" '.[191] In great part, for Wittgenstein, this is because important connections with testing, evidence and other epistemic cognates simply do not hold in religion. In religion, he says, 'we don't talk about hypothesis, or about high probability, nor about knowing'.[192] This is a grammatical remark on Wittgenstein's part. If such talk had a place in religion, religion would be something else, superstition perhaps or bad science, but not religion. Once again, on this issue as on others, Wittgenstein's intuitions are close to Kierkegaard's, even though the locus of Wittgenstein's reflection, religious discourse, is very different from Kierkegaard's.

Neo-Wittgensteinian intuitions on this issue, as on others, are in basic accord with Wittgenstein's First-Perspective viewpoint. Phillips, who has developed a characteristically Neo-Wittgensteinian view on this issue, is as suspicious of religious knowledge as Wittgenstein. True, he allows himself to speak of knowledge in connection with religious belief in God, but he clearly has something very special in mind. For instance, at one point he suggests that knowledge of God is to be equated with worship.[193] At another point he says that 'to know God is to love

Him'.[194] What he means is that to know God is to come to understand the potential of religious love: as he says, 'seeing that there is a God . . . is synonymous with seeing the possibility of eternal love'.[195] But while Phillips speaks of knowledge of God, he is in basic agreement with Wittgenstein, for he insists that, as he puts it, 'there is no *theoretical* knowledge of God'.[196] That is, there is no knowledge *about* God, no propositional knowledge about God, as a Being over and above the world, to whom the concept *God* applies.

Phillips observes, a little ruefully, that 'contemporary philosophy of religion has benefited little from Wittgenstein's later epistemology'.[197] For Phillips questions in philosophy of religion about the nature of religious belief, rationality, and so on are to be answered by looking at the religious language-game, at the use of religious language in the religious 'context'. And for Phillips, as we have seen, there is no legitimate question about the justification of religious criteria, once they are identified. The philosopher's task is not to justify religious criteria, it is to understand them. Earlier in this chapter we looked at this aspect of Phillips' thought in relation to religious rationality, but he applies it generally to religious concepts and specifically to religious knowledge: if we look at the religious context we will see that religious knowledge is worship or love of God. Philosophers go wrong, Phillips believes, when they ask whether knowledge of God is possible and then proceed to question the applicability of religious concepts to reality.

In Phillips' thinking such an epistemological approach has things absolutely reversed. He quotes Peter Winch:

> Our idea of what belongs to the realm of reality is given for us in the language that we use. The concepts we have settle for us the form of experience we have of the world. . . . The world *is* for us what is presented through those concepts.[198]

Thus there is no meaningful question about knowing that these concepts really apply to the world. Earlier we saw that, for Phillips, the religious language-game internally defines rationality and evidence. Now we see that, for him, as for Winch, it defines the 'world' of the religious. This of course fits with what Phillips said about religious pictures and the impossibility of evaluating religious pictures. Phillips accepts the implication that 'the saint [or believer] and the atheist do not interpret the same world in different ways. They see different worlds'.[199] For Phillips, and for Winch, there can be no question about whether either the saint knows that there is a God or the atheist knows that there is no God. Such questions ask if the concept of God applies to the world, and asking this wrongly presupposes that the worlds of the saint and of the atheist are not defined by their concepts.

Phillips' thinking on religious knowledge is consistent with his thinking on religious reasons or evidence. If there is no 'external' evidence, if there is only 'internal' evidence, then it is natural to conclude both that there can be no religious knowledge that religious concepts apply to reality and that 'There is a God' does not make a cognitive claim whose truth is independent of what religious people say and do. Here, on the issue of religious knowledge, Phillips once again extends Wittgenstein's thought without doing violence to it. Although whether he has paid heed to all of Wittgenstein's thought pertinent to this issue is another matter.

The Second Perspective

The Second Perspective on this issue gives some place in religion to religious knowledge, and usually not an insignificant place. Those with the Second Perspective do not exhibit the First Perspective's suspicion of the hope to attain religious knowledge, and they perceive no antithesis between believers' having religious knowledge and their lives' having religious depth. For the Second Perspective the commitment of believers and their religious practice are not vitiated by their having religious knowledge: one's commitment to God is not lessened by one's knowing that there is a God, it is strengthened they will say; and prayer is not made arid by the knowledge that one's prayer is heard, it is made more serene.

Typically, or often, those with the Second Perspective on the knowledge subissue see all knowledge as comprising a unity; in part this means that they regard the body of all knowledge as consistent. This of course is not to say that for the Second Perspective all knowledge has the same source. And, it does not mean that there is general agreement among those with the Second Perspective on the source, or sources, of religious knowledge. In fact, within the tradition of the Second Perspective there are radical differences. For some, those who follow Aquinas' main line of thought, religious knowledge can have a 'natural' source. For others, who follow a strong strain in Protestant thought, religious knowledge must have a uniquely religious source, the action of the Holy Spirit. Among contemporary or modern philosophers and theologians who have the Second Perspective on this issue, as we might expect, we find appeals to various distinct sources of religious knowledge. Four such sources may be noted: demonstration, miracles, revelation, and experience.

If we construe 'demonstration' broadly, then not all who have defended some form of logical demonstration of God's existence would, like Aquinas, claim that a demonstration can yield knowledge of God's existence. Proponents of the teleological argument, for instance, might well claim that while it supports religious belief it does not give us *knowledge* of God's existence. But Alvin Plantinga would, I think, say that following a logical demonstration can bring one to religious knowledge. Plantinga, who defends the ontological argument in one version, does not go so far as to claim that the ontological argument indeed demonstrates God's existence. He makes the lesser claim that it is rational to accept the ontological argument in one version. So, for Plantinga, a study of the argument may yield only the knowledge that it is rational to believe that there is a God, but, especially from a Second-Perspective standpoint, this is well worth knowing. (I leave aside as too *recherché* the possibility that for Plantinga the argument, instead of yielding knowledge, yields only a rational belief that it is rational to believe that there is a God.)

Miracles also have been seen as a source – a welcome source – of religious knowledge. Miracles of course may be thought of in various ways, and not all religious thinkers who believe and discuss their significance would regard them as avenues to religious knowledge. Still in orthodoxy, for a long time, miracles along with fulfilled prophecy were taken to prove Christianity.[200] Even today in certain theological traditions miracles are regarded as significant for religious knowledge, especially those miracles that involve a violation or breach of the laws of nature. Such miracles, or certain of them, are taken to corroborate Scripture by those who follow at least one strain of contemporary theological thought.

A different source of religious knowledge is revelation. It is possible to argue that revelation, in particular the revelation of Scripture, is to be accepted because the historical miracles establish its Divine source. But it is also possible to regard revelation as an independent source of religious knowledge. This is the position taken by Emil Brunner in his *Revelation and Reason*. In Brunner's view miracles should only be ' "signs" or suggestions, or indications' for anyone who believes in Jesus Christ: they are 'in no case', he says, 'the basis of belief'.[201] It is true, he allows in a footnote, that the 'proof from miracles' once played a large part in orthodoxy, but only through confusion; now miracles are seen to be less a support and more a burden for apologetics. For Brunner we put things backwards if we regard miracles as support for belief. Take the miracle of the resurrection: Faith in the Godhead of Jesus Christ is not based on the resurrection, he says; rather, belief in the resurrection is the result of belief in the Godhead of Jesus. Finally revelation, Brunner says, is 'the source of all the knowledge of faith'.[202] Revelation is of God, and God reveals himself through theophanies, angels, dreams, oracles, visions, locutions, through natural phenomena and historical events, and through guidance given to human beings and through the words and deeds of the prophets. The Bible itself is not only a record of revelation, it is revelation.[203]

Although revelation for Brunner is or gives knowledge of God (especially in His final self-manifestation in Jesus Christ), this knowledge is unlike 'ordinary knowledge', which is always knowledge 'of an object'. Unlike ordinary knowledge, knowledge of God given by revelation creates 'community' and brings us to 'communion with Him', a communion characterised by love.[204]

Revelation is, Brunner says, 'a knowledge that is unexpected'. It is not gained by our own efforts; it is a gift, with the character of a sudden event.[205] For Brunner, 'revealed knowledge is poles apart from rational knowledge'. But Brunner sees no essential conflict between revelation and reason; indeed, he allows, whoever forms sentences, including sentences found in the Bible, uses reason. Revelation's enemy is not reason; it is the 'irrational arrogance of those who pride themselves on their intellect' and the 'irrational self-sufficiency of reason'.[206] Not surprisingly, then, for Brunner faith has no interest in the proofs for the existence of God, and in any case, he affirms, echoing Pascal and Buber, the proofs do not prove the existence of the 'Living God of Faith'.[207] Here as elsewhere Brunner to some extent has First-Perspective intuitions. He not only rejects miracles as a source of religious knowledge but he rejects them as any support for belief (in accord with First-Perspective intuitions on the fourth subissue). Yet in regard to this issue – about the place of knowledge in religion – Brunner's viewpoint is resolutely Second-Perspective. Though he may disagree with fundamentalism about miracles as a source of religious knowledge, and though he may disagree with the Thomistic tradition, and Plantinga, about proofs as a source of religious knowledge, he is as clear as he can be that there is religious knowledge of God – but its source, its only source, is revelation.

Other religious thinkers consider another source – religious experience – to be a significant source of religious knowledge. H. D. Lewis, as we have seen, regards experience of God to not only be possible for individuals, but to be possible for individuals in a variety of forms. However, it is perhaps John Baillie, in his book *Our Knowledge of God*, who most clearly and emphatically espouses religious experience as a source of religious knowledge.

Baillie agrees with Brunner that God does not come to be known by logical argumentation of any kind.[208] For Baillie God is not an object to be inferred, but a Presence to be encountered. Without the experience of an encounter with God argumentation is pointless; with it argumentation is a superfluous addition. As Baillie puts it at one point, 'our knowledge of God's reality' does not come to us 'as the result of an inference of any kind, whether explicit or implicit, whether laboriously excogitated or swiftly intuited'; rather it comes 'through our direct personal encounter with Him in the Person of Jesus Christ His Son our Lord'.[209]

For Baillie, as for Buber, God is encountered as a Person, as a Presence. In religious experience for Baillie we nevertheless come to have knowledge of God, specifically of His reality, but of more as well. Significantly, for Baillie, we come to have knowledge of God as moral authority. Knowledge of God first came to him, Baillie reflects, 'in the form of an awareness that I was "not my own" but one under authority, one who "owed" something, one who "ought" to be something which he was not'.[210] This awareness, he feels sure, came from 'the spiritual climate of the home into which I was born'.

This moral dimension of religious experience, or encounter, is central, even paramount, for Baillie. Because it is Baillie believes that 'all peoples' have an awareness of the Divine, at least to some extent.[211] Lewis in *Our Experience of God* is broadly sympathetic to Baillie's perspective, as we can well understand. However Lewis is concerned with Baillie's tendency to consider 'an uneasy conscience' to be a religious encounter with the Divine. Such an equation, Lewis argues, supports Baillie's view that all have had experience of God at the cost of a 'grave attenuation' of what Christians understand by a religious encounter with God in Christ.[212] But, as we have seen, Lewis would agree with Baillie that our experience of God does not come apart from other experience[213] – such as Baillie's experience in his childhood home. Both Lewis and Baillie hold that experience of God is imbedded in our everyday experience.

In a similar way Baillie is not so very far from Brunner, even though Baillie's central categories are *knowledge* and *experience* and Brunner's central category is *revelation*. Their closeness comes out in those instances when Baillie refers to his or another's encounter with God's Presence as 'revelation' or God's 'reveal[ing] Himself'.[214] Both Baillie and Brunner are, as it were, looking at the same religious phenomenon, but Brunner focuses on one side (God's revealing Himself) and Baillie focuses on the other (a human being's experiencing an encounter with God). For both the result is knowledge of God.

Finally in this section let us turn again to the religious thought of John Hick. As we saw in the last section, Hick in *Faith and Knowledge* considers the nature of religious experience and its relation to the freedom of faith. In addition Hick examines *knowing*, *awareness*, and related concepts as they pertain to the believer's epistemic relation to God.[215] According to Hick's analysis, certain or 'infallible' knowledge – religious or otherwise – is not obtainable. But for Hick religious knowledge can be obtained; however it is or involves faith.

Hick's analysis merits our attention. Although we cannot in this context examine it in great detail, we can and should examine its outline. For Hick there are three levels or spheres of human experience; in order of ascending inclusion they are: the natural, the moral, and the religious. In each sphere, Hick finds, if perceptions are to be made, an act of interpretation is required. In the moral sphere, for Hick, our perception of our responsibilities and obligations requires a 'voluntary' interpretation of the significance of an ambiguous 'given', namely those moral situations in which moral judgements must be made. In the same way in the natural sphere our perception that there are material objects and our perceptions of what they are – hats and books and such – require that we interpret a given, although in this sphere the interpretive act is nearly vestigial and less truly voluntary. (In fact, as we saw in the last section, for Hick our experience of the material world is 'compelled'. This, however, does not mean for Hick that there is no interpretive act at this level of experience; it means that 'the margin of cognitive freedom is here a narrow one'.)[216] In the religious sphere the structure of experience is the same: once more an ambiguous given – this time all of life – must be interpreted as to its significance. It can be interpreted religiously (that is, theistically) or non-religiously, Hick allows. Neither interpretation is necessitated or ruled out by his analysis. But if in the religious sphere the interpretive act is religious, then it corresponds to faith. In this way faith is, or is involved in, religious knowledge of God's existence. For, just as an act of interpretation is allowed and even required by our moral knowledge of our obligations and our natural knowledge of the material world, so too an act of interpretation – faith – is required by and makes possible a believer's religious knowledge. True, we do not have 'infallible knowledge' in the religious sphere, but then we do not in the other spheres either. In each, given experience, knowledge claims can be reasonable, and in this sense knowledge is available. Thus, for Hick, we can have religious knowledge for the same reason, or the same kind of reason, that we can have moral knowledge and knowledge of the material world.

We see, then, that Hick endeavours to clarify religion's basic epistemic concepts through a descriptive analysis of the use of epistemic concepts both inside and outside religious belief. Characterised in this way his philosophical approach may seem Wittgensteinian. In fact, though, his method and procedure are distinct from those of Neo-Wittgensteinians like Phillips and Winch. They are for several reasons: (i) Hick accepts the apologetic thrust of his analysis, in contrast to the Neo-Wittgensteinian renunciation of any apologetic effort, (ii) Hick looks at secular as well as religious use and does not compartmentalise them as distinct 'language-games', and (iii) Hick emphasises that religious belief makes a cognitive claim held to be true by believers independently of anyone's believing or disbelieving it.[217]

It is a virtue of Hick's analysis, I believe, that it addresses secular as well as the religious use of *knowledge* and cognate concepts. At least his analysis thereby avoids some of the problems that relate to Neo-Wittgensteinian 'internal' constructions of, for instance, rationality. Moreover Hick has not lost sight of what in the last section I called the 'moral dimension' of religious belief. It is perhaps another virtue of his analysis that it attempts to bring together in an intelligible way the decision-element of faith (as a voluntary interpretive act) and the cognitive requirements of religious knowledge (the need for suport or grounding for religious knowledge claims). Those with the First Perspective on this issue may, like Kierkegaard, clearly recognise the moral dimension of faith, but they deny religious knowledge; on the other hand those with the Second Perspective proclaim the possibility of religious knowledge, but especially if, like Aquinas or Plantinga, they offer a philosophical account of religious knowledge with a natural source, they often do so without finding a place for faith's moral dimension. Hick's Second-Perspective philosophical analysis, successfully or unsuccessfully, attempts to give a place to religious knowledge that is compatible with, and even dependent on, faith's moral dimension.

Beyond these virtues (as they seem to me to be), to what extent is Hick's analysis of religious knowledge correct? I shall take up this question, as well as related questions about, for instance, the Neo-Wittgensteinian internal views of rationality and evidence, in the last two chapters.

Now let me state what seem to me to be the strengths of the two perspectives on the knowledge subissue.

Strengths of the First Perspective. The First Perspective rightly insists upon the central place in religious belief of passion and emotional commitment, and it reminds us of the role of will in religious commitment and faith; it thereby brings before us and makes us recognise both the prima facie tension between faith as committed belief and the attitude of knowledge and the prima facie tension between faith as an act of will and the requirements of religious knowledge.

Strengths of the Second Perspective. Those with the Second Perspective recognise that many believers have a deep conviction that their fundamental beliefs about the universe are true and even, at times, proclaim their knowledge. To the extent that the Second Perspective posits religious knowledge it avoids making faith an arbitrary choice or a matter of taste or mere convention. Moreover, those with the Second Perspective who allow that religious believers at times are certain avoid condemning believers to an irrational certainty without knowledge.

III CONCLUSION

I believe that many religious persons, especially those who have thought about their religion, find themselves attracted to one or the other of the two perspectives that I have explored in this chapter. In fact – and this is the main thing that I wanted to bring out – *both* perspectives are attractive, both appeal with good reason to aspects of religious sensitivity. Consequently it is not surprising that some philosophers, like Robert Herbert and John Hick, tend toward one perspective on some issues and toward the other perspective on other issues. And it is not surprising that some philosophers, like Kierkegaard and Wittgenstein, show an ambivalent tendency toward both perspectives on certain single issues. In this chapter I have stressed their dominant First-Perspective tendencies, but both Kierkegaard and Wittgenstein display Second-Perspective intuitions as well. Kierkegaard in *Fear and Trembling* projects a Biblical model of faith appropriate to Job and Abraham (Abraham is Kierkegaard's example), which is very different from his *Postcript* model and in which the 'knight of faith' is portrayed as knowing.[218] And Wittgenstein at one point in *Philosophical Investigations* admits as meaningful the question whether a picture applies to reality.[219] When we extend this strand of Wittgenstein's thought to religious pictures we find countenanced the possibility of knowing that a religious picture applies to reality.

It remains, however, that the two perspectives are antithetical and opposed almost with animosity at many points of contact. The two perspectives pull in different directions, and hence they pose a philosophical problem of the deepest and truest sort for a believer, a problem at once philosophical, theological, and personal. For non-believers too a problem is posed, at least for those who gaze with wonder or perplexity at belief in God or who, confronted by the faith of their fathers, are concerned to argue for the rejection of belief. It behooves us, then, whether we are believers or non-believers, to resolve or in some way to come to terms with the problem that these opposed perspectives create, that is, the problem of the cognitivity of religion. In the remainder of the book I shall address this task.

I conclude this chapter with an invitation to the reader to turn to the final paragraphs of sections (1)–(5) above and to review the strengths of the two perspectives on each of the five subissues. Doing so will help keep vivid the richness of the two perspectives and their multifarious points of contact and antithesis.

2 The Third Perspective

I INTRODUCTION

In the first chapter we looked at two religious perspectives on the issue of cognitivity, each of which appeals to religious intuitions and each of which in some way captures a part of the truth, although a tension exists between the two. There is also a Third Perspective on religious cognitivity that is identifiable within the Judaeo-Christian heritage. This is not to say that it is limited to that heritage, and in fact it is not. Given the aetiology of the concerns of this book, however, I shall focus on the Third Perspective in its Judaeo-Christian manifestation, as I have done for the first two perspectives. Nevertheless at times I shall point out how the Third Perspective applies to other religious traditions. In the Judaeo-Christian heritage the Third Perspective is embodied in the reflections of certain though not all mystics, in the sensibilities of the authors of various devotional works, and pre-eminently in the Psalms. Also the Third Perspective is found in other styles of religious reflection and expression. Those philosophers of religion and religious thinkers who look to the kind of religious experience that informs the Psalms, to the extent they do so, stand over toward the Third Perspective. And this is so despite whatever sympathies they may have for the First or Second Perspective. In this way John Baillie and H. D. Lewis, for instance, reflect a disposition toward the Third Perspective. It remains, though, that in the Judaeo-Christian tradition the home of the Third Perspective is in the Psalms and, secondarily, in certain mystical and devotional works. At least this is true so far as written religious expression is concerned. One could also say that the home of the Third Perspective is found in the lives, the sensibilities, and the self-understanding of many individual believers.

I do not mean to say that the Psalmist[1] or any mystic or indeed any religious writer has set forth the Third Perspective as a defined perspective in contrast with the first two. I do not believe that any has. Although several mystics, and others, have, I think, instinctively reacted against aspects of the first two perspectives. Still the framework of the Third Perspective has not been set forth, not fully, and not so as to bring out its contrast with the first two perspectives. In this chapter and the next I hope to do two main things: to delineate the Third Perspective and to present its framework. In this chapter I shall try to set out what I perceive to be at the heart of the Third Perspective, a type of religious discovery. In the next chapter I shall fill in the framework of the Third Perspective, and bring it into relief against the First and Second Perspectives. This I shall do by applying the Third Perspective to each of the five subissues of the general issue of cognitivity. If all goes as I hope, the result will be that the Third Perspective, mediating between the other two, will mitigate their differences and lessen their opposition while respecting their strengths. In this way perhaps a contribution will have been made to the task I identified at the end of the last chapter, that of resolving or lessening the issue of cognitivity.

We shall begin this chapter with a renewed discussion of religious rationality, but not because a concern with rationality is at the heart of the Third Perspective: it is not. I have two reasons for choosing the avenue of rationality. First, the question of religious rationality is an aggravated issue between the First and Second Perspectives, and the Third Perspective bids fair to resolve their differences on it. Second, the rationality concern naturally introduces a consideration of what I have said is at the heart of the Third Perspective, a type of religious discovery; this type of discovery, as we shall see, has significant implications for rationality and the nature of rationality.

II   RATIONALITY AND DISCOVERY

(1) Some Turns in the Concept of Rationality

In philosophy there is a main traditional way of understanding rationality as it applies to belief, a way not only evident in the writings of philosophers of various stripes but embodied in the way most of us a lot of the time use the word 'rational'. In this traditional conception of rationality, there is an essential connection between one's holding a rational belief and one's having evidence for what one believes. Moreover, when the traditional understanding of the connection between rational belief and evidence is unfolded, that connection is seen to contain several elements. These two seem to be necessary elements: (i) when belief is rational, the strength of belief is proportionate to the evidence for it, and (ii) when belief is rational, one investigates to see what evidence there is for and what evidence there is against the belief before embracing it. The home of this conception, it should be observed, is *investigation* or intellectual enquiry. Its paradigmatic application is to the verification of hypotheses or, more humbly, to the confirming of suspicions and tentative thoughts, as is done in various intellectual pursuits and in everyday life. The model of rationality projected by this traditional view is what we may call an enquiry-model.

This of course is the view of rationality held by W. K. Clifford (James's adversary) and also, to a great extent, the view held by 'rational believers' and 'devout sceptics'. But also this view of rationality, if it is not held, is not objected to by several of the religious thinkers that we have discussed on both the First-Perspective and Second-Perspective sides. On the Second-Perspective side George Schlesinger would no doubt accept it. Plantinga, the author of *God and Other Minds* and *The Nature of Necessity*, also seems to accept it. (As we shall see shortly, however, the later Plantinga has a changed view.)

Somewhat surprisingly perhaps, on the First-Perspective side Kierkegaard, Wittgenstein, and Phillips all accept this conception of rationality, or so it seems to me. Let us consider Wittgenstein and Phillips. To be sure, neither argues that religious belief *is* rational in this conception. Both reject the applicability to religion of 'rationality' *tout court*, but in doing so both seem to have in mind this conception and its enquiry-model of rationality. Wittgenstein says that religious belief is neither rational nor irrational in part because believers do not try to hold their beliefs with a conviction related to evidence – pretty clearly a reference to one of the elements of the traditional conception. Phillips has what I called an *internal* view of religious rationality (and an internal view of religious evidence as well). According to Phillips, rationality relates to religion, but (like religious reasons or evidence) it has an internal meaning determined by religious practice. However this is not to say that Phillips challenges the traditional conception of rationality. Rather, he restricts its scope. And, given his concerns, he need restrict it only so that religion is excluded. While for Phillips there is no one paradigm of rationality and, instead, each different context (science, art, etc.) has its own rationality, in saying this he does not challenge the application of the traditional conception and its enquiry model to contexts other than religion. In fact he implicitly allows the traditional view to reign outside religion.

I think that Wittgenstein and Phillips are correct to be suspicious of applying this traditional conception and its enquiry-model of rationality to religious belief. Perhaps it applies to some forms of Judaeo-Christian belief, for instance the 'hypothetical faith' discussed by King-Farlow and Christensen, but it does not apply to the religious tradition of the Psalms. At least to this extent the First-Perspective intuitions of Wittgenstein and Phillips seem to be right. However, if I may say of Phillips what he says of John Wisdom, I do not believe that he has gone far enough. To the extent that he and Wittgenstein – at least the Wittgenstein of *Lectures on Religious Belief* – keep before themselves exclusively this conception of rationality they fail to consider other ways of thinking of religion's rationality. They have not gone far enough in that they have not questioned whether there are legitimate alternatives to the enquiry-model of rationality *both inside and outside religion*, which is to say legitimate alternatives other than Phillips' internal sense of religious rationality.

Are there alternative ways of thinking of rationality that may be more suitable to religion? Several have thought so. Let us look at three such views, each of which to some extent challenges the exclusivity of the traditional conception and its enquiry-model of rationality.

The first is that of William James. While James for the most part accepts the traditional conception of rationality, he tries to clarify it, or to modify it, in an important way. James's addition to the traditional conception is this: If after investigation we find that evidence is insufficient to decide an issue of belief, and the issue is 'forced', so that we must decide one way or the other, then it is 'lawful' to decide on the basis of 'passional need'. James's addition, though, works a significant change in the traditional conception: it allows a belief to be rational, under certain circumstances, when sufficient evidence is lacking. I shall not here repeat the earlier discussion of James's view of rationality (see Chapter 1, section (1) for that); rather I shall now take a more critical look at his view, especially in its application to religious belief.

The main problem with James's pragmatic justification of belief is one that is familar: in general pragmatic reasons do not provide a rational justification for belief; instead, when an issue is 'forced', they provide a rational justification for *acting as though* a belief were true. This criticism applies to James's view as it relates to belief generally and as it relates to religious belief specifically. To help crystallise the point of the criticism consider the following case. A man is lost in a mountain range in the desert. If he remains where he is he will soon die. He knows that the settlement of Last Chance is somewhere nearby, but he does not know where. But, in any case, only one route is open to him. So he has two choices: remain where he is (and die of exposure) or begin walking along the route open to him (in the hope that it will lead to Last Chance). In these circumstances, it will be allowed, pragmatic considerations make it rational for him to choose to walk along the route open to him and to act as though it will lead to Last Chance. But this is not to say that it is rational for him to believe that this route does indeed lead to Last Chance – he still has no reason to think this. In the same way, in religion, pragmatic reasons would seem to justify, not religious belief, but, at most, acting as though religious belief were true.

On James's behalf, however, it can be argued that there are exceptions that elude this criticism. James in one of his essays brings forward such a case.[2] We are to imagine a mountaineer climbing in the Alps. He finds himself in a position from which he can escape only by making a terrible leap across a chasm, and he must make the leap or perish. The rational thing for him to do, we will agree, is to leap. But, moreover, we are asked to allow, his really believing that he will leap the chasm will help him to succeed. His believing it to be true will help make it true. In such a case as this it does seem arguable that it is rational for the mountaineer to believe that he can make the leap (and not just to act as though he could). It even seems rational for him to believe this in the face of strong evidence to the contrary; for, we are allowing, his belief will help increase what chances he has to make the leap, and the greater his conviction the better his chances. However this kind of case does not help James argue for the rationality of *religious* belief. It does not because if this kind of case is an exception to the criticism it is only because in this kind of case someone's believing that something is true helps to bring about the desired state of affairs and hence the truth of the belief. And nothing like this is the case regarding religious belief in God. With anything like a traditional understanding of religious belief, belief in God does not help bring about the reality of God's existence. The more analogous case is the one we had at first – the lost-in-the-desert case – and there the criticism seems to hold. Of course regarding religious beliefs James appeals to pragmatic reasons of a different sort – our passional needs – but still he appeals to pragmatic reasons. As such it appears that they would provide, at most, a rational justification for acting as though religious belief were true, not a rational justification for religious belief.

It seems to me that this criticism of James's view of religious rationality is very strong. It does, however, make an assumption, namely, that acting as though a belief were true is distinguishable from holding a belief to be true, distinguishable from actually believing it. This assumption has been challenged by some. As King-Farlow and Christensen construe James's best case, James denies this assumption and, in effect, defines believing that a proposition is true as being measurably willing to act on that proposition.[3] It is true that if James does not say this he very nearly does.[4] Is this equation correct? I think not. Surely in the lost-in-the-desert case the man lost can say, and correctly say, 'I have no idea whether this is the way to Last Chance (I do not hold that belief), but I had better proceed as though it were (I will prudently act as though that belief were true).'

James's (or King-Farlow and Christensen's) equation then seems dubious. But to the extent that it is shown to be dubious, other things being equal, the above criticism is shown to be correct. Stephen Davis, though, argues that James's 'right to believe' doctrine can be rewritten to avoid the equation of belief and the tendency to act.[5] Davis' reformulation states that when a decision between two hypotheses is forced and cannot be made by a person on the basis of evidence (that is, 'public evidence' in Davis' sense), still 'with full epistemological justification he can choose between the hypotheses on some basis other than evidence and can tentatively (i.e., with his mind still open) accept the hypothesis chosen and act as if it were true'. And for Davis tentatively accepting the hypothesis chosen does not entail, nor is it entailed by, acting as if it were true. For Davis both are justified.

Does Davis' reformulation resuscitate James's pragmatic justification of religious belief? To begin with, it would seem that if Davis' reformulation succeeds in keeping apart accepting a belief and acting as though a belief were true, then once more pragmatic considerations will justify only the latter, for the reasons that we have seen. However, Davis holds that considerations other than evidence could justify a *tentative* acceptance of a belief with a mind open to any evidence found in the future. By 'tentative acceptance' Davis does not mean a necessarily weak acceptance. He is aware that religious believers often hold their beliefs with great conviction. But if such a 'tentative acceptance' is justified by our passional needs (or other non-evidential bases Davis mentions – expediency, flipping a coin),[6] it would seem to be nothing beyond the *lack of rejection* of a belief in the absence of evidence, which is very far from conviction. Nevertheless, for the sake of argument, let us follow Davis and allow that pragmatic reasons can make it rational to believe with conviction. Still, limiting consideration to James's pragmatic reason, our passional needs (as opposed to Davis' wider category of non-evidential, private bases), this justification will not address religious belief when, in the self-understanding of believers, their belief amounts to religious knowledge. It will not address those believers who are certain in their belief *because* they believe that they have come to know God. Thus, even with this generous application of James's rationale, it will not apply to many believers. In particular, it will not apply to those in the Psalmist's tradition, whose certainty, in their own understanding, does not derive from their passional need to belief, but rather from what they regard as their experience of God's presence.

Finally, then, it seems that James's pragmatic justification of religious belief does not adequately address religious belief. To the extent that it applies to religious belief (as opposed to those situations in which one's holding a belief helps bring about the truth of the belief), it seems that what is justified is not religious belief, but, at most, acting as though religious belief were true. And even if, following Davis, we allow that pragmatic reasons can justify a tentative belief in God, religious belief that is held to be certain will not necessarily thereby be justified; moreover such a justification does not apply to the religious belief of those who are certain because in their self-understanding they have come to know God through their own experience.

James and those sympathetic to his approach are not the only ones to give an account of rationality that would challenge the exclusivity of the traditional conception and its enquiry model of rationality. A second attempt to give an alternative account of rationality does not stress the difference between religious and scientific attitudes toward belief (as James does), but instead emphasises how, at bottom, religion and science both must rely upon faith. Raphael Demos has developed such a view.[7]

Religion, Demos allows, accepts it that God exists without deductive demonstration and without empirical evidence. In this sense the belief that God exists is without rational justification and is an article of faith. It is an 'ultimate belief' or a 'basic belief' that does not rest on evidential support. But, Demos argues, science is in the same epistemological boat. True, science seeks evidence to verify its hypotheses. Nevertheless it has ultimate beliefs that are presupposed by its conception of evidence. It assumes that sense experience can be relied upon to confirm a theory and that those data that reflect reality are intersubjective. Moreover, for Demos, it must assume that there are persons, that is, other reporters of sense experience. Science also accepts Occam's principle as an ultimate belief. And, along with common sense, it accepts it as an ultimate belief that memory is trustworthy. In addition, notoriously, science accepts the principle of induction without non-circular grounds. For Demos these ultimate beliefs or presuppositions are without evidential support just as the religious belief in God is. So both science and religion have 'faiths', that is groundless propositions that must be accepted on faith.

Demos does not conclude that since science is rational therefore religion is. In fact he draws no general conclusion about the rationality of religion. But, given his argument, it would follow that religion in accepting ultimate beliefs is no more irrational than science. In this way Demos in effect presents a defense of religion's rationality which rests not on special grounds found by enquiry, but on the necessity of there being for both religion and science some ultimate beliefs which do not rest upon evidence.

Some would question whether all of the beliefs that Demos regards as ultimate for science are indeed without evidential support. Some perhaps would even maintain that none of the propositions that Demos identifies is ultimate in his sense, not even the principle of induction. However, even assuming that science has ultimate beliefs, problems remain for Demos' account. One problem that Demos himself raises is that of distinguishing true from false faiths, true from false ultimate beliefs.

But there is another, and to my mind, more serious problem regarding Demos' account of religious belief, a problem related to the concern of Neo-Wittgensteinians and others that religion not be made theoretical. Given Demos' account, both religion and science have ultimate beliefs, beliefs without evidential grounds. However, by putting religion and science in the same epistemological position, his account is disastrous for religion. Sophisticated scientists might accept it that science has ultimate beliefs and proceed to use the principle of induction, or to rely upon other ultimate beliefs, because doing so serves their ends: doing so allows them to conduct research, make what their fellow scientists agree are discoveries, and even to contribute to the development of technology. They have a kind of pragmatic justification, not for saying that their ultimate beliefs are true, but for using them as rules for scientific activity. And being sophisticated they are not embarrassed by this. Their claim, after all, would not be that their ultimate beliefs are true, but that using them works – as it patently does. They could even be unconcerned about their truth – as long as they work. But religious believers cannot be so sophisticated, not if they are to retain something close to traditional belief. Those believers who followed what William James called the 'Mind-cure movement'[8] gloried in the healthy effects of healthy religious belief. They even took these effects to be reasons to believe. Still, if I am not mistaken, they were not so sophisticated as to say, 'For all I know or care there is no God, but believing in God works wonders for me.' If Demos' account were correct, and religious faith were like scientific faith, the reflective believer, on analogy with the sophisticated scientist, should end by saying just this. Demos presents a new view of rationality that departs from the traditional view, and he marshals his view to give comfort to religion. But it is not religious belief that receives the comfort. It rather is a kind of non-belief, analogous to the sophisticated scientist's attitude toward science's ultimate beliefs, which construes them not as beliefs but as useful rules.

The third view of rationality that we should examine is one

articulated and discussed by Alvin Plantinga in his work since *God and Other Minds* and *The Nature of Necessity*. In *Gods and Other Minds* and in *The Nature of Necessity* Plantinga defends belief in God, or the rationality of belief in God, by investigatively gathering and marshalling support for the belief that God exists. However in two recent essays he takes a different tack.[9] In these essays he discusses *foundationalism*. This is the view that a belief is rational only if it is evident with respect to the beliefs that form a foundation for a person's 'noetic structure'.[10] A belief can be evident with respect to a person's foundational set of beliefs in two ways, either of which will make it a rational belief. First, it can be supported by the beliefs in the foundational set; in this case foundational beliefs are *evidence* for the belief in question. Second, the belief in question can itself be a proper part of the foundation, a 'properly basic belief'. (Thus, to use one of Plantinga's examples, his belief that $72 \times 71 = 5112$, which is based on other beliefs, including the beliefs that $1 \times 72 = 72$ and $7 \times 2 = 14$, is not basic; while his belief that $2 + 1 = 3$, which he does not accept on the basis of any other beliefs, is basic and presumably properly basic.) Plantinga in these essays is especially, even exclusively, interested in the second way that a belief can be rational and in the possibility that religious belief might be rational in this way. To an extent his categories are like those Demos uses: both speak of 'basic beliefs', and for both basic beliefs do not rest on other beliefs. But for Demos science and religion – areas of human endeavour and commitment – have ultimate or basic beliefs, while for Plantinga it is persons, or their noetic structures, that have basic beliefs. This is a difference that makes a difference.

Plantinga's central question is: might not one's belief in God itself be in the foundation of one's noetic structure? (Plantinga means the belief that God exists, and in discussing his view I shall follow his usage.) Might not belief in God – belief that God exists – be a properly basic belief? At any rate this is the central question in one essay. In the other he allows that 'it isn't the relatively high level and general proposition *God exists* that is properly basic, but instead propositions detailing some of his attributes or actions'.[11] Examples of such beliefs, supplied by Plantinga, are: 'God is speaking to me', 'God has created all this [the universe]', 'God disapproves of what I have done', 'God forgives me' and 'God is to be thanked and praised.' But since each of these, as Plantinga says, 'self-evidently entails that God exists', the issue is not shifted much. Plantinga for the most part, for the sake of simplicity, discusses the issue as though it were over whether belief in God's existence is properly basic. If belief in God's existence is properly basic, then it will be rational, not because it is supported by evidence, but because it is part of the foundation of a noetic structure.

But, Plantinga appreciates, many would object to the idea that belief in God might properly be in the foundational set of beliefs for a noetic structure. According to what Plantinga calls 'classical foundationalism', in order for a proposition to be properly basic for a person it must be either self-evident or incorrigible, or, for the ancient and medieval form of classical foundationalism, it must be self-evident or 'evident to the senses'.[12] Plantinga maintains, though, that we are under no obligation to accept either principle. Neither is self-evident nor deductively established. Modern foundationalists may accept it that only propositions that are self-evident or incorrigible can be properly basic for a person, but in fact they have no reason at all for accepting this.[13] It is a belief they simply adopt as basic (despite the fact that, since it itself is neither self-evident nor incorrigible, it violates the very principle it embodies). Why then cannot belief in God be properly basic for believers? Plantinga finds no reason why it cannot be.

The main problem with Plantinga's new idea regarding religious rationality is one that he himself identifies. As he puts it, it is this: 'If belief in God is properly basic why can't *just any* belief be properly basic?' And he allows the objector to ask, 'What about voodoo or astrology? What about the belief that the Great Pumpkin returns every Halloween? Could I properly take *that* as basic?'[14]

Plantinga, however, argues that allowing belief in God is properly basic does not commit one to accepting just any belief as properly basic. Even though there is no strict criterion that excludes belief in the Great Pumpkin as properly basic, we can fairly reject it. We can for the same reason that someone who does not accept the positivists' strict criterion for meaning could still reject as nonsense 'Twas brillig; and the slithy toves did gyve and gymble in the wabe'. Just as no criterion is necessary in the second case, none is necessary in the first case.[15]

Plantinga's point has a point, I think. But it applies better to the Great Pumpkin belief than to the others he mentions. It may be granted by all that, even without a formulated criterion for properly basic beliefs, 'The Great Pumpkin returns every Halloween' can be fairly rejected as a properly basic belief. After all, no one believes in the Great Pumpkin. The other cases, voodoo and astrology, which Plantinga drops from discussion are different. These are beliefs held by people; they are live beliefs and present something more of an issue. Even harder to dismiss is the belief that there is no God. The real issue here might be put this way: Why should not 'There is no God', instead of 'There is a God' be counted properly basic – or can one be properly basic for one person and the other properly basic for another person?

This last possibility seems to emerge as a real possibility for Plantinga in the light of his argument that criteria for properly basic beliefs must be reached from below rather than from above.[16] That is, such criteria should not be presented as *ex cathedra*; they should emerge from a relevant set of examples of beliefs that we accept as rational and proper. And, Plantinga says, 'the Christian community is responsible to *its* set of examples'.[17] not to other sets of examples that others accept. But if so, and if we can say the same for the community of atheists, then belief in God will be properly basic for one group and belief that there is no God will be properly basic for the other.

Thus 'There is a God' and 'There is no God' could be rational for different persons. At first this does not seem alarming. In fact it is almost a commonplace that a belief can be rational for one person and its contradictory rational for another person. 'The world is flat' was a rational belief for antiquity, though its contradictory is the received rational belief today. This epistemological phenomenon is explained by the fact that different persons, at different times or in different circumstances, may have access to different parts of the relevant evidence. In such cases if both parties came to be acquainted with all of the evidence available to all parties, then, other things being equal, one party on pain of irrationality will have to adjust his or her belief. As we might put it, in such cases both of two contradictory beliefs are contingently and biographically rational (for the rationality of at least one belief, if persisted in, may be changed by new evidence coming into the ken of the holder of the belief), but they are not flatly and absolutely rational (so that the rationality of each is established regardless of what new evidence emerges).

However, if we start with different sets of examples of rational belief, one set accepted by one group, one set by another, and these different sets in effect embody different criteria for rationality from which there is no appeal, then on this view contradictory beliefs will be flatly and absolutely rational. And it is in this position that I think Plantinga ends up.

Finally, then, it seems to me that Plantinga's view of religious rationality has trouble escaping from the toils of relativism, and this means that belief in God, if basic, may be rational for religious believers, but only in the same closed and internal way the belief that there is no God may be rational for atheists. Perhaps some religious believers would count their belief rational in just this way, but I am sure that at least some would not.

And so, if I am right, Plantinga's later view of rationality, like the views of James and Demos, presents problems when it is applied to religious belief. I would like to conclude this section, however, with some reflections on the shift in Plantinga's thinking and on the new role he gives to grounds. At the end of one essay he says this:

> The mature believer, the mature theist, does not typically accept belief in God tentatively, or hypothetically, or until something better comes along. . . . The mature theist *commits* himself to belief in God; this means that he accepts belief in God as basic.[18]

The rejection of hypothetical belief, the stress on commitment: these are in accord with First-Perspective intuitions (just as relativism seems to be more of a First-Perspective problem than a Second-Perspective problem). Yet Plantinga retains a good part of his Second-Perspective orientation. He is, after all, still seeking a defence of religious rationality. And, moreover, he has not closed the door completely on religious evidence. For Plantinga saying that belief in God is properly basic does not mean 'that there are no justifying circumstances' for belief in God.[19] In this sense properly basic beliefs need not be groundless. As Plantinga understands Reformed thinking, Calvin and Reformed theologians allow that belief in God, though basic, does have grounds. 'Calvin', Plantinga says,

> holds that God 'reveals and daily discloses himself to the whole workmanship of the universe,' and the divine art 'reveals itself

in the innumerable and yet distinct and well ordered variety of the heavenly host.'[20]

But Plantinga does not call these grounds evidence since, for him, evidence takes the form of a further belief or proposition, and these grounds are experiential as opposed to propositional (let us not worry unduly about whether what Plantinga allows as grounds can be recast as propositional evidence).

Just here something instructive begins to emerge, it seems to me: sooner rather than later reflection on the nature of rationality as it applies to religious belief brings us back to reflection on the nature of *evidential support* as it applies to religious belief. For Plantinga belief in God, if basic, may have grounds but no evidence. For Malcolm and Wittgenstein, on the other hand, religious belief is groundless (and for them there is no important difference between evidence and grounds). At the same time H. D. Lewis finds no problem in speaking of evidence for religious belief. All of these thinkers (as well as others, like John Hick and Robert Herbert) have a sense of the importance of the kind of religious experience referred to by Calvin, which is the kind of experience embodied in the Psalms. The question is: What is that significance, and how does it bear on religious rationality and on evidence for religious belief? The Third Perspective, as we shall see, has an answer to this question.

(2) Realisation-Discoveries

We find then, it seems to me, that the two hard issues of the nature of rationality as it relates to religion and the nature of evidence as it relates to religion are joined, and joined in such a way that not much progress can be made discussing one in isolation from the other. Consequently I shall pursue the two together. However, rather than take up the issue of rationality and its logical connection to evidence in a direct way, I want now to turn our attention to a neglected category in religious epistemology, the category of *discovery*. For, as I believe we shall see, this new category provides a fruitful way of understanding both religious rationality and religious evidence, as well as the connection between them.

Of course there are discoveries and there are discoveries. Not all have special import for religion, or rather not all have the import that I want now to explore. Only one discovery-type fits the recurring experience of the Psalms. Since I want now only to provide the grammar of this discovery-type – and since this discovery-type is not limited to the Psalmist's discovery – I shall use non-religious examples to introduce it and to bring out its nature.

In order to develop an example of the kind of discovery needed, let us consider an episode in *The Possessed*: Stavrogin's confession to Father Tikhon. Father Tikhon is a holy man, a retired bishop who lives a monastic life (although this element is not important for our purposes). Stavrogin visits him in his cell ostensibly to confess how he brought about the suicide of a child. Years before he had seduced, or as well as seduced, a young girl and then had stood by silently while the child grew ill and depressed and, in a matter of days, took her own life. He presents himself to Tikhon as ready to suffer for his crime by publishing a full account. It is not that Stavrogin is sorry for what he has done; in fact he is not penitent. He is proud of his shamelessness and has written his confession to confront and astound the world with his audacious morality. But Tikhon, after reading the confession and observing its tone, and after talking with Stavrogin, becomes aware that his motive is more complex than this. It involves as well his being afraid and ashamed of penance; and, at the deepest level, it is formed by a need and a wish for forgiveness. Tikhon sees this and nearly brings Stavrogin to confess it. Stavrogin in the heat of his emotion does say that his 'whole aim' is to 'forgive myself myself', but he says it as though this would be some triumph of pride. At all costs he cannot allow himself to recognise his need and his wish for forgiveness from others.

In Dostoyevsky's novel Tikhon knows Stavrogin's motives better than Stavrogin, which is an instance of a not unheard of, if uncommon, state of affairs. Stavrogin never quite recognises his motives for what they are. Having come to Tikhon seeking to wring 'respect' from him, he cannot allow that Tikhon has correctly identified his deepest motive as a wish for forgiveness. At any rate this is one way to understand Stavrogin. Given this understanding of Stavrogin, it would remain open that he might ultimately acknowledge his motives – not just to others but to himself. If he can hide his motives from himself, he can discover them. The model of discovery that we are seeking is not exemplified by Tikhon's discovery of Stavrogin's motives, but is exemplified by Stavrogin's discovery, the discovery of his own motives that he did not make in Dostoyevsky's novel, but could have made.

If Stavrogin had made a discovery of his own motives, it would have been utterly unlike the discovery that a hypothesis, experimental or non-experimental, is confirmed. Stavrogin entertained no hypothesis that his deepest motive was a wish for forgiveness. He addressed no such issue. He unequivocally rejected any such notion. Yet all that he needed in order to discover his motive was before him and familiar to him. It was more familiar to him than to Tikhon. The data of the familiar pressed upon him, as it were; but he resisted seeing them for what they were. He needed new eyes, or his old eyes, so that he could see the significance of facts already familiar to him. The discovery that Stavrogin needed to make would have been made had he overcome his blindness and seen the significance of those familiar facts as an embodiment of his wish for forgiveness.

Such a discovery would, in type, contrast with a scientist's discovery that an experimental hypothesis is verified and with John Wisdom's issue-settling discoveries.[21] To be sure Stavrogin, the scientist, and Wisdom's issue-settlers would make a discovery of the truth. And none of them would come to a baseless belief with no reasons in its support. Nevertheless distinctly different models of discovery apply. The scientist with his experimental hypothesis would investigate, gather evidence, and weigh it to discover whether his hypothesis is confirmed. Wisdom's issue-settlers would intellectually pursue the issue before them. Stavrogin would do neither of these things. Rather, if he were to make his discovery, he would come to realise the significance of what is already before him, ordered and familiar. The evidence needed by the scientist is clear in its significance as evidence once it is before him, but first he has to find it. The evidence needed by Wisdom's issue-settlers is before them, but they need to order it. The evidence needed by Stavrogin is already before him, but he cannot see its significance as evidence, nor will further intellectual ordering make it clear. His failure is not one of enquiry. It lies elsewhere. The difference between this imagined Stavrogin before he has discovered his deepest motive and after he has is that, before, he fails to see because he is blind to the significance of what is familiar to him while, after, he undeniably sees the significance of the familiar. Stavrogin's failure to discover, or to be aware of, his own deepest motive is a failure in sensitivity – a word that Tikhon uses. Both an *investigative failure* and *insensitivity*, or *blindness*, are cognitive failures, but they are different sorts of cognitive failures.

Our imagined Stavrogin's discovery, the discovery that Stavrogin could have made, contrasts with every kind of investigative discovery. It is rather, a perhaps sudden, perhaps unexpected, *realisation* of the significance of the familiar. Accordingly I shall call such a discovery a *realisation-discovery*.[22]

One other example. A man is jealous of his son, but he is unaware of his jealousy. In fact he violently denies it, or would if it were suggested to him that he is jealous of his own son. Thus he investigates no suspicion, for he has none to investigate. For the same reason he gathers no evidence, although he would not have far to look. The facts that would confirm another's suspicion of his jealousy are already familiar to him. But he does not see them in their significance as indications of his jealousy. He assiduously construes these facts as indications of his son's ability to irritate him when he is tired, or in some other way discounts them. Then something happens. Perhaps he reads a novel depicting a relationship like that between himself and his son, or something else occurs. In any case he comes to see the significance of the uneasiness he feels around his son and of much else that had vaguely disturbed him. He discovers that he is jealous of his son by realising the significance of his own actions and feelings toward his son.

It may not be too far off the mark to suggest that the home, or a home, of realisation-discoveries is in the realm of human relations. Also, often if not always, when a realisation-discovery is made one's self-image is at stake. There is, I think, a wide range of things to which human beings can be blind, and this is so, I suggest, because there is a wide range of things that can be important to the self-image of one person or another. In any case a person's prized self-image, or some element of it, often plays a role in that person's resistance to making a realisation-discovery – as in both of our examples. The significance of this fact for making the religious realisation-discovery I shall explore later in this chapter.

Now, however, in case it is not already clear, let me try to bring out how the Psalmist's experience of God's presence is, in his eyes, a realisation of the meaning of what is familiar to him. The Psalmist lifts up his eyes to the hills and finds his strength renewed and his help from the Lord. The Lord keeps his going out and his coming in (Psalm 121). In Psalm 19 we find:

> The heavens are telling the
> glory of God;
> and the firmament proclaims his
> handiwork.

And in Psalm 42:

> Deep calls to deep
> at the thunder of thy cataracts;
> all thy waves and thy billows
> have gone over me.

The Psalmist beholds the works of the Lord (Psalm 46). He beholds that God the Lord speaks and summons the earth from the rising of the sun to its setting (Psalm 50). It is the Lord who opens his lips that his mouth may show forth his praise (Psalm 51). So that he may say (Psalm 93):

> The Lord reigns; he is robed
> in majesty. . . .
> The floods have lifted up, O Lord,
> the floods have lifted up their
> voice,
> the floods lift up their roaring.
> Mightier than the thunders of
> many waters,
> mightier than the waves of the
> sea,
> the Lord on high is mighty!

It is the Lord who works wonders, whose thunder is in the whirlwind, whose lightnings light up the world (Psalm 77). And it is the Lord to whom the Psalmist says (Psalm 104):

> . . . how manifold are thy
> works!
> In wisdom hast thou made them
> all.

The Psalmist does not reason from indications of design in the world. He does not conduct an experiment or discover a phenomenon unaccountable by known physical laws. He merely beholds the hills, the heavens, and the deep and finds there the presence of the Lord. He looks upon what we all look upon – what the fool in the Psalms looks upon too – and he realises what it means: that there is a God whose presence creation bespeaks. At any rate so he believes he realises. The point at present is not to argue that the Psalmist has indeed made a discovery of God's presence. It is to bring forward a discovery-model which applies to the Psalmist's experience and does justice to the discovery that, in his own eyes, he has made and makes again and again. While the Psalms include much besides expressions of the Psalmist's experience of God's presence, they are vibrant with the Psalmist's sense of the presence of God. His realisation and deeper realisation of God's presence is the constant and recurring theme throughout.

Phillips, referring to the Psalms, says that '*any* event can lead the believer to God'[23] Yes, and non-believers too – if their eyes are opened. Malcolm said something similar: that the wonders and horrors of nature can be responded to religiously or non-religiously.[24] But Phillips and Malcolm, from their deeply First-Perspective positions, do not contemplate that believers and non-believers can discover the presence of God in the wonders and horrors of nature or in the events of their own lives.

Now, in the remainder of this section, let me try to connect the type of discovery mirrored in the Psalms with the themes of evidence and rationality. When a realisation-discovery is made by someone – by Stavrogin, the jealous father, or by the Psalmist – that person comes to see the significance of what has long been familiar to him. Those who make realisation-discoveries come to see the significance of the familiar as that which establishes what they had not thought or had not fully realised or had even denied. Their discoveries, if they are discoveries, involve gaining an appreciation of a grounding for their new or old belief, and this grounding is evidential. It is distinct from a psychological cause for one's belief (such as, fear or desire), and it is distinct from pragmatic reasons for acting as though a belief were true.

Still, for many, the word 'evidence' is too contaminated to be used in religious contexts. In part this is because it is associated with Paley and Deism. And too its use *seems* to imply doubt or investigative neutrality.[25] In fact the use of the word implies neither, I would argue, at least not always. Though *I* known and am certain, I can speak of evidence as a concession to another's doubt. Also when we speak of *conclusive* evidence we allow that all real doubts have been answered. In enquiry-contexts, it is true, evidence is pursued and cited with tentativeness, and as long as the enquiry continues such a tentativeness is properly required. But in realisation-contexts a realisation is made, or rather, has been made; no enquiry is being conducted. In such contexts, if one points to that through which one came to one's realisation, tentativeness, investigative neutrality, and doubt are not required on one's part. Indeed they are ruled out.

It seems to me, then, that if we bear in mind the different colorations that evidence takes on in enquiry-contexts and in realisation-contexts, there is no great problem in speaking of *evidence* in connection with the Psalms and the Third Perspective. The Psalmist's evidence is all that through which he comes to realise or more deeply realise God's presence. Yet nothing turns on the word. We can use as well *experiential grounding* or even *manifestations* in place of 'evidence'. In what follows, with these caveats, I shall most often use 'evidence' and its cognate, 'grounding', when speaking of realisation-contexts.

Regarding rationality I believe that a distinction paralleling that just introduced regarding evidence is required. There is, I suggest, an *enquiry-rationality* and a *realisation-rationality* (or *blindness-rationality*). Enquiry-rationality is the kind of rationality focused on most often in philosophical discussions. It locks into the traditional conception of rationality discussed in section (1), which applies to various modes of issue settling. It is enquiry-rationality that is violated when, for instance, a person knows what would count as evidence, but fails to look hard enough, or fails to take into account counter-evidence, or fails to look for counter-evidence. These are investigative failures and can, often justifiably, bring down on one's head the charge of irrationality – that is, the charge of enquiry-irrationality. But what are we to say of Stavrogin and the jealous father before their discoveries? Were they rational? I think that we can see that in a sense they were not. But they were not enquiry-irrational, for they were not conducting any enquiry. Though they exhibited a cognitive failure, a kind of failure of understanding, it was a cognitive failure of a different kind. The source of their irrationality was their blindness. Being blind to what was relevant to their wrong beliefs, they believed irrationally. Accordingly I think that we may properly speak of a blindness-caused irrationality and a blindness-free rationality in realisation-contexts.

Granted it may not be wise to insist on using the word 'rational' *tout court* to describe this kind of rationality; like 'evidence' it may be too closely associated with enquiry-contexts. Nevertheless, I think that it is appropriate to use 'rational' in realisation-contexts if its sense is properly qualified. It is because *if* a realisation-discovery has been made by a person, then that person's belief is indeed grounded. Earlier (Chapter 1, section (1)) we saw that Mavrodes distinguishes between rational belief and an individual's rational belief (or believing). Using that distinction, and recognising that evidence or grounding need not be hypothetical, it seems allowable, even mandatory, to say that one who has come to believe something via a realisation-discovery has a rational belief (that person's belief is rational). Of course if we take as a requirement of all rationality the requirement of enquiry-rationality that supporting evidence be discernible to all disinterested investigators, then we will demur. Many do this. Kierkegaard thought this way, it seems. And, given the vast areas of application of enquiry-rationality, such thinking is understandable. Still, it is not necessitated. And if I am correct about enquiry-contexts and realisation-contexts, it is too narrow. I distinguish, then, between enquiry-rationality and realisation-rationality, and I suggest that we can properly apply the latter and its opposite, realisation- or blindness-irrationality, to realisation-contexts.

In this way, directing our attention away from enquiry and toward realisation, we find not only a discovery-type appropriate to a central strain of religious belief, but an architectonic reordering of the concepts of *evidence* (or *grounding*) and *rationality*. Or rather – for this is what it really is – we find a reminder of how these concepts apply to realisation-contexts. More must be said about rationality and evidence in the Third Perspective, and I shall say more about them in Chapter 3. But, for the present, perhaps I have said enough about how these concepts apply to the Third Perspective.

III   RELIGIOUS DISCOVERY

(3) Settings for the Religious Realisation-Discovery

In the Psalms there are many references to different settings for
the religious discovery. In the last section, in the quotations from
the Psalms, we saw several (the Psalmist lifts up his eyes to the
hills, he beholds the heavens, the lightning and thunder, he
beholds his going out and coming in, his own act of praising God,
and as a whole the manifold works of creation). These settings,
and similar settings, recur in Judaeo-Christian religious literature. The tradition of the Psalms does not begin and end with the
Book of Psalms.

Paul in his letter to the Romans says, 'Ever since the creation of
the world [God's] invisible nature, namely, his eternal power and
deity, has been clearly perceived in the things that have been
made.'[26] Undeniably this echoes the Psalms (especially Psalms 19
and 104 among those cited before). Paul is in effect proclaiming
the possibility of all making the religious discovery. But by their
wickedness, Paul says, men suppress the truth and their minds are
darkened.

The tradition of the Psalms is particularly strong in various
mystical and devotional works. In the twelfth century Richard of
St. Victor wrote *The Twelve Patriarchs*, a personification allegory in
which the twelve sons of Jacob, as well as his one daughter, his
wives Leah and Rachel, and their handmaids, are given a
symbolic sense. Richard lets each figure represent a faculty or
virtue and presents an allegory which depicts different stages in
spiritual growth. The details of Richard's psychology of spiritual
development, though worthy of reflection for their own sake, are
not germane to the present concern. What is germane is his
treatment of Joseph, who symbolises self-knowledge, and Benjamine, who symbolises contemplation or knowledge of God. 'The
rational soul', Richard says,

discovers without doubt that it is the foremost and principal
mirror for seeing God. For if the invisible things of God are
seen, being understood by the intellect by means of those things
which have been made, where, I ask, have the traces of
knowledge been found more clearly imprinted than in His
image?[27]

The reference of course is to Romans, the passage we just saw. Richard does not deny that we can discover God through all things which have been made. He is maintaining only that knowledge of ourselves, of our 'rational souls', which are in the image of God, is a *pre-eminent* ground by which God may be discovered. But it is Benjamine who represents knowledge of God, and, Richard says, when Benjamine is born Rachel, or reason, dies. 'Therefore,' he concludes, 'let no person suppose that he is able to penetrate to the splendour of that divine light by argumentation.'[28] Richard, then at once recognises the discovery of God found in the Psalms and that it has nothing to do with 'argumentation'.

A religious thinker who very clearly stands in the tradition of the Psalms is the great Franciscan theologian and mystic, St. Bonaventura. In *The Mind's Road to God* Bonaventura entreats his readers to 'open your eyes . . . prick up your spiritual ears, open your lips, and apply your heart, that you may see your God in all creatures, may hear Him, praise Him, love and adore Him, magnify and honor Him'.[29] The wise, Bonaventura says, can say with the Psalmist (Bonaventura says 'Prophet'), 'Thou hast given me, O Lord, a delight in Thy doings: and in the works of thy hands I shall rejoice' (Psalm 91.5, Douai-Reims Bible). For Bonaventura the man who is 'not illumined by [the] splendor of created things is blind'.[30] And when such a blindness is lifted the 'signs' of God's presence in 'all creatures' and in His 'doings' cannot but be seen: the significance of the familiar becomes evident.

Although Bonaventura urges us to open our eyes and says that we should strive to see God, he does not mean to imply that one can, solely through one's own efforts, see God in the panoply of the world. As he puts it, man is 'bent over by his own sin', and his natural powers are insufficient without regenerating grace.[31] The grammar of realisation does not entail that realisation-discoveries can, or that they cannot, be attained by our own efforts. It is compatible with the grammar or logic of the model that we have identified that one can try to open one's eyes or that such efforts are pointless or that such efforts, while not pointless, must be insufficient. For Bonaventura, in his categories, more is needed than 'the light of nature and of acquired science'.[32] The more that is needed for Bonaventura, as a Christian, is Christ as mediator. However, again, this is not entailed by the discovery model itself; nor is it ruled out.

Although *The Mind's Road to God* contains much more than a simple appeal to the Psalmist's experience, including an adumbration if not a statement of the ontological argument,[33] it is imbued with the spirit of the Psalms. For Bonaventura the sensible world is a mirror (*speculum*), as are our natural powers, through which we can come to see God. The metaphor of a mirror was also used by Richard of St. Victor. In addition, for Bonaventura, there is a ladder of the mind's ascent to God. These metaphors are not found in the Psalms and may, to an extent, go beyond the Psalms, as Bonaventura's Neo-Platonism surely does. Nevertheless, at least sometimes, and even often – when Bonaventura speaks of our being blind and of our opening our eyes to see – the discovery model that applies to *The Mind's Road to God* is the same realisation-discovery model that applies to the experience embodied in the Psalms.

One finds echoes of religious realisations with a realisation-discovery structure throughout the history of Judaeo-Christian religion, and many other examples could be provided.[34] Also one can find echoes in literary works that strictly are neither devotional nor mystical, and in this sense are secular, but which are strongly religious in tone. For instance Dostoyevsky portrays Father Zossima, Alyosha's mentor in *The Brothers Karamazov*, as having made a realisation-discovery of the presence of God while he was still 'in the World'.[35]

The tradition of the Psalms, which is the home of the Third Perspective in the Judaeo-Christian heritage, is not limited to the written word. It is reflected as well in the consciousness of individual believers. However, in order to see this, we must bear in mind the grammar of realisation-discoveries in general and of the religious discovery specifically. Generally what prevents a person from making a realisation-discovery when there is one to be made is blindness. This is a grammatical point about all realisation discoveries. Often, if not always, what causes blindness is a resistance to seeing what is there to be seen created by one's prized self-image or some element of it. This too is a grammatical point about all realisation discoveries. These general grammatical points have specific corollaries relating to the religious discovery. Within the tradition of the Third Perspective, in Judaeo-Christian terms, what keeps human beings from making the Psalmist's discovery of the presence of God is blindness to the presence of God. And what causes this blindness is attachment to self, or lack of self-denial, which in Judaeo-Christian terms is sin, that is, turning from God. Often in mystical and devotional literature the denial of self is heeded, even though the Psalmist himself does not use this expression. He says instead, 'there is nothing upon earth I desire besides thee' (Psalm 73.25). The, or one, Biblical source is Luke 9.23–.24: 'If any man would come after me, let him deny himself and take up his cross daily and follow me. For whoever would save his life will lose it; and whoever loses his life for my sake, he will save it.' In the developing tradition Johann Arndt speaks of denying onself and even of hating one's life, that is, one's lustful and prideful life. St. Bernard says that to love all, even oneself, for the sake of God one must be forgetful of self and be emptied of oneself. St. Bonaventura says that none can be made blessed unless he ascend above himself.[36] The denial of self in Judaeo-Christian religion can take various concrete forms. It need not be ascetic. It need not involve a monastic retiring from the world. In all its forms, though, it in same way involves denying one's will or redirecting one's will towards God or making one's will one with God's will. At its core there is one thing that dying to self always is in the Judaeo-Christian heritage, at least within the tradition of the Third Perspective: it is always dying to self outside a relationship to God.

Bearing in mind this role for denial of self, we can identify phenomenologically a number of settings for the religious discovery within the experience of individual believers. These are settings in which there is some form of getting beyond oneself or self-forgetting. Religious realisations of the Third-Perspective sort come or seem to come in settings where one's deepest concern is directed away from oneself.

One such setting is the experience of grief. H. D. Lewis in *Our Experience of God* says that crises can precipitate a leap that takes the mind beyond finite things[37] I think that this may be so. Grief is a kind of personal crisis and in moments of grief, in moments of pure, incandescent grief at another's death, one's heart can turn from oneself to the other. And in such a moment, within that forgetfulness of self, the condition for a religious realisation may be found. In such a case the 'leap' that Lewis mentions is more exactly a discovery or a rediscovery. Another setting is that of awe and wonder. Settings of awe and wonder are of course unmistakably present in the Psalms (in for instance Psalms 93, 99 and 104). Also there is the setting of acknowledgement of personal guilt. And there is the setting of love or sympathy, where one's heart is moved and one sees another as oneself.

Again, the present point is not that the Psalmist or any person has made a religious realisation of God's presence, whether in the settings just noted or in any other. My effort in this section is to bring into relief settings for the kind of religious discovery that I have identified. Whether such religious discoveries have indeed been made I shall explore in the next section.

Before I turn to that issue, there is one further signal element of the grammar of religious realisation that I should bring out. A religious realisation-discovery is a discovery of God's presence, and this is to say that it is a discovery of a *relationship* to God or to the Divine. It is not a discovery of particulars of dogma, like 'God is Triune' or 'God became temporal 2000 years ago'. Also a discovery of God's presence is not merely a discovery that God exists. In fact typically when believers more deeply realise God's presence they do not even in part discover that God exists. The Psalmist does not discover God's existence: he more deeply realises God's majesty, love, and power. Only those who deny that there is a God would discover God's existence in making a religious discovery, and then they would by realising that there must be a God to whom they now see they stand in a relationship and whose presence they can no longer deny.

The grammatical point I wish to make here is this: given that the religious realisation is a discovery of a relationship to God, the religious realisation is not limited to Judaeo-Christian religion or even to theistic religion. To the extent that there is or can be a realisation of a relationship to the Divine outside the Judaeo-Christian tradition, the religious discovery-model before us applies to other religions as well. It is not essential that the Divine be called 'God' or 'Allah'; it may be and has been called 'the Numinous' or 'Reality'. Of course the nature of discoverable relationships to God will to an extent determine the nature of the concept of the Divine. If one discovers that one stands in a relationship of goodness and love to the Divine, then the Divine must be a Being of goodness and love (thus God's attributes may be said to be more deeply realised). However it may well be, so far as the realisation-discovery model goes, that individuals in different traditions have discovered slightly, or significantly, different relations to the Divine and so have characterised the Divine differently. There may be realisation-discoveries in the

Christian, Hindu, and Buddhist traditions, all of the same Reality, but of different relations to that Reality, which lead to or allow different conceptions of the Divine Reality.[38]

This last point is not unrelated to what John Hick has maintained in his recent writings.[39] Hick has suggested the possibility that those in different religions may have experience of the same Reality but conceive of it differently. Though Hick speaks of experiencing Reality and knowing Reality, he has not appealed to the category of religious discovery that I have presented here. He could though, I believe (although if he did so there might be a tension with other views he holds, such as his view of faith as interpretation and his conception of the nature of religious knowledge). In any case we should be clear that the possibility of a religious discovery of a relationship to the Divine is not limited to the Judaeo-Christian tradition.

(4) The Issue of Whether Religious Realisation-Discoveries Have Been Made

Now, finally in this chapter, let us turn our attention to the issue of the reality of religious discovery. The concern here is not whether the Psalmist, certain mystics, and ordinary believers have had experiences that phenomenologically are like realisations or deeper realisations. They have. Let us take that as established. The issue here is whether any of their supposed realisations were indeed realisations.

Before I go any further, however, let me say that I do not intend to resolve this issue. Rather, I shall endeavour to make clear, or clearer, the nature of the issue by bringing into the open its grammar or logic. For it does indeed have a logic. In fact, as I hope that I shall be able to show, once we are clear on the logic of the issue we shall be clear that the issue could not possibly be resolved by anything that I might bring forward. Yet the issue has a determinable logic.

In general the difference between the person who is blind to what there is and the person who is not is, at its heart, a cognitive difference. This holds specifically regarding the religious discovery. The difference between the person who believes that he has discovered God's presence and the person who denies that there is such a discovery is, then, not merely a matter of different attitudes or different ways of life (although these too are involved, and not merely accidentally). The issue of whether the Psalmist or any person has made the religious discovery is the issue of whether any religious person has realised the significance of the familiar, not just regarding those painful truths to which most of us, like Stavrogin and the jealous father, blind ourselves, but regarding all that there is. The issue of whether anyone has made the religious discovery is in general type a cognitive issue of blindness; and it exhibits the general logic of such issues. Beyond this it is an issue of that particular blindness referred to by St. Bonaventura regarding all of existence. The question raised is: Who is blind to the familiar and who has seen aright? Are those who fail to discover the presence of God blind, or are those who find the Psalmist's experience in their own lives blind with eyes that see too much, reading into the universe a significance not there to be found? Issues of blindness generally, and in the particular case of religious discovery, have a traceable logic, an identifiable structure. That structure deeply involves the concept and reality of self-deception.

Often, although perhaps not always and certainly not necessarily, the root cause of the sort of blindness operating in realisation-contexts is self-deception. In fact many who have spoken of blindness in connection with religion have been aware of its connection to self-deception, although they have not always named self-deception as such. Paul in Romans says that men's minds are darkened; the Psalmist speaks of the corruption of the fool who denies God in his heart (Psalm 14). Nor have those who deny or would deny the religious discovery been unaware of the relevance of self-deception. Nietzsche, speaking of the conviction of faith in *The Antichrist*, allows that it is indistinguishable from a lie, a lie with which one lies to oneself; and by 'lie' he says that he means wishing not to see what one does see, wishing not to see as one sees. Earlier in the same work he says explicitly that 'everything in [the New Testament] is cowardice, everything is shutting-one's-eyes and self-deception [*Selbstbetrug*]'.[40]

Freud too was aware of the possible role of self-deception in religious belief, and, going beyond Nietzsche, he developed an analysis of religious belief that accounts for it in terms of wish-fulfilment. Several of Freud's works bear on religion, including *Totem and Taboo*, *Moses and Monotheism* and, most importantly for our concerns, *The Future of an Illusion*. Freud seems to have held two distinguishable if interrelated theses about religious belief. One is an historical thesis about the origins of the cultural phenomena of religion, developed in psychoanalytic terms with great emphasis on the Oedipean situation. This thesis, developed in *Totem and Taboo* and *Moses and Monotheism*, is a highly speculative account of the history and prehistory of religion and need not concern us. The second thesis is a psychological account of how belief in God arises in the lives of individual believers. It is this thesis, developed in *The Future of an Illusion* and addressed specifically to theistic belief, that is pertinent to the issue before us.

In *The Future of an Illusion* Freud maintains that religious belief, belief in God, is an 'illusion'. An illusion, for Freud, is a belief derived from human wishes, motivated by wish-fulfilment, and held with disregard for its relation to factual proof.[41] Belief in God, Freud thinks, derives from human beings' helplessness and their need for protection and security – which a projected cosmic father can provide.[42] He goes on to say that religion is 'the universal obsessional neurosis of humanity', which arises 'out of the Oedipus complex, out of the relation to the father'.[43] However Freud's reference to the Oedipus complex is not essential to his psychological thesis. If it were his thesis would apply to males only. Understood in terms of a wish for protection his thesis applies to all believers who seek the protection of a cosmic father. Moreover some Freudian writers, filling out Freud's thought, have placed an emphasis on the function of the religious father-image in relieving guilt (by confession and penance). This function too may be subsumed under the wish for protection, if we allow protection to include relief from anxiety (as Freud does). And, of course, as William Alston points out, such guilt need not be restricted to the Oedipal situation.[44] A formulation of a general Freudian account of individuals' religious belief, then, might be something like this: religious belief is an illusion, a belief in a cosmic father-figure arising from a sense of helplessness and a need to feel protected.

Freud was clear that illusions can be true, and he did not argue that religious belief is false.[45] But he felt that there was no reason at all to believe it to be true, and he thought that once we discover our motives for religious belief 'our attitude to the problem of religion will undergo a marked displacement'.[46] Thus a Freudian psychological thesis does not entail that there is no God. But still, if religious belief in God is always an illusion in Freud's sense, then it would follow that there is no religious discovery of God's presence. Rather what seems to the religious in the tradition of the Third Perspective to be a realisation of God's presence would be a projection of a perhaps unacknowledged wish for protection from the vicissitudes and anxieties of life.

While Freud does not discuss self-deception as such in *The Future of an Illusion* he clearly allows it a central role in the formation of religious belief. For it is self-deception that would lead the religious to read into the universe, in the absence of all support, what would fulfil their wish for protection, the presence of a protective Father. The connection between blindness and self-deception regarding religious belief that we find in the Freudian view is this: human beings feel a *need* for security, they *wish* for the protection of a heavenly Father, and accordingly they deceive themselves into 'seeing' what they fervently wish to see, the presence of a protective Father. Nietzsche is cannily close to Freud here. In *Thus Spoke Zarathustra* he says:

> Weariness that wants to reach the ultimate with one leap, with one fatal leap, a poor ignorant weariness that does not want to want any more: this created all gods and afterworlds.[47]

For Freud and Nietzsche self-deception produces a blindness that sees too much. It reads into the natural world a supernatural presence in the face of, or at least independently of, reality.

On the other side is St. Bonaventura, among others. Bonaventura, as we have seen, also spoke of blindness. In *The Mind's Road to God* one who fails to find 'traces' of God's presence in the world is blind. Such blindness sees too little, and its source, Bonaventura tells us, is sin and 'cares'. But sin and cares as much as a wish for protection are a candidate for a cause of self-deception.

We encounter at this point a kind of stalemate. On the one side there are critics of religion, like Freud and Nietzsche, who directly address the Third Perspective and the issue of religious discovery and attribute to the religious blindness and self-deception. On the other side the religious, or those with the Third Perspective, attribute blindness to those who fail to make the religious discovery and allow that their blindness may arise from self-deception. However more can be said, for there is more to the logic of the issue of religious discovery than we have yet seen. In order to bring it out, though, we shall have to take a closer look at the nature of self-deception.

Self-deception of course is not limited to religious belief and discovery. Consequently we can draw upon its less problematical manifestations to characterise its nature. The possibility of self-deception exists or may exist whenever there is a realisation-discovery that could have been made by a person but was not, and whenever a person regards himself as having made a realisation-discovery of what others deny or do not see. While realisation-discoveries can have any of a wide range of subjects as content, they have a natural home, as I observed, in the area of human relations and feelings. The case of Stavrogin, who fails to realise his own wish for forgiveness, is typical, as is that of the jealous father who fails to realise that he is jealous of his son. Both fail to realise the significance of the familiar. And in each case their blindness may be said to be caused by self-deception.

What, then, is the nature of self-deception? While there have been many useful discussions of self-deception,[48] at its heart the phenomenon remains paradoxical. In deception of another, one person knows, or believes, something and leads another to believe otherwise. In self-deception, however, one and the same person is both the deceiver and the deceived. The paradox is this: In self-deception the self-deceiver both believes, as the deceiver, and does not believe, as the deceived. If self-deceived, one and the same person may know and not know a truth, may be aware and not be aware of something. In one sense self-deceived persons are aware but in another sense they are not aware: they are *implicitly* aware, but *explicitly* unaware.[49] One as the deceiver, the other as the deceived. The paradox of self-deception is undeniable, and I do not deny it. But still the state can be characterised, despite its paradox. It even has a logic, and using the just noted distinction between levels of awareness we can proceed to describe the state and logic of self-deception.

Let us begin by observing that the self-deceived person is, at one level, unaware because he or she suffers from a blindness that is in some way self-induced. The jealous father, who may be flagrantly jealous of his son, maintains to himself the fiction that he is a good father through failing to recognise the obvious signs of his jealousy. But his failure is not an unintentional failure. Self-deceived persons are not *simply* unaware. They *refuse* to recognise the evidence for what it is. They, as it were, blind themselves to the significance of the evidence. Yet in a sense, at one level, they are aware of the evidence and of its import. As Terence Penelhum says, 'the self-deceiver is not ready to *acknowledge*, even though his behaviour and his actions will tend to show, his recognition of the import of the evidence . . .'.[50] And, we can add, he is not ready to acknowledge the import of the evidence even to himself, although, again, in a sense, or at one level, he is aware, as his demeanor may show.

We should note, then, an intentional or deliberate element in self-deception. It is not a simple, unintentional overlooking of evidence; it is not an innocent ignorance of, or lack of acquaintance with, the evidence. Self-deception involves a refusal to see evidence as evidence, even though it is familiar. In this way self-deceived persons contrast with naive persons, who innocently fail to see the import of evidence with which they are familiar. Naive persons will see the import once it is pointed out to them; self-deceived persons will resist seeing the evidence for what it is. Similarly self-deceived persons stand in contrast to persons who have made an error in judgment in sizing up the evidence. Errors in judgment are not deliberate, while self-deception is. Also self-deceived persons are different from the cautious person who is in a state of intellectual indecision, and from the person who believes as a result of wishful thinking. The cautious person does not have enough evidence but is prepared to acknowledge it and its import when it is forthcoming; persons who believe as a result of wishful thinking believe on the basis of inadequate evidence, but they too are prepared to acknowledge evidence against what they believe when they find it.

Nor, of course are self-deceived persons the same as those who know full well and lie. This is the position of persons who deceive others but not themselves. Self-deceived persons are sincere in a way the liar is not. They are sincere, but selectively blind. It is not that they see and lie; it is that they fail to see. They blind themselves. But of course for self-deceived persons to see and blind themselves – to hide the truth, or what they take to be the truth, from themselves – they must have seen it in some sense; and here is the paradox again. While self-deceived persons are aware in one sense, in another they are not. They are implicitly aware that some displeasing proposition is a truth, and implicitly aware of what supports it, but having glimpsed the Gorgon's head they avert their gaze and hide what they have seen from themselves and thus are explicitly unaware of the truth and of its support.

Self-deceived persons, then, at one level may be and often are aware of evidence against their belief, but at another level they fail – refuse – to recognise the significance of this evidence. If we allow that, at one level (that of explicit awareness), self-deceivers hide from themselves the significance of evidence, then we can explain how self-deceived persons can be acquainted with, even familiar with, the evidence and yet not believe: they fail to see (to be explicitly aware of) the significance of the evidence as evidence. We can even explain how, at one level (that of implicit awareness) they can be aware of the import of the evidence and yet not believe. Furthermore we have a way of characterising how self-deceived persons can overcome their self-deception without new evidence: they finally, in one way or another, come to see (to be explicitly aware of) the evidential significance of what was familiar to them all along.

There is another feature of self-deception, which is crucial to the logic of discovery and self-deception. It is this: self-deception is motivated; self-deceived persons have a motive or purpose for deceiving themselves. Most writers on self-deception have recognised and in one way or another described this feature, which of course is in accord with Freud's analysis of religious belief as an illusion, that is, a belief motivated by wish-fulfilment. Herbert Fingarette, for instance, says that the self-deceiver 'persuades himself to believe contrary to the evidence in order to evade [an] unpleasant truth' that, Fingarette later tells us, relates to the 'personal identity [he] accepts'.[51] Alan Drengson sees the motivation of self-deception as more inclusive. 'People deceive themselves not only out of concern for truth or moral and personal integrity,' he says, 'but also in order to avoid facing up to some truth that is painful or as a result of fear and/or desire.'[52] Amelie Oksenberg Rorty says of the self-deceiver that he has an 'interest . . . associated with preserving or changing his identity, the sort of person he is, or conceives himself to be'.[53] And John Turk Saunders characterises the motive of the self-deceiver simply and succinctly as: 'To gain satisfaction; to avoid distress.'[54]

We should note here a certain disagreement about the *range* of the self-deceiver's motivation. Even so, there is general agreement that something the person, as that person, is attached to is at stake: his image of himself as a father, a cherished belief about the world upon which he or she is psychologically dependent, etc.

Again there is a certain disagreement about whether the 'motive' involved strictly is a motive. Fingarette distinguishes between a motive and a purpose and maintains that, while a motive may or may not be present, a purpose always is. However, what he means by a purpose (evading an unpleasant truth) others would label a motive, I suspect. Rorty too sets aside the word 'motive'; she prefers the notion of an 'interest'. She is quite clear, though, that, in her thinking, the self-deceiver engages in self-deception because of, and not merely coincidentally with, his 'interest'. In short, while there may be some hesitation about the adequacy of the word 'motive', there is general agreement that, integral to self-deception, there is a motive or purpose or interest or, most broadly, a psychological reason, which operates in the sphere of motivation. (Henceforth I shall refer to this element as a motive or purpose or, alternatively, as a reason.)

All of those cited, then, would agree that a motive or purpose is more than accidentally connected to self-deception. Even Penelhum, who in one place suggests that a motive is not necessary for self-deception, concedes that there being a motive is 'usual' and cases lacking a motive would be 'odd'.[55] Accordingly one strong piece of evidence that a person is deceiving himself is the presence of a motive in the range defined by Fingarette and the others; and, furthermore, if such a motive or purpose is lacking, that is conclusive evidence, or for all intents and purposes conclusive evidence, that self-deception is not present. Here, again, I believe all those cited would agree, including Penelhum. The importance of this fourth feature of self-deception for the issue of religious discovery will emerge shortly.

Now after this brief but essential excursus into the nature of self-deception let us return to the question of whether anyone has made the religious discovery. If the Freudian view we have identified is correct, then religious belief is born of self-deception. If so, then the religious who think that they have discovered God's presence really have not, for they have failed to see aright and have allowed their beliefs to be dictated by their wish for protection. But regarding religious belief the issue of self-deception addresses both sides: Is the person who 'discovers' God's presence self-deceived (as we would think following Freud); or is the person who 'fails' to make this discovery self-deceived and blind to what the other has seen (as we would think following Bonaventura)? As we have just seen, it is always conceptually in place to look for a motive or purpose for self-deception. So it is in place to look for motives for self-deception among those who regard themselves as having discovered God's presence and, as well, among those who have not made the religious discovery.

Both Freud and Nietzsche appropriately identify motives for the self-deception of the religious. However one can allow that their views hold for some religious believers while maintaining that they do not hold for all. One might agree with Freud that the wish for protection is a motive for belief and that some religious belief is so caused, and yet maintain that some religious belief is not so caused. The pointed and exact question that Freud raises is *not*: Is religious belief an illusion or is it not? The more exact question is: Is it always an illusion? If religious belief is caused by the wish for protection in only some believers, then it still may be that other believers have made the religious discovery. And I think that there are indications that some religious belief is not created by the wish for protection. It would appear not to be in those believers who pray with St. Francis Xavier:

> O God, if I worship Thee for fear of Hell, burn me in Hell; and if I worship Thee in hope of Paradise, exclude me from Paradise; but if I worship Thee for thy own sake, grudge me not thy everlasting beauty.

Such believers, if their prayer is true, seem to be poor candidates for Freud's wish-fulfilment analysis. Similarly they do not seem to hold their belief out of weariness, Nietzsche's suggested motive: their wish is to do God's will with an acceptance of whatever that entails. It is arguable then that the motives for belief identified by Freud and Nietzsche, though they may account for the origin of religious belief in many, are not universal. And when Freud's and Nietzsche's motives are not to be found in believers, Freud's and Nietzsche's psychological accounts of the origin of religious belief are not applicable and so do not rule out religious discovery.

But two points should be noted here. First, it could be maintained that there are other motives for the self-deception of the religious. Perhaps this is true. Although Freud's category of 'protection' may be so broad that it covers the spectrum (protection from the anxiety of guilt, from the fear of punishment, etc.). Second, it could be maintained that even in a believer like St. Francis Xavier the motive provided by a wish for protection is the operative cause of belief, despite his prayer. The very self-deception that would read God's presence into the universe could blind one to one's true motives. It would be hard to deny this point.

We have acquainted ourselves with Freud's and Nietzsche's proposed motives for self-deception among religious believers. What of the other side? We need not look far for unconscious reasons, or motives, not to recognise that one stands in a relationship to God or to the Divine. As we saw in the last section, in the tradition of the Third Perspective what prevents human beings from discovering the presence of God, and one's relationship to the Divine, is attachment to self. Let me now expand this theme.

Notoriously the relationship to the Divine that one would discover if one made the religious discovery carries with it responsibilities that are not appealing to all. The religious ideal is expressed in Christian terms as 'taking up the cross'. In Judaeo-Christian terms it involves conforming oneself to God's Law. What is involved in recognising one's relationship to God in the Judaeo-Christian tradition and in conforming to God's Law is much more than living by a code. It involves a recognition of God's absolute demand on one and the awesome, even terrible, aspect of that demand. It is, if the relationship is fully acknowledged, a giving up of selfhood to God.[56] So it is that St. Paul tells the Corinthians that he would not have the love they must have if he but gives away all that he owns or if he but delivers up his body to be burned (1 Corinthians 13.3). And Jesus tells the lawyer, 'You shall love the Lord your God with all your heart, and with all your soul, and with all your strength, and with all your mind; and your neighbour as yourself' (Luke 10.27). As we are told in the Gospels, whoever would save his life must lose his life. True, there is a life to be gained: a life that is lived in an acknowledged and deepening relationship to God. However in a real sense it is more convenient and gratifying to believe that there is no God to whom one stands committed and who makes absolute demands upon one, for then one's life is one's own in a way that it is not for the religious person.

For the Third Perspective the requirements of living one's life in a relationship to God identifying one's will with God's will, and the life that we are required to give up, provide an ample motive for the unbelieving to avert their gaze from the evidence of God's presence. And this reason, be it noted, provides what could be a universal motive for self-deception on the part of unbelievers, even if to a great extent it is an unconscious motive. Perhaps it is not a happy thing when we come to see that an issue of great moment turns on the force of motives that may be unconscious. As Phillips says, few of us are happy with the idea that 'if we are not the victims of bad unconscious reasoning and hidden causal forces, those who disagree with us must be'.[57] But nevertheless if there is a religious discovery to be made it may be precisely such unconscious motives that prevent us from making it. It is an insight shared by the Third Perspective and the anti-religious who attack the Third Perspective on its own ground that the blindness that sees too little or too much may be caused by what those who are blind cannot see within themselves.

At this point a good part of the structure, or logic, of the issue of religious discovery has emerged. We can recapitulate that logic as a progression of questions. When there are those who are deemed to have made the religious discovery the evident first question is: Has a discovery been made? The second question that arises, then, is: Who is blind to the familiar, those who believe they have made a discovery or those who have made no such discovery and, it may be, say there is none to be made? This question leads immediately to the third: Who is self-deceived? For, while self-deception is not the only conceivable cause of blindness, it is closely associated with the resistant blindness operative here. And this question, in its turn, leads to the fourth: Who has a motive or purpose for self-deception? However, we should add, it is not sufficient for self-deception that there be a *possible* motive (whether or not the possible motive is universal): the motive must also be operative in an individual. Conversely, if it could be established that there were no operative motive, self-deception would be ruled out.

Now let us see where we are. It is one thing to trace the logic of realisation-discoveries, and it is another to determine whether by that logic the religious discovery, or any specific realisation-discovery, has been made. In fact can the question 'Who is self-deceived?' even be pursued? Yes, by seeking a possible motive for self-deception. Say that there is a possible motive, or that a motive cannot be ruled out, can the issue be pursued further? Yes, in some cases. It will even yield to investigation in some cases. It will in those cases where there are neutral observers who, as it were, stand outside the issue. For instance, in the example of the father jealous of his son, whose motive for self-deception is clear (namely his keeping intact his image of himself as a good father), a neutral observer could with justification conclude that the father is deceiving himself if he, the father, is familiar with the signs of his jealousy, appreciates how such signs would indicate jealousy in *others*, and is unable to spell out any difference between his own case and those of others. But this conclusion cannot very well be reached by the self-deceived father himself, of course: he cannot through investigation discover his own self-deception for the same reason that he cannot see the jealousy about which he deceives himself. He can see one only if he can see the other, and while he may come to see both it will not be as the outcome of an investigation, but through the lifting of his blindness.

In the case of the religious discovery the same holds. However in the case of religious belief and discovery there are no neutral observers. For the religious discovery, being about the general significance of all that is – and hence the significance of our very lives – involves us all. Nor would there be neutral observers from non-theistic cultures. There would not be, if we allow (as we should) that the religious discovery may result in the discovery of a relationship to Reality not necessarily conceived of as a personal God, as in forms of Buddhism. Granting this, the possibility of a religious discovery in some form is before everyone in every culture. There is no person neutral and unaffected who might disinterestedly investigate a hypothesis about the religious discovery, even if there were one to investigate. This does not quite mean that there is nothing to be done by those in the midst of the issue. One can ask 'Am I blind?' and even 'Am I self-deceived?' and hope for light. Maybe one can seek light too, even if not through an investigative pursuit. One can endeavour to entertain as possible what is unthinkable. And, through effort or luck or grace, blindness and self-deception can be overcome.

To sum up: There is a traceable logic applicable to the religious discovery. It is the logic of realisation-discoveries generally. But, because we are all involved in the issue of religious discovery, it is not possible for us to settle by investigation whether, by that logic, the religious discovery has been made. Even so we can be clear that, where it is self-deception that would have caused blindness, *if* no conscious or unconscious motive for self-deception exists in a person who is regarded to have made the religious discovery, then this is strong even conclusive evidence that self-deception is not present and the religious discovery has been made. Furthermore, even if it can never be investigatively settled whether anyone has made the religious discovery, the logic of realisation-discoveries makes it understandable how one can come to realise God's presence without the investigative corroboration of others. We would miss the entire substance of the issue of religious discovery if we persisted in thinking of all discovery as a result of enquiry, where what is at issue is correct reasoning or the thoroughness of investigation. In its depths the issue of religious discovery is about freedom from self-deception, or at least the kind of blindness to the familiar that self-deception causes (for self-deception is not necessarily its cause); it is not about investigative thoroughness. From Freud's vantage point it is about freedom from neurotic manifestations of the unconscious. From the vantage point of the Third Perspective we may say that it is about purity of heart.

Palpably there is a *cognitive* issue about religious discovery. Making or not making the religious discovery is not merely a matter of choosing to believe or choosing not to, nor is it merely a matter of taking up or rejecting a way of life with its internally regulating images. There is a kind of evidence or grounding within realisation-discoveries, and after my earlier caveats I make no apologies for my use of 'evidence' in the just completed discussion. Alasdair MacIntyre in discussing religious belief and Freud's analysis of it suggests that Freud has dogmas as much as Christianity and both are unverifiable.[58] This may be. He also suggests that it is logically inappropriate to ask for evidence for either. This may be too. For the sort of evidence that one asks for and receives is the public sort clear to all when presented, which enters the lists on one side or the other in the investigation of a hypothesis. But not all evidence or grounding is of this public sort.

Nor is the issue of whether the religious discovery has been made the same as the issue of the correct interpretation of the world as a whole. To say that faith is an interpretation of the world as manifesting God's presence is not, in itself, to say that there is a religious discovery of God's presence. This is so even though what some among the religious regard as a discovery of God's presence others may regard as only an interpretation (and possibly a wrong interpretation if they do not describe it as a discovery). Discoveries are unlike interpretations. Interpretations can be conscious or unconscious, right or wrong. And there can be competing interpretations. The theistic and atheistic interpretations of the world are just such competing interpretations. When there are competing interpretations there is an enquiry-issue about which is correct, and it would seem that this issue should be settled before one take one's own interpretation to be correct. No such issue exists regarding the religious discovery. There is of course an enquiry-issue about whether the religious discovery has been made, one which is uniquely unsettleable, as we have seen. But the religious judgement that one has made the religious discovery does not wait upon the resolution of this enquiry-issue, for that issue does not arise for those who live their lives daily in God's presence. On the other hand if the religious concede that they are but interpreting the world religiously, and there are other interpretations, then it seems incumbent upon them to wait before they confidently accept their interpretation as correct.

John Hick, as we have seen (in Chapter 1), regards religious faith as interpretation, and – appropriately, given the issue of competing interpretations – he gives a place to eschatological verification, which will decide between the religious and non-religious interpretations of the world and, in his more recent thinking, also will decide which of the various religious interpretations have which part of the truth.[59] It may be significant, however, that Hick says in *Faith and Knowledge* that

> the believer can already have, on the basis of his religious experience, a warrant as to the reality of God. He may already know God in a way which requires no further verification.[60]

And he immediately adds that 'to the extent to which the believer actually has a present consciousness of God . . . the life of heaven will not fundamentally change his cognitive relation to his Maker'. When Hick says this it seems to me that he comes close to presenting the believer's experience of God's presence as a discovery. Perhaps then he would allow that as religious persons who have had the Psalmist's experience understand themselves they have made a discovery, while for others they are only interpreting the world and their experience. This, in any case, is the self-understanding of believers in the tradition of the Third-Perspective.

IV CONCLUSION

In this chapter I have begun to present a third religious perspective, one which goes back to the Psalms but is not limited to the Psalms. Central to this perspective is a discovery of God's presence, and I have tried to show how in type this discovery is a realisation-discovery. As such it exhibits the general logic of realisation-discoveries and carries implications for both rationality and evidence, although this is not to deny that the religious discovery is a unique discovery. In several ways it is. For one thing it is about the significance of all that there is. I have not argued that the religious discovery has ever been made, but I have tried to shed light on that issue. There is an issue here, a cognitive issue with a logic that can be examined, although this is not to say that there is an issue for the religious who live in the midst of their discovery. Moreover if any religious persons have made the religious discovery, then they have made the religious discovery: their having done so does not require that others resolve the issue of whether they have truly discovered God's presence. Still, for others, there is an issue here. It is an issue of blindness. And regarding it Freud and Bonaventura are a long way closer to the heart of the matter than are Hume and Paley.

Now finally in this chapter I would like to draw out some implications of the Third Perspective for philosophical concerns by considering a question asked by religious sceptics, and by other philosophers as well, about religious belief. It is implicitly asked by Kai Nielsen in his book, *Scepticism*, where it has this form: What would it be like for the fundamental claims of religion to be true?[61] In the light of the Third Perspective, and the religious discovery at its core, we can offer an answer to this question. However it is not a verificationist answer, either of the sort Nielsen wants or of the sort Hick offers. On the other hand we need not appeal to a form-of-life dependent concept of evidence. What would the world be like if the fundamental claims of religion were true? The world would be a place in which human beings could in reality here and now make the religious discovery.

Often contemporary religious sceptics hold that religion with its reference to a transcendent Reality must have either no cognitive status or a confused cognitivity. In response many with the Second Perspective try to show that God's existence is, to a greater or lesser extent, an enquiry issue, and as such has a legitimate cognitivity. Neo-Wittgensteinians, from a First-Perspective position, allow that there is another choice: an internal cognitivity. What we have seen in this chapter is that if we turn our gaze from enquiry-contexts we will discern yet another alternative, which we might call realisation-cognitivity. This is no technical creation. Realisation is at home in the world, and importantly it is at home in a recogniseable tradition of religious belief.

But neither this account of the Third Perspective's religious discovery nor the fact that the religious discovery has been made, if that is a fact, gives us a method whereby one can repeat the religious discovery and so confirm whether it is a true discovery. There is no such method. Without exception realisation-discoveries are not made as the result of pursuing an investigative methodology, not of any sort. Thus the logic of the religious discovery, while it gives us a way of understanding how the presence of God can be plain and open for the religious, provides no new test or criterion for the presence of God. Rather, following the grammar of the religious discovery, we are invited to look upon what is already familiar to us: the firmament, the deep, our own lives. And, if we are given new eyes, we shall see what was there to be seen all along.

This does not represent a retreat into mystification. As we have seen, the religious discovery at the heart of the Third Perspective has a grammar, or logic; and the issue of whether the religious discovery has been made has a logic. While not all have made the religious discovery, even those who have not can understand its logic and the general logic of realisation-discoveries. In accord with the logic of the religious discovery, which is the grammar pertinent to realisation-discoveries generally, the religious have an explanation of why some have not made the religious discovery. Also, given the logic of the issue of whether the religious discovery has been made – which again is just the logic that applies generally to such issues about realisation-discoveries – there is even an explanation of why the issue of whether the Psalmist or any person has made the religious discovery, though it can be raised and pursued, cannot be settled.

In a sense, then, this discussion must point beyond itself. Finally there is nothing more to be said. But *why* this is so can be clearly said. I am reminded of something M. O'C. Drury has written about Kierkegaard and Wittgenstein. Drury says that for him one idea is central in all of Wittgenstein's thought, and that idea he also finds in Kierkegaard's writings. As Kierkegaard put it, it is this: the majority of us try to understand more and more about things, but finally there is a critical moment when everything is reversed and the point becomes to understand more and more that there is something which cannot be understood. As Wittgenstein put the idea it is this: 'We show the unspeakable by clearly displaying the speakable.'[62] One idea or two ideas, the spirit is the same; and, allowing one idea, it is applicable to the logic of the religious discovery. To understand the possiblity of the religious discovery is to understand that there is something beyond the reach of that understanding we employ when we garner facts and by so doing learn more and more about the world. And, in regard to Wittgenstein's expression of the idea, by clearly displaying the logic of the religious discovery we show or point to what that logic and any discussion of it, by the nature of the case, cannot demonstrate.

3 The Framework of the Third Perspective

I INTRODUCTION

In addition to the realisation-discovery at its centre there is a framework of intuitions that fill out the Third Perspective. In this chapter I shall draw in that framework. As the religious discovery itself has a grammar so it has grammatical implications, strong or weak, for the interconnected issues of religious cognitivity that we have identified. Drawing in the framework of the Third Perspective is mainly a matter of tracing these implications. In Chapter 1, I drew in the First and Second Perspectives, and identified their strengths, by presenting a range of First- and Second-Perspective stances on the five subissues of the general issue of cognitivity. Here I shall try to bring into focus the framework of the Third Perspective that rests upon, but also complements, the religious discovery by applying the Third Perspective to these same five subissues.

Also, by following this procedure, I shall be able to contrast the Third Perspective with the First and Second Perspectives. Given that the five subissues are in essence issues between the First and Second Perspectives, and given the background of the second chapter, even if the first two perspectives were not explicitly mentioned, the contrast would come out to some extent. However very often I shall make explicit significant points of difference as well as significant points of similarity (going well beyond the few comments I made along these lines in Chapter 2). Moreover I do not want to lose sight of the strengths of the first two perspectives. And so, also in this chapter, I shall try to show how the Third Perspective can accommodate the strengths of both of the first two perspectives. If the Third Perspective can do this, then *ipso facto* it can begin to resolve the five subissues and so begin to resolve the issue of cognitivity as a whole.

II THE THIRD PERSPECTIVE ON THE FIVE SUBISSUES

(1) The Rationality Subissue: What Is the Value of Rationality for Religion?

Those with the Third Perspective may or may not directly address this issue in its own terms. (One will search long to find any pronouncement in the Psalms on rationality.) Still one can draw out the implications of the religious discovery for rationality. To do so, however, it is necessary to bear in mind that the religious discovery is a realisation-discovery. Consequently enquiry-rationality is not applicable to the Third Perspective's religious discovery, and this means that neither the adequacy of argumentation nor the care exercised in weighing considerations nor the thoroughness of investigative evidence-gathering is relevant to the rationality of the Third Perspective. On the other hand, realisation- or blindness-rationality does apply to the Third Perspective.

This is not to say that those with the Third Perspective have raised and discussed the issue of the blindness or lack of blindness of those who regard themselves as having made the religious discovery. Typically devotional writers and mystics with the Third Perspective see no issue here: confident of their own discovery they regard those who fail to see God's presence as blind. The issue as it faces others, though, can be raised, and its logic traced, as we have seen. But, again, it is not the concern of the Psalmist or even of Bonaventura to do this.

In any case, the question before us at present is not whether it is valuable for the Third Perspective to pursue the issue of the rationality of religious believers; the question is whether for the Third Perspective rationality is valuable. And it is. For blindness-rationality is just the overcoming or lifting of blindness that enables one to make the religious discovery. In fact sometimes in the tradition of the Third Perspective it is acknowledged as valuable, although it is not called 'blindness-rationality' or 'realisation-rationality' in religious literature; rather, it is called 'opening one's eyes' or 'having one's eyes opened' or, in reference to the state that may allow this to happen, 'purity of heart'.

The religious realisation-discovery and that blindness that

prevents one from discovering the presence of God are significantly related to what I have referred to as the moral dimension of
faith. This is the dimension of faith that involves the will and
willfulness. It is this aspect of faith that Kierkegaard takes to be all
of faith in the *Postscript* and, as we have seen, that John Hick and
Robert Herbert heed. Blindness-irrationality, particularly when
it is a matter of self-deception, involves willfully averting one's
eyes lest one see what one cannot bear to see. Enquiry-
irrationality, on the other hand, might involve nothing worse than
a lack of investigative care – a fault, but a fault of a different order.
The cognitive fault of blindness-irrationality, when it arises from
self-deception, is not insincerity, it is closer to a lack of honesty to
oneself. The fool of the Psalms says to himself that there is no God.

Let us in this connection recall the 'devout scepticism' that I
discussed in Chapter 1.[1] Devout sceptics may wish to believe in
God, but they are prepared to believe only after their honest
doubts have been laid to rest. They would rather honestly and
devoutly doubt than dishonestly believe. In taking this stand
devout sceptics seem to be the soul of rationality: when adequate
evidence for God's existence is forthcoming, then, but only then,
will they believe, regardless of how eager they may be to believe
without it. Notice, however, the rather different light that is cast
on the rationality of devout scepticism from the standpoint of the
Third Perspective. Devout sceptics seem paradigmatically
rational as long as we apply to them enquiry-rationality (and
allow that public evidence appropriate to an investigative effort is
lacking). But if we apply blindness-rationality to them, then
things are different. Devout sceptics then emerge as blindness-
irrational. They do, that is, if there is a religious discovery of
God's presence to be made, as the Third Perspective affirms.
There is a story of an agnostic philosopher, recounted by H. H.
Price, to whom the question was put: 'What would you say if God
himself suddenly appeared among us in this room?' The
philosopher, it is said, replied, '"God", I should say, "why did
you make evidence for your existence so inadequate?"'[2] But the
evidence is not inadequate, the Third-Perspective believer would
say. It speaks as loudly as the evidence for one's own life. It is only
that, for one reason or another, many are blind to it in its
significance as assurance of God's presence. For the Third
Perspective religious doubters, including devout sceptics, are
blind to what the religious, some of the religious, have seen. Thus

they are blindness-irrational; although, as I have tried to stress, this does not strictly entail that they are self-deceived. Have religious doubters willfully deceived themselves into doubting God's presence? Or might it be that God's presence is evident and inescapable to the Psalmist and others while many, though not self-deceived, are in their age blind to what the Psalmist could not but see? In the latter case those who do not see God's presence are not self-deceived, although this is not to say that their blindness is in no way willful (on which more in section (3)).

For the First and Second Perspectives the issue of the value of rationality for religion is over enquiry-rationality. As I have argued, both contemporary thinkers with the First Perspective and contemporary thinkers with the Second Perspective tend to focus on the traditional concept of rationality, which projects an enquiry-model of rationality. But as the existence of the Third Perspective makes clear, this focus is not required. Still the hold of the enquiry-model is strong. Thus Phillips, in *Religion without Explanation* argues that both critics and defenders of religious belief are confused because both use the language of the indicative mood and matter of fact.[3] He says that instead we need to appreciate the character of what is before us in religious belief. We need to remind ourselves of the familiar characteristics of religious belief. In this Phillips echoes Wittgenstein. But, it seems to me, Phillips has not followed his own advice. Or, at best, he looks at the religious belief of only some believers.[4] I suggest that the critics and defenders Phillips has in mind *and* Phillips wrongly think of the 'paradigm' of rationality as enquiry-rationality (proof-seeking, hypothesis-proving, and so on). The cure is not to make religion non-cognitive in the way Phillips sometimes does, or to resort to internal rationality and evidence. Rather the cure is to pay heed to the working epistemological concepts in various strains of Judaeo-Christian religious belief, and this includes the strain I am pointing to in this and the previous chapter.

Kierkegaard too, in renouncing 'reflection', 'reason', and 'speculation', is thinking of enquiry-rationality, or at least not thinking of blindness-rationality. However, though this is so, in the light of Kierkegaard's thought a problem or question arises for the Third Perspective. For Kierkegaard in the *Postscript* the object of faith is the absolute paradox. The absolute paradox is a contradiction (that the eternal became temporal in the Incarnation), and of necessity, it would seem, it cannot have support; and so, it seems to follow, faith must be irrational in even the blindness sense. The question here is this: Can the religious discovery relate to the absolute paradox; and if so, how?

It must be confessed that it is hard to see how it can as long as the object of faith is precisely *that* the eternal God was born as a temporal man in a particular place at a particular time. But two obervations are worth making: First, the eternal-becoming-temporal may be religiously understood in other ways consistent with but different from the Christian Incarnation. It may be understood to mean that the eternal God acts in and is present in the temporal world or that the eternal, the Divine, through grace, is expressed in the temporal lives of men and women. In these constructions the eternal-becoming-temporal is more understandable as a candidate for a religious discovery of the significance of the familiar. Second, the religious discovery is more than a discovery that there is a God; it is a discovery of a relationship to God. Kierkegaard's *Postscript* definition of faith makes faith the embracing of an absolutely uncertain *proposition*. Yet at the same time faith for Kierkegaard is a God-relationship. Could one discover a relationship to the absolute paradox (or to the eternal-become-temporal God) without discovering that the absolute paradox is true? Perhaps we should here recall Kierkegaard's idol worshipper who has faith in God though his eyes rest upon an idol (see Chapter 1, section (2)). If the idol worshipper by virtue of his infinite passion can embrace the absolute paradox without having the Christian conception in his mind, then one can discover a relationship to the absolute paradox (or to the eternal-become-temporal God) without accepting the Christian conception. Just as one's holding the true conception of God is not necessary for one to believe in the true God, so one's holding the true conception of God is not necessary for one to discover a relationship to God.

But let us remind ourselves of the three reasons that we found Kierkegaard has in the *Postscript* for requiring faith to be irrational. First, to seek reasons is to try to reduce the passion of faith. Second, the absolute paradox is a 'contradition' and so can have no support. Third, faith requires the possibility of an offence to reason. Taking the second first, we have just seen that the absolute paradox can be understood in such a way that its truth is open to religious discovery, and in any case a relationship to the

eternal-become-temporal God, perhaps under a different conception, is open to religious discovery.

Kierkegaard's other two reasons derive from his enquiry-
conception of rationality and reasonableness. Kierkegaard's first
reason for requiring faith to be irrational – that to seek reasons is
to try to reduce the passion of faith – relates directly to *investigating*
and *gathering* evidence, and to the tentativeness of attitude such
'approximation' efforts require. But no such attitude as this is
required in those who make the religious discovery. Since no
investigative effort is undertaken, no such attitude is required.
True, one who makes the religious discovery may have sought
God, may even have hungered and thirsted after righteousness.
On the other hand one may make the religious discovery while not
seeking God and while even denying that there is a God. In
neither case is enquiring after reasons for belief what enables one
to make the religious discovery. Of course in making the religious
discovery one in a sense comes to have reasons for one's belief:
God's presence is discovered in His creation. But this is not to say
that one sought reasons, and it certainly is not to say that
enquiring after reasons is necessary for one's making the
religious discovery.

Kierkegaard's third reason is that faith requires the possibility
of an offence to reason. Once more Kierkegaard's concern is with
enquiry. Overcoming blindness-irrationality, or blindness, and
coming to see God's presence leaves the possiblity of offence to
'human reason' intact if reason is identified with enquiry-
rationality (an equation Kierkegaard clearly makes). Those who
have made the religious discovery still cannot present public
evidence, evidence apparent to all, either to others or to themselves. They can only point to the familiar. There is nothing to
convince others – short of their own religious discovery. Thus
those who have made the religious discovery invite the intellectual
disdain of others, and their own too when they take a literally
common sense posture: in this way the possibility of an offence, an
offence to enquiry-rationality, remains before the believer.

Already, at this point, we can begin to see how the Third
Perspective can negotiate between the First and Second Perspectives. The issue between the First and Second Perspectives, so far as
rationality is concerned, is over enquiry-rationality. Realisation-
rationality is not addressed by either perspective. Thus if the First

Perspective will limit its rejection of rationality to enquiry-rationality (the investigative seeking of evidence, enquiring into the basis of belief before believing, and so on) and the Second Perspective will substitute realisation-rationality for enquiry-rationality (which perhaps is easier for some versions of the Second Perspective than for others), the two perspectives can, on this issue, draw closer together.

(2) The Cognitivity-of-Belief Subissue: Is Religion Cognitive at Its Core?

At the centre of the Third Perspective is the discovery of a relationship to the Divine, or of God's presence, as it is expressed in the Psalmist's tradition. Those who make the religious discovery discover, or rediscover, that they stand in a relationship to God or the Divine. Such a discovery, though it is of a relationship to God and not of the truth of a proposition about God, would make no sense if religious belief were not cognitive. Even though the object of the discovery at its deepest level is not a proposition but a relationship to the Divine, the discovery's having that object presupposes the truth of both the proposition that there is a God and the proposition that one stands in a relationship to God. To deny this connection would be to deny that a relationship to God has indeed been discovered, and it would be to deny that the religious discovery results in that personal knowledge of a relationship to God which, for the Third Perspective, is its spiritual fruit. In short it would be to deny the truth of the self-understanding of those in the tradition of the Third Perspective. For this reason the Third Perspective gives a deep place to cognitive belief. I do not mean that those with the Third Perspective typically address this issue and explicitly affirm the cognitive nature of their belief. For the Psalmist and others in the tradition of the Third Perspective no such issue presents itself. Those with the Third Perspective implicitly – naturally and without second thoughts – understand that they are in a relationship to God or the Divine, that this proposition is true, and that it is true by virtue of a correspondence with the deepest reality in the universe.

On the second subissue, then, the Third Perspective is very close to the Second in its essential response: at its core religion is and must be cognitive. At the same time, it seems to me, the Third Perspective draws close to the First Perspective in that it can speak to First-Perspective concerns, at least some of them.

The Third Perspective, I think, must be sympathetic toward Kierkegaard's rejection of 'objective belief', that is, the idea that religious belief is precisely a matter of holding the right, the true, beliefs about God. For the Third Perspective, the religious discovery is of a relationship to God and religious faith is living in accord with that relationship. To the extent that Kierkegaard sees faith as a God-relationship, despite his giving no place to the discovery of a relationship to God, his intuitions are not that distant from those of the Third Perspective.

Again, while for the Third Perspective religious belief is deeply cognitive, it is not for this reason a 'question of science'. At least to this extent the Third Perspective is in accord with Wittgenstein's intuitions in his lectures on religious belief. To say that religious belief is cognitive and even deeply cognitive is not to say that religious belief is a matter of enquiry, and for the Third Pespective religious belief grounded in the religious discovery clearly is not a matter of enquiry. For the Third Perspective, as for the First, religious beliefs are not hypotheses, not even non-experimental hypotheses. But the Third Perspective, unlike the First, or some of its versions, does not embody the presupposition that if religious belief is cognitive, then (if it is not merely a matter of the relations of ideas) it must be a kind of hypothesis. Thus it is not forced to deny cognitivity to religious belief.

A further reason that some with First-Perspective intuitions, notably Phillips, tend toward a non-cognitive understanding of religious belief is that they perceive something to be wrong with attributing existence to God. For Phillips God is not an object among objects, like a planet, which exists and whose existence might be discovered, but toward which we might then be indifferent. To an extent the Third Perspective shares this perception and concern. The religious discovery is not the discovery of God's *existence*, it is the discovery of God's presence and of one's relation to the living God in whose presence one finds oneself. Only when the one who makes the religious discovery is one who has denied that there is a God is God's existence also discovered, and then only secondarily. But of greater concern to Phillips is what he takes to be an implication of allowing that God exists or that the concept even applies to God. Phillips seems to think that (i) if we say that God exists, then we make our belief factual and this entails that possibly God does not exist, and (ii) if we say that God exists, then that makes God a contingent object and this means that even if God exists now possibly at some time He will not or did not exist. Both of these implications run counter to what many religious believers understand God to be, as Phillips sees it. And of course he is right.

However, drawing upon and elaborating the intuitions of the Third Perspective, we can reply to Phillips' concerns, I believe. First we should observe that the proposition that God exists does not itself carry the implication that for all we know God might not exist. What carries this implication is the tentative hypothesis that God exists, which when articulated amounts to: 'I am justified only in tentatively believing that God exists, and it is possible that this belief is wrong.' But God's existence could be certain, and it is certain if anyone has come to know in the Psalmist's way, through experience of the presence of God, that the living God exists. Those who have made the religious discovery count as certain God's existence and their relationship to God (even if precisely what that relationship requires of them is at times in question). Similarly if a relationship to the *eternal* God is discovered, it is certain that God has always existed and always will exist (from everlasting to everlasting). For the Third Perspective to speak to Phillips' concerns in this way it is true that the offending implications must be construed as 'for all we know possibly at some time God will not or did not exist'. However I believe that these are precisely the concern or should be.

A related concern that Phillips has is that, if we allow that existence applies to God, then we allow the possibility of an atheist's coming to believe indifferently and theoretically that God exists without confessing a religious belief.[5] Clearly, if one makes the religious discovery, one does not come to an indifferent belief that God exists. As I have tried to emphasise, the religious discovery is of a relationship to God, and as such it necessarily is a personal discovery. The knowledge that non-believers would gain from it – that the living God exists and that they stand in a relationship to that God – necessarily rules out religious indifference. We can even say with Phillips that if it is truly acquired it must be confessed. There may be a mode of religious belief that shuns existence in the way Phillips and others suggest. I do not deny this, although I should say that such a notion sounds odd to me. The point here is only that the Third Perspective can speak to those First-Perspective concerns with existence which lead some to deny that 'God exists' is a legitimate cognitive belief.

But the Neo-Wittgensteinian First-Perspective resistance to the cognitive status of religious belief has other roots. Intertwined with the reasons just discussed, another reason why Phillips tends to deny cognitivity or full cognitivity to religious belief is that, for him, there is no finding out in religion. If there were, Phillips seems to think, whether there is a God would be a *matter of fact* about which one could say, 'I couldn't care less.' Here the concern is with the implications of finding out that something is so. Phillips seems to see a necessary gap between discovery and response. Religious belief, he sees, is indistinguishable from religious response, but a discovery that something is so does not necessitate any feeling response, so discovering that something is so has no place in religion. This of course is in line with a lot of philosophical thinking, going back at least to Hume, according to which fact and value are in distinct camps. However much Phillips has been influenced by this way of thinking, it holds best for enquiry-contexts and the investigating of various hypotheses. One who finds out through investigation that there is one more planet may well be indifferent to that fact (this is Phillips' example). But such a discovery in ordinary circumstances would be made by investigating a hypothesis. The religious discovery is not like this. In part because it is a realisation-discovery and in part because it is the realisation-discovery that it is, there is no gap between discovery and response where it is concerned. If one does not say 'My Lord and my God', that shows or as good as shows that the discovery of God's presence has not been made. Perhaps Phillips would say that no 'matter of fact' is discovered then. This may be so – depending on what is packed into the concept of *matter of fact*. What *is* discovered, in the self-understanding of Third-Perspective believers, is a relationship to God; and, again, this necessitates that truths about reality are discovered. The Third Pespective, however, holds no brief for calling these 'matters of fact'.

It seems to me, then, that the Third Pespective can speak to at least some First-Perspective concerns about the cognitivity of religious belief, especially certain Neo-Wittgensteinian concerns which have led those with them to deny the cognitive status of religious belief. I propose now to turn attention to the connections between religious practice and cognitive belief. As we explore these connections I shall have occasion to refer to Kierkegaard, and I believe that we shall see that Kierkegaard in some writings is closer to giving a deep place to cognitive belief than might be thought given his *Postscript* views.

It is a matter of the grammar of the religious discovery that it does not result in a theoretical belief. If it did it would have no place in the Psalmist's tradition. For in that tradition religious faith in God is a way of life, not belief that various religious propositions are true. It is not, in Kierkegaard's language, 'objective belief'. The Third Perspective, the perspective of the Psalmist's tradition, then, recognises the essential place of what broadly may be called religious practice – including the role of belief, commitment, religious passions, specific religious activities, and the life-regulating role of faith. For the Third Perspective as for the First, religion is *essentially* a way of life. But from the standpoint of the Third Perspective a view of religion that stresses religious practice should not sever practice from cognitivity. Rather it should be alive to the deep connections between specific religious practices, emotions, attitudes, etc., and the cognitive. Here we may say that the Third Perspective is again closer to the Second.

What, though, are these connections? Let me comment on several. First, consider belief in God (and I shall now address the question I raised in Chapter 1 about the connection between belief in God and cognitive belief). The connection between belief in God and cognitive belief, specifically the belief that God exists, seems plain within the Third Perspective. For those in the Psalmist's tradition there is a belief in the existence of the God who is believed in. They do not balk at saying that there is a God; they are not in the position of believing in God while failing to affirm the existence of the God in whom they believe. The Third Perspective on this specific matter is closer to Calvin than to Malcolm. It agrees with Calvin that faith in God is more than belief that God exists; but while it is more it must contain the belief that God exists. It must to make logical and emotional sense. At the same time the Third Perspective agrees with Malcolm that the indifferent belief his atheist comes to by following the ontological argument is not a religious belief; and, for the Third

Perspective, it is not such a belief in God's existence as this that is presupposed by belief in God.

Commitment to God is similarly understood. Commitment to God, for the Third Perspective, again requires a belief that there is the God to whom one is committed. However we should not read too much into this grammatical comment. Roger Trigg says: 'The belief [in God and His existence] is distinct from the commitment which may follow it, and is the justification for it.'[6] In making this claim Trigg, proceeding from a Second-Perspective starting point, perhaps goes too far; and I shall offer a Third-Perspective emendation, with the spirit of which the First Perspective would tend to agree. It is not that commitment may (or may not) follow belief. Belief – if it is full religious belief, that which would follow the religious discovery – is not accidentally connected to commitment in this way. A lack of commitment demonstrates a lack of belief. Nevertheless Trigg is right when he says that belief can be a reason for commitment and so is distinguishable from commitment. This point is clear if we take a specific instance of religious commitment as it could occur in an individual's life: one might become a medical missionary because of one's belief in God (and how one understands God's will). Yet becoming a medical missionary is not belief in God; for the next believer commitment to God might well take a different form.

The same general point holds for religious emotions. Let us consider two that are not unimportant for the Psalmist's tradition: trust and awe. Religious trust is precisely trust in God, and, as such, as a matter of conceptual and emotional sense, it presupposes a belief in God's existence and a belief in God's goodness. Religious awe and wonder also have a connection to the cognitive, but here the connection is more difficult to make out. It is because one thing that we might call 'religious awe' is that sense of awe one can feel before having belief in God, which helps lead one to religious belief. But since such awe is felt before one believes it clearly does not presuppose a cognitive religious belief. However, once one has attained belief one may well retrospectively describe the context of awe in a way that requires cognitive belief. No longer is awe merely awe before the starry heavens above and the moral order within, it in retrospect is seen as awe before God's creation. And of course if religious awe and wonder are the awe and wonder found within religious belief, which is that expressed by the Psalmist again and again, then the full description that the believer would give is 'awe and wonder before God's creation' or 'before the Divine', and now the connection with cognitive belief is clear.[7]

Also specific religious activities are essentially connected to the cognitive (and at this point I shall turn to the question I raised in Chapter 1 about the connection between specific religious practices and religious belief). Consider prayer. In offering petitionary prayers Third-Perspective believers (but not Third-Perspective believers alone) ask for something. What is asked for may be mercy or forgiveness, or that the sins of God's children be taken from them, or that God's light not be taken from them. An evident cognitive belief connected to the practice of prayer in each case is that God can grant what the prayer names. At least this connection is evident to the Third Perspective. In fact, it is worth noting, this connection holds even for the prayer that God's will be done. This prayer does not ask for anything specific, like mercy or forgiveness, and certainly it does not ask for anything like recovery from an illness or protection on a journey. But, as Peter Geach observes, it is in the context of the Lord's Prayer a petition that God's will be done on earth as it is in heaven.[8] It is not a prayer of resignation. Of course 'May Your Will be done' can be a prayer of acceptance of what may come, and this prayer is not without significance in the tradition of the Third Perspective. But here too there are evident connections to cognitive beliefs in God's existence and in the existence of the Divine will.

In apparent opposition to this understanding of petitionary prayer Phillips, from his First-Perspective position, has argued that in the case of prayer 'petition' does not mean what it means in ordinary discourse. In *The Concept of Prayer* he says:

> When deep religious believers pray *for* something, they are not so much asking God to bring this about, but in a way telling Him of the strength of their desires.[9]

It is not clear that Phillips quite means what he seems to be saying, for he immediately goes on to say:

> They realise that things may not go as they wish, and they are *asking to be able to go on living* whatever happens.[10]

And, if this is right, believers are after all asking God to bring it about that they have the strength to go on living. Perhaps Phillips means that in proper prayer (prayer of the deeply religious) what contributes to personal aggrandisement is not asked for. This may be so and is in accord with the religious sensitivities of the Third Perspective.

But on balance, given other things he says, it seems that Phillips holds that the deeply religious just do not ask God to bring about anything. Except in a revised sense they do not ask God for anything. Perhaps this is the way prayer is understood in some tradition, that to which Phillips consistently appeals. In such a tradition, since there is no real asking of God, the cognitive belief I just identified – that God can grant what is asked for – would drop out.

At the same time, though, I want to emphasize how close some of Phillips' First-Perspective observations about prayer are to the Third Perspective. Phillips is exactly in accord with Third-Perspective intuitions when he says that prayer for something is not to be understood as an incantation or magic rite.[11] Saying a prayer is not like wielding an instrument. It is not for Phillips and it is not in the tradition of the Third Perspective. Yet there is an asking in the Third Perspective, though it is an asking in accord with God's will – as when Anselm prayed in the *Proslogion* that God would give understanding to his faith 'as far as thou knowest it to be good for me'. Again Phillips is right not only for the believers he has in mind but for the Third Perspective when he allows that to ask for help in overcoming envy is already to have begun receiving help from God. And Phillips is right, too, in being suspicious of asking God for such benefits as good health or prosperity. But from the standpoint of the Third Perspective such prayers are deficient not because they ask God for what it is believed He can grant, but because they ask God for what one wills despite what God may will.

Within the Judaeo-Christian heritage prayer is sometimes characterised as a colloquy or conversation of the soul with God. St. Francis de Sales in the *Treatise on the Love of God* reminds us of this way of understanding prayer,[12] a way that does no violence to the Third Perspective. (Perhaps we should call to mind here Phillips' comment that when deep religious believers pray for something they are telling God of the strength of their desires.) Such prayer is mystical, St. Francis goes on to say, because it is secret and hidden; it takes place in that mental solitude 'where the soul alone treats with her God alone'. St. Francis does not mention Dionysius at this point, but he pretty clearly is drawing upon Dionysius' mystical tradition (prayer, St. Francis says, is mystical theology). But this does not put him utterly at odds with the Psalmist's tradition, and, indeed, he goes on before the chapter is done to quote passages from the Psalms in which the Psalmist cries out to God. In prayer of this sort the effort 'is to speak to God and to hear God speak in the bottom of the heart'. Such prayer may be wholly non-petitionary. And all prayer, whether petitionary or not, when profound, may be an effort to speak to and hear God in one's heart, and in this way to draw near to God. The Third Perspective not only allows this understanding of prayer, it welcomes it as wholly congenial to its sensibility. The idea that one can discover God in the movement of one's heart, as St. Bernard did, is at home in the Third Perspective. However this understanding of prayer is, if anything, more intimately interwoven with cognitive belief. For in the understanding of the believer, with whom does the soul discourse if it is not with God? And from whom does the soul receive inspiration, as St. Francis says it does, if it is not from God?

Let us consider other religious practices. 'Regulating', in Wittgenstein's sense, may also be considered a religious practice. For Wittgenstein in *Lectures on Religious Belief* religious beliefs or pictures are used by believers to regulate in all of life. Now to the extent that regulating one's life with a picture is using a story to guide one's life, no cognitive belief is required for the practice. For instance one can use the story of the good Samaritan as a life-guiding parable without believing that it is true. Under this construction regulating is understood in a First-Perspective way – and Wittgenstein and R. B. Braithwaite are quite close. But, given this construction, Wittgenstein's own example of the Last Judgment is a bad or at least misleading example. It is because the religious belief in the Last Judgment is a belief, not a story. If religious believers regulate their lives *by* keeping before themselves the prospect of being judged in a Last Judgment, the regulating function would seem to be different from and even based on a cognitive belief in the Last Judgment.[13] I believe that within the tradition of the Third Perspective there is a place for what Wittgenstein calls 'regulating'. But for the Third Perspective there need be no effort to isolate belief's regulating function from cognitivity. Indeed for the Third Perspective the regulating function of religious belief rests upon its cognitivity. This is not to say that the belief in a Last Judgment is a particularly significant belief in the tradition of the Third Perspective. In fact, it seems to me that generally it is not (perhaps, though, its importance varies from believer to believer within that tradition). Much more important – or rather, of paramount importance – is trying to live as God wills in a God-relationship. It is this effort that regulates the life of the believer in the tradition of the Third Perspective. But this effort is essentially cognitive. For believers cannot consciously try to live in accord with a God-relationship – discovered or not – without believing that there is a God and that they stand in a relationship to God.

For the Third Perspective *dying to self* is essential to the believers' relationship to God. Also, as we saw in the last chapter, dying to self is crucial to the religious discovery itself. Clearly this religious category is important for the Third Perspective. And so let us now ask, to what extent is dying to self to be understood cognitively? If we look at that self-renunciation or dying to self which is crucial to the Third Perspective, then I think that we will see how this religious element is essentially connected to cognitive belief in God, not as a matter of logic, or not merely as a matter of logic, but as a matter of the coherence of a lived religious life within the tradition of the Third Perspective. Let me give three reasons why this is so.

First, the *object* of self-renunciation. For the Third Perspective, self-renunciation cannot be out of a concern for self or a desire for compensation. By its nature self-renunciation cannot have such an object. Self-renunciation (or that love of which self-renunciation is a part) may be *in* God, as Simone Weil says (and strictly objectless), or *for the sake* of God, as St. Bernard says (and so have a Divine object).[14] Either way, though, self-renunciation is a renunciation of self outside a relationship to God. In this way, within the self-understanding of the Third Perspective, in order for believers to appreciate what is involved in one's not having an object in renouncing the self, or one's having only a Divine object, it is required that believers acknowledge the reality of God over and above their self-renunciation. If they do not, they no longer can make religious sense of their own spirituality. They would end up, not renouncing their lives outside a relationship to God, but renouncing their selves for the sake of self-renunciation.

A second reason. Self-renunciation involves doing *God's will*. It is often spoken of as doing or being one with God's will. And this means that God has a will and that we can be far from it or close to it in our lives. Dying to self in God is a oneness with God's will in the tradition of the Third Perspective. Again, religious persons in the tradition of the Third Perspective cannot make sense of trying to do this without a belief in God's existence and in God's will, which with God's grace they will approach in their lives.

A third reason. Religious self-renunciation is distinct from *other sorts* of self-renunciation, but for religious belief, especially in the Psalmist's tradition, this distinction can be drawn only in reference to a God-relationship. Consider the self-renunciation of the suicide or the suicide-in-life, one who feels that life is worthless and wants nothing so much as to be shed of it. Perhaps he is an ambitious man who has failed to realise his ambition. And here let us use an example provided by Kierkegaard, who is more alive to the cognitive element in religion than other First-Perspective thinkers and who, on this point, is more in accord with the Third Perspective. Kierkegaard's example is of one who says, 'either Caesar or nothing', and then fails in his ambition.[15] Because he has failed he renounces his ambition and himself. He comes to hate himself. He is, Kierkegaard says, in despair over himself; for he is not the person he would be. Indeed, Kierkegaard says, the formula for all despair is to despair over oneself, in despair to will to be rid of oneself. Why is this despairing self-renunciation not religious self-renunciation? It even uses the religious language of 'hating' oneself. The difference is not, or is not merely, that in one there is no hope and in the other there is. Religiously there is a greater difference, but that difference requires a reference to a relationship to God. (Kierkegaard calls despair a 'disrelation-ship'.) One who has died to oneself in God is one with God's will. One who despairingly renounces oneself finds no solace in God's will. Note that an overt behavioural difference is not crucial. The person who hates his life despairingly may be religious in manner and appearance. But still, from a Third-Perspective viewpoint, the difference between him and one who has died to self, or in his heart seeks to die to self by seeking God's will, could not be greater: one has a proper relationship to God, the other a 'disrelationship'. One hates himself, as for his unrealised ambition. One hates his self outside a God-relationship. Once again reference to a relationship to God is essential to understand the religious point.

What we see then is that, for the Third Perspective, religious practice broadly construed – really the religious life – and the cognitive are inseparably united: cognitive belief is so closely woven with specific religious practices that it cannot be separated without destroying the fabric. The point here, we should be clear, it not that religious practice is *based* on cognitive belief; it is that cognitive belief is implicit in religious practice, as religious practice is understood by the Third-Perspective believer. Thus to the extent that the First-Perspective, or the Neo-Wittgensteinian, objection is to the idea that religious practice is based on cognitive belief, and not to the idea that cognitive belief is implicit in religious practice, perhaps here too the First Perspective and Third Perspective can draw together.[16]

However perhaps a word of qualification is called for. I think that it should be noted that a non-cognitivist view of religious practice, toward which Neo-Wittgensteinian philosophy of religion tends, is closer to the truth for what might be called *abiding relationships*. Yet, even so, such relationships at bottom have an essential connection to the cognitive and so, finally, are better understood from a Third-Perspective standpoint. But I should explain what I mean by an 'abiding relationship'.

In the Judaeo-Christian tradition, in the Bible and ancillary literature, a religious relationship to God is sometimes described in terms distinct from, though compatible with, the language of faith and belief. For instance, in 1 John 4.16 we are told that 'he who abides in love abides in God, and God abides in him'. In Micah 6.8 what is required of man is that he should 'walk humbly with . . . God'. And in the first letter to the Corinthians St. Paul speaks of himself as an 'imitator of Christ' (1 Corinthians 11.1). Taken collectively these relationships might be called *abiding relationships*. Entering into such a relationship is not so much a matter of believing as it is a matter of accepting God in one's life (as it would be put from a Judaeo-Christian standpoint).

Many relationships are such that we need not acknowledge them to be in them, and such an abiding relationship to God would be of that sort. Moreover, it should be appreciated, such a relationship could be entered by those within the Judaeo-Christian tradition and those outside that tradition. Such a relationship both a Christian and, say, a Buddhist could enter by virtue of the place each gives to love of humanity or compassion for the world. While a love of God might require a conscious belief in God, and explicit faith surely does, a love of humanity in itself could still constitute a relationship to God. Would such a Christian and such a Buddhist be in precisely the same abiding relationship? For one the ideal is love of neighbour and love of God, for the other the ideal is compassion for the world. How they think of God or whether they think of God is not that important for this question. What determines whether the Christian and the Buddhist are in the same abiding relationship is the sameness of their practice of love or compassion. To the extent they abide in the same practice, to the extent the Christian's love is the Buddhist's compassion, they abide in the same relationship. However, strictly, we need not decide whether the Christian and the Buddhist are in the same abiding relationship in order to see that each is in some abiding relationship to God defined by love or compassion.

Of course this is not to say that the religiousness of either the Christian or the Buddhist consists solely in being in some abiding relationship to God. Each is surrounded by a different panoply of ritual, tradition, style of contemplation, and more. In addition, the Christian, at least in the Psalmist's tradition, importantly has explicit faith in God while the Buddhist does not, and the Buddhist importantly seeks Nirvana for all sentient beings while the Christian does not. Yet, despite these not unimportant differences, each may be in an abiding relationship to God, even the same abiding relationship to God; and such an abiding relationship, since the Buddhist has attained it, would not require one's cognitive belief that there is a God or that one is in a relationship to God. However, this is not to say that cognitivity is not essentially involved. It is, and let me now say why it is.

In the first place, abiding relationships cannot be coherently described unless some cognitive beliefs are presupposed. While one may be in an abiding relationship without knowing or believing that one is, a coherent description of an abiding relationship requires the positing of some religious truth. Thus, describing any person as being in an abiding relationship to God posits the religious truth that there is a God. And if what is described as an abiding relationship to God is indeed a relationship to God, then it is true that there is a God. Could some abiding relationships be delineated in non-theistic terms, say in Buddhist terms? Perhaps so. Perhaps there could be delineated in Buddhist terms an abiding relationship to dharma that is essentially

identical to an abiding relationship to God. If abiding relationships can be described in Buddhist as well as Judaeo-Christian
terms, then, while our saying that both a Christian and a
Buddhist are in abiding relationships would leave open the
precise nature of the Reality to which they are related, still a
Reality or Divine would be posited.

Second, while one need not realise that one is in an abiding
relationship to God to be in such a relationship, one *can* realise it.
And an abiding relationship can be the relationship discovered in
the religious discovery. If to walk humbly with God it is not
necessary to believe in God, still it is allowed. And if one had
discovered a relationship to God in which one is to walk humbly
with God, then it is in essence an abiding relationship that one has
discovered.

While it may not be that the Psalmist himself held that there are
abiding relationships to God that could be entered both by those
who embraced belief in God and those who did not, the tradition
of the Third Perspective, and the tradition of the Psalmist
specifically, can consistently recognise the possibility of abiding
relationships. Of course within the Judaeo-Christian heritage
such a recognition would be relatively new, but that is understandable. Before the Common Era there was a great concern
with keeping the commandments of the Lord and not turning to
false gods. Later, and on into the Middle Ages, the Christian
Church, much concerned with heresy, was not inclined to look for
right relationships to the Divine in other religious traditions.
However, more recently, in the spirit of ecumenism, Christians
and others have sought ways of understanding how different
religions with opposing belief structures can each in its own way
engender a right relationship to Reality. The tradition of the
Third Perspective can accommodate this contemporary effort. It
can in two significant ways. First, as we saw in the last chapter,
the model of religious discovery that applies to the discovery at the
heart of the Third Perspective in its Judaeo-Christian manifestation, the discovery made by the Psalmist, can be applied to other
religious traditions; and, second, the Third Pespective can
recognise that religious persons both inside and outside the
Judaeo-Christian heritage are profoundly related to the Divine by
virtue of their being in an abiding relationship to the Divine.

Now let me try to sum up the implicit view of the Third
Perspective on the cognitivity of religious belief. The Third

Perspective must give the cognitive a deep place in religion in order for the religiousness of Third-Perspective believers – their beliefs, their practice, their strivings, their self-understanding – to make sense. Yet the Third Perspective is very far from denying a number of First-Perspective insights. It does not deny the Kierkegaardian insight that religious belief is not a matter of merely proclaiming, or believing, to be true a body of doctrine, not even the central religious statement that God exists. Also the Third Perspective does not deny the Neo-Wittgensteinian point that religious belief is not theoretical. It agrees that to realise there is a God in the religious sense is not to discover that there is one more existent but rather to see the possibility of new meaning in one's life, the possibility of a new life. For the Third Perspective that new life is in a relationship to God or the Divine, and the religious discovery is of that relationship.

(3) The Understanding Subissue: Is It Possible to Understand Without Believing?

Unlike the First and Second Perspectives, the Third Perspective has no strong tendency to give one reply to this question to the exclusion of the opposite reply, although it has what is perhaps a greater sympathy with the First Perspective. Before I try to draw out the Third-Perspective response we should remind ourselves of the issue between the First and Second Perspectives. The question at the centre of that issue is whether a person can stand outside religion, understand it, and yet not believe. How this question is answered has implications for the coherence of religious scepticism on the one hand and for the possibility of loss of faith on the other. The First-Perspective tends to deny that anyone can understand without believing (or at least without having a sympathy for religious belief), and accordingly rejects as incoherent religious scepticism. Also the First Perspective, or strong versions of it, reject as grammatically impossible a loss of true faith, after which a former believer would understand while not believing. The Second Perspective tends to affirm that one can understand without believing. Consequently it accepts as fully coherent religious scepticism and finds no difficulty in understanding the possibility of loss of faith, as well as the possibility of conversion and the occurrence of dialogue between believers and non-believers, which, like loss of faith, have the prima facie implication that one can understand without believing.

Each perspective has its strengths, but how can the insights of both be accommodated? What is needed to lessen the tension between the First and Second Perspectives, and to accommodate the insights of each perspective, it seems to me, is to recognise a distinction between levels of understanding. Understanding can be better or worse, deep or shallow, and so the concept readily lends itself to the kind of distinction that is needed. I do not mean to suggest that we ought to create such a distinction out of whole cloth; rather, we ought to see if there is not in religious thinking some such distinction already acknowledged. The distinction needed should, moreover, respect the special character of religious belief: its life-involving quality and its moral dimension. There is, I believe, such a distinction; and it is implicit in the tradition of Third-Perspective belief.

The distinction that we need is cited and developed by Kierkegaard, not the Kierkegaard of the *Postscript* but the Kierkegaard of *The Sickness unto Death*, in which, as we have already seen, he is closer to the Third Perspective. In *The Sickness unto Death* Kierkegaard raises the question: 'Does the Socratic definition of sin as ignorance go far enough?' Kierkegaard argues that it does not.[17] Kierkegaard has great respect for Socrates, whom he says elsewhere he approaches with 'palpitating enthusiasm',[18] but still he believes that Socrates, who looked for truth within the seeker and gave no place to turning toward God, has not gone far enough. It is when Kierkegaard tries to say why Socrates has not gone far enough that he brings forward the needed distinction.

'To understand and to understand' are certainly two things, Kierkegaard says, following Socrates' thinking. The individual who stands up and says the right thing shows that he understands it, but then when he proceeds to do the wrong thing nevertheless he shows that he has not understood it. The first understanding is verbal, perhaps eloquently verbal, but merely verbal. The second is not. So far there is no problem for the Socratic idea 'that to understand / and to understand are two things'. But Socrates has not gone far enough. Or rather, Kierkegaard says, we must go a little further back than Socrates goes. For Kierkegaard it is true, as Socrates says, that if a person does not do what is right this shows that he does not understand what is right. 'But,' Kierkegaard says, 'Christianity goes a little further back and says, it is because he will not understand it, and this in turn because he does not will the right.' There is more to Kierkegaard's discussion (relating, for instance, to the nature of sin), but at this point we can extract from it the distinction we need. There is on the one hand that understanding that we demonstrate verbally by first stating and then expounding a truth. And on the other hand there is that understanding that we show in our actions, the lack of which derives from our not willing to understand.

We should be clear that Kierkegaard is not saying that one who acts against his advantage has not really understood what is to his advantage. Kierkegaard, I believe, would agree with Dostoyevsky[19] that human perversity can easily account for individuals' seeing their advantage and willfully choosing the opposite, merely to assert their will. Kierkegaard's point is that if a person professes a moral or religious truth and then acts as though he or she has not heard it, that truth has not been understood, and it has willfully not been understood.

Applying Kierkegaard's distinction to the issue about belief and understanding, we can allow that those who are not believers, even skeptics, may well attain the first kind of understanding through a study of religious belief and practice, or through mere cultural acquaintance, while the second kind of understanding is attainable only with belief or a turning towards belief. In this way, using this distinction, we can begin to make out how the tension between the First and Second Perspectives may be resolvable. But a number of distinctions between religious understanding and understanding will allow us to say this much. Kierkegaard's distinction, however, has special features that suit it particularly well for the Third Perspective and its abiding intuitions and, as we shall see, allow the Third Perspective to resolve the tension between the First and Second Perspectives in a uniquely Third-Perspective way.

There are two signal features of Kierkegaard's *Sickness unto Death* distinction that are noteworthy. First, the distinction is *essentially* a distinction between levels of understanding religious belief itself: it is not a distinction between understanding religious belief and understanding something else, and it is not a distinction between understanding and understanding-with-an-affective-response. Second, Kierkegaard acknowledges the role of the will in attaining true understanding. This feature is especially significant for the Third Perspective and is in accord with its deepest intuitions. Let me say something about each feature.

With this distinction Kierkegaard steadily maintains the cognitive difference between the non-believer and the believer. Even though sceptics understand well enough to deny the existence of God, there is yet something they do not understand about the very belief they deny. This is different from what Kierkegaard says at one point in the *Postscript*. In the *Postscript* Kierkegaard imagines a 'pagan philosopher' to whom Christianity is preached, not as a doctrine, but as a challenge to become a Christian. Kierkegaard asks, 'Has he then not been told what Christianity is so that he could choose?' Yes, he has, Kierkegaard allows. He goes on to say:

> The possibility of knowing what Christianity is without being a Christian must therefore be affirmed. It is a different question whether a man can know what it is to be a Christian without being one, which must be denied.[20]

This distinction is not the one we find in *The Sickness unto Death*. Here, in the *Postscript*, the believer understands what Christianity is, what the religious believe, but he does not yet understand something else, what it is to be a Christian (the believer's subjectivity). There is something to Kierkegaard's point, but we should appreciate that it is different from his point in *The Sickness unto Death*.

Also Kierkegaard's distinction in *The Sickness unto Death* is different, in this respect, from the distinctions that Second-Perspective thinkers might use to differentiate between sceptics' understanding of religious belief and believers' understanding and involvement with their belief. Earlier we saw that Roger Trigg, in reflecting on belief and understanding, and on the views of Wittgenstein and Phillips on belief and understanding, draws a distinction between 'what is meant by prayer' and 'what prayer means to someone'. This distinction, extended to belief in God would be between (i) what belief in God means and (ii) what it means to someone to believe in God. W. D. Hudson, as we also saw, distinguishes between (i) making an assertion that there is a God and (ii) sharing in the believer's explanatory, commissive, and affective use of religious pictures. For those Second-Perspective thinkers who extend Trigg's distinction to belief in

God, sceptics can understand what belief in God means but not what it means to be a believer. For those Second-Perspective thinkers who use Hudson's distinction, non-believers can understand the assertion that God exists, but they cannot share in the explanatory, commissive, and affective force of the belief. I submit that there is something to both of these Second-Perspective constructions, as there is to Kierkegaard's *Postscript* distinction (which is not so different from Trigg's). There surely is a significant difference between the non-believer and the believer in regard to understanding what it means to a person to believe in God, or what it is to be a Christian, and in regard to sharing in the non-cognitive uses of belief in living a religious life. But there is another, more fundamental difference between the non-believer and the believer precisely in understanding religious belief itself, It is a virtue of Kierkegaard's *Sickness unto Death* distinction that it resolutely focuses on this difference.

The second noteworthy feature of Kierkegaard's *Sickness unto Death* distinction is the role that he attributes to the will in one's coming to true understanding. For Kierkegaard social believers and even sceptics can come to understand religious belief at the level of understanding accessible to all by virtue of cultural exposure to the public meaning of the religious statements that express beliefs. But any understanding at the deeper life-involving level, if Kierkegaard is right, will involve the individual's ceasing to will not to understand.

Given these two signal features of Kierkegaard's *Sickness unto Death* distinction, it is particularly well suited for the Third Perspective, for it cuts between understanding and understanding precisely at the line where those with the Third Perspective would see one understanding divided from the other. For the Third Perspective there can be a purely social or cultural understanding of religious belief, and it is indeed of *what* the religious believe, as Kierkegaard's distinction maintains. This understanding is open to sceptics and all those who do not believe, and may not be surpassed by those nominal believers who are merely social believers. They understand, as their exposition of belief shows; but they do not understand, as either their lives show or, if their lives present an exterior religiosity, as the disposition of their hearts would show.

What for the Third Perspective is necessary for a true understanding of religious belief? With the First Perspective the

Third Perspective replies that there is no understanding without belief. But for the Third Perspective this is not to say that one must believe in order to understand, it is to say that one must understand in order to believe. With understanding there will be belief as surely as there will be seeing without blindness. For the Third Perspective true understanding and the religious discovery are bound together. Internal to the religious discovery is the disposition of the will, as we have seen. Perhaps the religious discovery is not always made precisely when the individual wills to understand (for this would deny that God can open the eyes of those who turn from Him). Still what prevents one's discovering God's presence is a disposition of the will. If blindness is the result of self-deception, it is a willful refusal to see. And if it is not the result of self-deception, it is still the result of willing not to understand. For the Third Perspective this willing not to understand is a defiance of will that turns toward self and away from God: in religious terms, sin.

Earlier (in section (1) of this chapter) I acknowledged that for the Third Perspective there may be some non-believers – namely devout sceptics – who, though blind, may not be self-deceived. Devout sceptics, we recall, may wish to believe and may even long to believe, but without evidence that they can identify for themselves they will not renounce their doubts, and so they withhold their belief. They are blind to God's presence, but in their case the cause of blindness is not, or may not be, self-deception. Yet, for the Third Perspective, even so, they too will not to understand, despite their wanting to believe. Consistent with their wanting to believe there can be an attachment to their self-sufficiency that amounts to willing not to understand. Here, however, we begin to encounter opaque or difficult areas in the logic of religious discovery. For do we not then find that, contrary to our assumption, devout sceptics are self-deceived after all? No, not necessarily. Unlike the self-deceived that we have considered, devout sceptics may truly wish to believe; and they may not deny with any of the vehemence of self-deception the possibility of evidence for religious belief. This, though, is not quite to say that they have simply made the intellectual error of assuming that religious evidence must be public evidence appropriate to hypothesis-confirming. For their failure of understanding may reside in the will. In this way, in accord with Third-Perspective intuitions, we see that there may be an underlying willful reluctance in all religious blindness, not just that caused by self-deception.

Now I think that we are in a position to see how the Third Perspective can in its own way accommodate the strengths of both the First and the Second Perspectives and so help the two to resolve their differences.

Regarding First-Perspective strengths, the Third Perspective shares with the First Perspective the root-intuition that those who do not believe do not understand, that non-believers, at the most profound level, fail to understand the belief that they reject. Thus the Third Perspective agrees with the First that there is a logical or grammatical connection between understanding and believing. But the Third Perspective goes beyond the First in helping us to understand the ligature of that connection. From the standpoint of the Third Perspective, it involves the role of the will; and that role in turn relates to the role of the will in making or not making the religious discovery.

At the same time the Third Perspective respects Second-Perspective strengths on the issue of belief and understanding. It recognises, with the Second Perspective, the possibility of loss of faith. In fact, for the Third Perspective, there are several versions of a loss of faith. First, there can be a loss of faith, or belief, on the part of the merely social believer or on the part of the non-religious believer who becomes convinced of God's existence by an argument. Social believers may lose their belief upon leaving the society of other social believers and entering a new setting in which they are exposed to anti-religious societal pressure. And non-religious believers may lose their argument-produced belief when confronted with a better argument against God's existence refuting the argument that produced their belief. Believers of each kind, both while believing and after losing their belief, understand what the religious believe, although only at the level of public meaning, that is, at the level of Kierkegaard's first understanding, that understanding which one can gain from proximity to a religious culture. But what about the harder case, where one with true faith in God, held with Kierkegaard's second kind of understanding, falls away from faith? It seems to me that the Third Perspective, without the accretion of theological assumptions, can allow that this might occur; and for the Third Perspective when it does, religious believers, ceasing to be religious believers, lose the religious understanding that they had.

Such a loss of understanding makes sense given what a loss of faith would be in one who has made the religious discovery. If one makes the religious discovery, then one comes to know that one stands in a relationship to the living God. But must this knowledge once attained endure to the end of life? This is in part a theological question and is not easy to answer. But as far as the logic of the religious discovery is concerned, I can see no reason to reply that it must. It is possible to discover, and to rediscover God's presence, given the logic of the religious discovery. But if one's eyes can be opened, cannot one's eyes be again closed? Can it not be, not merely that one begins to doubt in the absence of a renewed discovery, but that the discovery that was made comes to be smothered by a renewed sense of self, a reassertion of will? Nothing in the logic of the religious discovery rules this out. And if this should happen to Third-Perspective believers, their faith would be lost and they would no longer see a point to trying to live in the God-relationship that had recently claimed their lives. The religious way of life, recently their own, would appear as a pointless charade or fantasy going against their new intuitions. The very blindness that would prevent them from again seeing God's presence would banish that understanding they attained when they turned from self and ceased willing not to understand. True, in a sense they would continue to understand: they would continue to have Kierkegaard's first understanding; and this understanding, which in their new state they may hold is the only understanding they ever really had, would allow them to say coherently, 'Once I believed, now I do not'.

Also the Third Perspective is in basic agreement with the Second on conversion and the possibility of dialogue between believers and sceptics. For the Third Perspective non-believers, including sceptics, can be intellectually converted at the level of public meaning and go on to be converted to full religious faith through making the religious discovery. And, for the Third Perspective, this same first level of understanding makes dialogue between sceptics and believers possible. For the Third Perspective the sceptic can, at this level, have real understanding of what the religious believe. It is not, as Stuart Brown suggests from his First-Perspective viewpoint, that sceptics understand only to the extent that they can draw implications from belief, on the basis of which they can argue for the falsity of belief: there are many associations and amplifications of the meaning of religious belief in the public domain that the sceptic may understand. At the same time sceptics cannot penetrate to the second kind of understanding before there is a turning of their will. Yet dialogue is possible as a means whereby the sceptic and believer can come to a better mutual understanding. Of course dialogue at this level can, and perhaps more often than not does, lead to a deeper entrenchment of non-believers in their unbelief. Granting this, still dialogue can be a means whereby the invitation to faith is pressed and, indeed, it may operate as a catalyst or occasion for the removal of blindness. If any event can lead to the opening of one's religious eyes, it follows that dialogue can do so.

On this subissue, then, the Third Perspective is in substantial agreement with each of the other two perspectives. By bringing to bear such a distinction as Kierkegaard's between kinds of understanding it can, in its own way, accommodate the strengths of both the First and Second Perspectives, and so once more form a bridge between them.

(4) The Evidence Subissue: Is There a Place for Evidence, for Grounds, in Religion?

Given the keystone position of the religious discovery in the framework of the Third Perspective, the Third Perspective does, and must, give a significant place to evidence or grounding. This is so even though the Psalmist does not speak of evidence as such. For, while the Psalmist does not speak of evidence, he again and again points to what in his eyes makes God's presence manifest. And such manifestations of God's presence as those pointed to by the Psalmist are the evidence, or grounding, the discovery of which constitutes the religious discovery. As I observed in Chapter 2, the word 'evidence' is contaminated, for it is closely associated with enquiry-contexts. But the evidence or grounding grammatically necessary for the Third Perspective is not evidence arrived at through the investigation of an experimental hypothesis, nor in general is it any kind of enquiry-evidence. It is (if we need a category) realisation-evidence. It is that, in the midst of the familiar, which in a religious realisation-context one comes to see in its significance as evidence of God's presence. It is that which the Psalmist and other Third-Perspective believers behold with opened eyes in making the religious discovery.

Often objections to religious evidence are objections to enquiry-evidence. Much of the First-Perspective aversion to allowing evidence a place in religion is directed against investigative attitudes and evidence-gathering processes that are at home only in enquiry-contexts. Kierkegaard's objection to evidence, for instance, is in great part an objection to enquiry-evidence. The 'approximation-process' by which beliefs can be made more probable, and which, for Kierkegaard, makes religious belief impossible, clearly is an investigative, evidence-gathering process. Its required attitude of tentativeness and investigative neutrality is enough to put it at odds with the kind of faith attitude important to Kierkegaard in the *Postscript*. Also Kierkegaard objects to *speculation*. He perceives a profound opposition between the objective and subjective approaches to religion, and speculation is quintessentially objective. Insofar as one's approach to religion is a speculative concern to contemplate religion and arrive at its objective truth, the passion of inwardness is undermined.[21] But this objection to speculation, as far as it is just that, is an objection to an enquiry-attitude.

Wittgenstein, who says in *Lectures on Religious Belief* that it would 'destroy' religion if there were evidence, pretty clearly has in mind enquiry-evidence. For he takes it as proof that evidence plays no role in religion, despite what the religious may say, that there is no clear idea of confirming or disconfirming conditions – a test that is applicable to the investigation of hypotheses. Significantly, I think, Wittgenstein says that what he *normally* calls evidence has no role to play in religion. As I remarked earlier, in Chapter 1, this leaves a grammatical gap. And in Chapter 2 we saw the dimensions of that gap: if what we normally call evidence is enquiry-evidence, then the kind of evidence operative in the religious discovery is not spoken to at all and hence not ruled out by Wittgenstein.

Again two other philosophers with First-Perspective views on this issue, Norman Malcolm and Robert Herbert, focus on enquiry-evidence – specifically evidence that would count for or against a hypothesis – in their denial of religious evidence. Malcolm says that belief in God and other forms of religious belief 'are not hypotheses for or against which evidence can be marshalled'.[22] And Herbert, who, as we have seen, understands religious doubt as the will's insubordination, denies that doubt is a matter of the intellect's being brought by 'counterevidence' to weaken or abandon 'its "God-hypothesis"'.[23] (Later in this section I shall have more to say about Herbert and the role of the will *vis-à-vis* doubt and religious evidence.)

D. Z. Phillips too, I think, is focused on enquiry-evidence in his denial of the relevance of external evidence to religion (just as he is focused on enquiry-rationality in his denial of the relevance of external forms of rationality to religion). However he does allow that in religion there is *internal* evidence or reasons for belief. Earlier I gave his examples of such internal reasons. Here they are again:

> I have had an experience of the living God.
> I believe on the Lord Jesus Christ.
> God saved me while I was a sinner.
> I just can't help believing.

Notice that the first makes an apparently explicit appeal to religious experience and that the third makes an implicit appeal to what a believer has experienced. The second, however, is an appeal to Christ's authority, not to evidence. But it is the last 'reason' that is most revealing about Phillips' conception of *internal reasons*. Whatever it is to claim, or to confess, that 'one just can't help believing', it is not to give a reason in support of one's belief. It is to give a reason in one sense, of course. It is to give a psychological reason that explains, or begins to explain, why one holds a belief. In this particular case, a need of some sort seems to be confessed – confessed not in the sense that belief in God is confessed (that is, proclaimed from one's heart), but confessed as a weakness is confessed. In short this kind of reason is not an evidential reason in support of the truth of a belief, it is a psychological reason or cause that is offered to explain the aetiology of one's belief. Phillips' category of internal reasons runs together evidence for belief and causes of belief.

Phillips, as we saw in Chapter 2, acknowledges that any event can lead the believer to God. He even quotes the Psalms and refers to the Psalmist's sense that 'God is not only the God who sees the sparrow fall, but also the God who creates the darkness "wherein all the beasts of the forest do creep forth. The young lions roar after their prey and seek their meat from God".'[24] However Phillips seems not to recognise the distinction between: (i) any event can psychologically cause one to believe that there is a God, and (ii) any event can be the occasion of one's eyes being opened to God's presence. Or, if he is aware of it (as he surely must be), he deliberatly cuts across it. Perhaps, like Norman Malcolm in 'Is it a Religious Belief that "God exists"?' he wants to deny that the distinction between causes and evidence applies to religious belief. But Malcolm goes on in 'The Groundlessness of Belief' to acknowledge the distinction and to insist that while religious belief may be caused by anything, it can have no grounds in its support – which, I think, is in effect where one ends up if one treats psychological causes and evidential reasons as the same. It is not only Phillips' First-Perspective view on *internal evidence* that brings to grief the distinction between evidence that supports the truth of a belief and non-evidential causes that bring about a person's belief. Stephen Davis' Second-Perspective view on *private evidence* seems to as well. Still, both Phillips and Davis usefully encourage us to re-examine the concept of evidence in its application to religious belief.

When we do so, though, and look at the logic of the religious discovery, we find locked into that logic a place for religious evidence – but it is realisation-evidence. The Psalmist and other Third-Perspective believers regard themselves as seeing God's presence, the presence of the living God, all about them. Thus the religious discovery gives an essential place to experiential grounding, whether or not one terms such grounding 'evidence' or 'reasons'. And this experiential grounding is not, like a need to believe, a psychological cause of belief. At the same time, as we have seen, it is not evidence as it is often thought of, for it is not enquiry-evidence. For the Third Perspective the religious discovery made by the Psalmist does not depend on the facts of the world going one way or another: however the facts of the world go, if the world is God's domain, it is God's domain.[25] The religious discovery turns on one's seeing the religious significance of the familiar facts and surroundings of the world, whatever they may be. The individual who has made the religious discovery *has a reason* for his or her belief without *being able to give a reason*. Third-Perspective believers can point to evidence of God's presence, as the Psalmist did. It is all about them. But if *giving a reason* is presenting something that initially is unappreciated by one's hearer, which upon presentation, *ceteris paribus*, will be appreciated as a reason – if it is public in this way – then the person who has made the religious discovery is not in a position to give reasons.[26] In a real sense, for the Third Perspective, the issue between the religious and those who reject religion is not an issue over who is mistaken. To paraphrase Wittgenstein, neither religious believers nor non-believers are mistaken. The difference runs too deep for that. There is nothing overlooked that can be pointed out that will change one side or the other. But still there is a cognitive difference. Still we can understand one side having a wrong belief, a false belief. And we can understand those who believe what is false coming to see the truth, allowing that it is the truth, through making the religious discovery.

We can further clarify the Third-Perspective view on evidence (the view that I take to be implicit in the framework of the Third Perspective) by relating it to the First Perspective views of John Hick and Robert Herbert, both of whom recognise religion's moral dimension. In our earlier discussion, in Chapter 1, we saw that Hick's view on religious perception and the lack of coercion in religion implied a view on religious evidence. That view, I said, put a strain on the general concept of evidence because it disallowed that decisive religious evidence exists independently of an individual's choosing to regard the world religiously and having religious faith. If I am right, there are logically distinguishable sorts of evidence: enquiry-evidence and realisation-evidence. But all evidence, as evidence, has certain features that are so closely woven into the general concept that they may fairly be said to be necessary features. For instance, all evidence in some way provides support for the belief to which it is relevant (as psychological causes do not). And, in the same way, all evidence provides support independently of one's taking up the belief that is supported or one's choosing to see things in accord with that belief. It is because Hick's view of religious evidence runs counter to this last feature that I suggested his view on religious evidence comes down on the First-Perspective side.

In contrast to Hick's view on religious evidence the Third-Perspective view, we should be clear, does not require that one believe or freely choose to interpret the world religiously in order to discover religious evidence. For the Third Perspective the manifestations of God's presence become evident to persons when they make the religious discovery, and they make the religious discovery when their eyes are opened. One's trying to believe may (or may not) hasten the opening of one's eyes. On the other hand belief is not necessary for one's eyes to be opened; and often, for the Third Perspective, religious belief may *follow* the opening of one's religious eyes. It seems to me, then, that the Third Perspective keeps in place this feature of evidence, just as it maintains the logical distinction between evidence and psychological causes.

However the role of choice, or will, is not denied by the Third Perspective. In our earlier discussion of Herbert's view on evidence we encountered two First-Perspective concerns with evidence that relate to the role of will and the role of grace in religious belief. Herbert in *Paradox and Identity in Theology* maintains that (i) religious doubt is a matter of insubordination, a matter of will (as opposed to insufficient evidence) and (ii) religious conviction arises, not from evidence in nature, but from grace. I suggested that Herbert's views raised two questions about religious evidence: If religious doubt is a matter of will, is every role for evidence *vis-à-vis* doubt ruled out? And if grace is what brings one to faith, or conviction, is every role for evidence *vis-à-vis* faith ruled out? Now is the time to address these questions.

One question is about doubt and evidence; the other is about faith, or faith's conviction, and evidence. In each case, I suggest, a role remains for evidence – if evidence is the grounding one discovers in making the religious discovery. Let us take the case of doubt first. Herbert sees religious doubt as a matter of will, and the Third Perspective would agree. Religious doubt for the Third Perspective is doubt in the face of what is evident and manifest. It is not a merely intellectual doubt, but a doubt that derives from the non-believer's willful stance in relation to the familiar. If the non-believer's blindness is caused by self-deception then its willful nature is clear, but even if the non-believer's blindness is not caused by self-deception – a willful refusal to see – it is a matter of willing not to understand, and so turning from the religious discovery. Thus for the Third Perspective religious doubt's being willful does not rule out a role for evidence; rather religious doubt is willful in that the doubter has a lack of evidence just because he or she willfully turns away from what makes God's presence manifest.

Regarding faith and conviction, Herbert sees grace as that which brings one to conviction. For Herbert the conviction that God exists is established by God's miracle in those who have serious faith. If this is so, is evidence ruled out? Enquiry-evidence may be ruled out, evidence that is clear to all, or clearly lacking to all, once an enquiry is undertaken. But the evidence gained by the religious discovery comes not by enquiry, but after one's eyes have been opened. And how are one's eyes opened? Not by oneself, but by God, says St. Bonaventura; and not St. Bonaventura alone says this. In the Judaeo-Christain tradition, and in the tradition of the Third Perspective in particular, the religious often speak of discovering the presence of God through the grace of God. The realisation of God's presence and its sensible concomitants are spoken of as a gift. When it is said that one's eyes were opened to God's presence through God's grace, it may be meant that God's grace was required (and so one's own efforts were not enough) or it may be meant that God's grace irresistibly opened one's eyes perhaps even in spite of efforts to keep them closed. In either case grace is that which opens one's eyes that one may see the evidence of God's existence, or better, the evidence of God's presence. When grace brings one to conviction in this way grace does not rule out evidence. In fact it requires it. That is, it requires the grounding one comes to see when one's eyes are opened and the religious discovery is made. This, however, is not to say that the discovery model that applies to the religious discovery requires this role for grace, only that it allows it.

Now, finally in this section, let me say how the Third Perspective relates to the First and Second Perspectives on the issue of religious evidence. To begin with, it is in fundamental agreement with the Second Perspective that evidence has a place – and it is a deep place – in religion. For the Third Perspective religious belief does not require special pleading, and it is not such that it need be held in the absence of support. At the same time, regarding the religious discovery, it agrees with the First Perspective that evidence does not relate to religious belief as evidence, enquiry-evidence, relates to proving a theory. The Third Perspective, with the First Perspective, appreciates the moral dimension of faith and does not deny the role of will (about which more in the next section). It also recognises and understands the First-Perspective point that what can cause difficulties for belief can lead one to believe or even strengthen faith. The Third Perspective recognises this point without denying religious evidence or conflating it with causes of belief. It need not, and does not, deny that personal crises can create a need to believe and act as psychological causes of belief. But it appreciates that crises also relate to the religious discovery. They do in two ways. First, anything can be the occasion that opens one's eyes, and crises like grief can diminish the sense of self and in this specific way help lead to the opening of one's religious eyes. Second, since the presence of God is to be seen in all that is familiar, it is to be seen not only in the glories of nature and in the happy events of life, but in the horrible and horrendous events of life as well. In this way, or these ways, although the Third Perspective agrees with the Second that religious belief can be evidentially grounded, it heeds and embodies the strengths of the First Perspective.

(5) The Knowledge Subissue: Is There or Can There Be Religious Knowledge?

A place for religious knowledge is assured in the framework of the Third Perspective. This is so because discovery and knowledge are grammatically linked: all who make the religious discovery attain religious knowledge of that discovered. Of course within the Judaeo-Christian tradition, given its breadth, *what* is discovered may be variably expressed. And when the religious discovery is made in other religious traditions what is discovered may be expressed in terms at wide variance from the Judaeo-Christian tradition. Nevertheless in all cases of the religious discovery what one discovers, we may say, is that one is in a life-claiming relationship to the Divine or to Reality. True, that Reality may be differently conceived and differently articulated, but that one exists in a relationship to Reality – at least this – is the nucleus of knowledge attained in making the religious discovery.

In the Western theistic heritage, and in the tradition of the Third Perspective as it is found within that heritage, this Reality is a personal God. And *what* is discovered may be expressed as 'I am in the presence of the living God' or 'I have my existence in a relationship to God'. These are propositions. A part of what one discovers in making the religious discovery is that some key religious proposition is true, even though what one comes to understand with religious understanding may reach beyond the import of expressible propositions. However, allowing that a part, perhaps even the most significant part, of what is discovered cannot be expressed as a proposition should not lessen our insistence that, for the Third Perspective, knowledge is attained when the religious discovery is made and at least part of that knowledge is the knowledge that key religious propositions are true. In the Judaeo-Christian heritage the home of the Third Perspective is in the Psalms, or in the religiousness of the Psalms. For the Psalmist and for other Old Testament figures religious *knowledge* is a significant part of their spirituality. Unlike some with the First Perspective, Third-Perspective believers feel no discomfiture before Job's Biblical cry of faith 'I know my Redeemer liveth!'

But there are objections to religious knowledge, as we have seen, religious objections brought forward by various First-Perspective thinkers. Some of these objections derive from a non-cognitivist view of religious belief, as those associated with Phillips' thinking do. These objections I have spoken to indirectly in preceding sections. Others, however, do not rest on a non-cognitivist view. They now deserve our attention. Notable among the objections to knowledge in this class are the objections raised by Kierkegaard and the later Wittgenstein. Let me begin with a re-examination of Kierkegaard's thinking.

Kierkegaard's *Postscript* concern with *knowledge* as a cognitive state necessarily at odds with religious belief or faith has two sources, it seems to me. First, he sees knowledge (and its certainty) to be at odds with faith and its required struggle with uncertainty. Second, he has a strong, underlying objection to what I called the 'attitude of knowledge': the indifference of knowledge, its ties to investigation, its disinterestedness, and more. Starting with the first, I shall examine these two sources of his concern in order.

Given Kierkegaard's definition of faith and the implications of that definition as Kierkegaard sees them, there is in the *Postscript* an implicit argument against religious knowledge. Drawn out and made explicit, it is this:

> Faith requires risk.
> Risk requires uncertainty.
> So Faith requires uncertainty.
> But knowledge requires certainty.
> So faith and knowledge are exclusive.

Kierkegaard's implicit argument, we should observe, relates to both religious faith (faith proper) and non-religious faith. Given

Kierkegaard's thinking in the *Postscript*, the nature of faith itself puts it at odds with knowledge. The argument looks tight, but I think that it is not. Kierkegaard is right, it seems to me, that faith – religious or non-religious – requires some kind of risk. But we should ask this question: What is the nature of the risk of faith? Kierkegaard's *Postscript* definition of faith focuses on cases where what one believes is 'objectively uncertain' and so may not be true for all one knows. Accordingly the risk that Kierkegaard makes faith require is the risk that *what one believes is false*. For religious faith, or faith proper, then, the risk is that what one passionately embraces as the central truth of one's life is false. No doubt Kierkegaard presented this picture of faith to correct the complacent attitude of Christendom, which in effect said, 'Of course Christianity is true; everyone in Denmark knows that it is.' Kierkegaard wanted to put back into faith dread and passion; in the *Postscript* he does so by tying passion and inwardness to holding fast an objective uncertainty.

However another kind of risk also relates to faith: the risk of *failing to live within and losing an entered relationship*. In making the religious discovery one discovers a life-claiming relationship to God. But if one truly makes the discovery, then one must *participate* in the discovered relationship, and this is to say that one enters a relationship to God. In the tradition of the Third Perspective, as in the Judaeo-Christian tradition generally, the relationship entered by the believer is one of trust, obedience, and love. Trusting God is logically tied to certain beliefs about God, but trust is more than holding these beliefs: it is a profound acceptance of God. So too when God is obeyed and loved an acceptance of God and God's will is implied. When believers accept God in this way they expose themselves: they risk the trauma of not being able to live in, and finally, losing that relationship. This is no little risk. For if the relationship is truly entered, it is life-affecting, and its loss must similarly be life-affecting. As with human relationships, if the relationship is not taken up there is no risk of failing to live up to and losing the relationship. This risk, it should be appreciated, is run even when there is no risk that *what* one believes is false. It is a risk that relates to faith, not as a belief that something is so, but as a relationship. Kierkegaard of course emphasised that faith is a God-relationship, and he castigated 'objective belief'. Consequently it is ironic that the risk he ends up putting internal to faith is the risk that what is believed is false and not the risk of failing to live within and losing the relationship of faith.

The risk of faith, then, is not always as Kierkegaard presents it in the *Postscript*. Nevertheless I do not wish to deny that Kierkegaard's *Postscript* model of faith is coherent and may well have application to any number of believers and their faith. My point is that faith need not be in accord with the *Postscript* model, and when it is not it need not be antithetical to the certainty that religious knowledge requires. If I am right, Kierkegaard himself in *Fear and Trembling* presented a model of faith that requires knowledge, even though in the *Postscript* he is hard against religious knowledge.

The second source of Kierkegaard's concern with religious knowledge is his underlying objection to the attitude of knowledge. Here we find his concern with, for instance, the indifference and disinterestedness of knowledge. There is, I think, in the history and the practice of religion, of Christianity in particular, an identifiable thread of aversion to knowledge, and Kierkegaard to some extent echoes that historical aversion. However the exact nature of this religious aversion needs to be noted. The author of *The Imitation of Christ* sounds the theme of that work in the first chapter where he writes, 'All is vanity, except to love God, and to serve Him only'. It is better to be a 'humble rustic that serveth God, than a proud philosopher'; and 'cavilling and disputing about dark and hidden things' is folly, as is enquiring into the 'many curious things of men'. A 'humble knowledge of thyself is a surer way to God than a deep search after learning'. But 'learning' is not to be blamed. What is to be blamed is putting knowledge before 'a good conscience and a virtuous life'. And, as the author of the *Imitation* says in the Third Book, 'there is a great difference between the wisdom of an illuminated and devout man, and the knowledge of a learned and studious clerk'.[27] We find what is perhaps the most complete and finely drawn statement of a religious concern with knowledge in the prologue to *The Mind's Road to God*. There St. Bonaventura urges his readers to begin in prayer lest they should believe that

> it suffices to read without unction, speculate without devotion, investigate without wonder, examine without exultation, work without piety, know without love, understand without humil-

ity, be zealous without divine grace, see without wisdom divinely inspired.[28]

If we take these authors as indicative, as I believe we should, we find that what may be called the devotional criticisms of knowledge are not criticisms of knowledge in itself. The religious concern evinced here is not with knowledge per se, but with attitudes associated with seeking, collecting, possessing, and defending knowledge. There is no question about the value of self-knowledge or wisdom devoutly received. Even learning is given a place, as long as it is not proudly held or put before love.

What then of Kierkegaard's objection to the attitude of knowledge? A closer look at Kierkegaard's writings reveals that often his criticism of religious knowledge is similarly inspired. In the *Postscript* Kierkegaard's rejection of knowledge has very much to do with attitudes *associated* with knowledge. Accordingly Kierkegaard's objections to what I have called the 'attitude of knowledge' are in reality, or should be, not to religious knowledge itself, but to attitudes that may or may not be, but often are, associated with seeking, collecting, possessing, and defending knowledge. In short his objections to indifference, disinterestedness, abstraction, and the rest appear to be objections to *enquiry-attitudes*.[29] In places in the *Postscript*, where Kierkegaard is not addressing the 'objective tendency' to investigate and to prove, he relents and moderates his opposition to knowledge. I do not mean merely that he allows 'subjective knowledge': this category of 'knowledge' seems to come to no more than intense subjectivity. Beyond this, in one place, after he has denied that one can 'observe' God, he says that when the potential of spirit in an individual has been 'awakened in inwardness to become a God-relationship ... then it becomes possible to see God everywhere'. This is the language of discovery, although Kierkegaard does not say so and quickly drops the theme. But if, as I suspect, his objections to the attitude of knowledge really are to enquiry-attitudes, then he need not deny the religious discovery and its knowledge on the basis of such objections.

Wittgenstein also has objections, grammatical objections, to religious knowledge. In fact they are very similar to Kierkegaard's, although Wittgenstein of course proceeds from reflection on religious discourse, as opposed to reflection on the subjectivity of faith. However some attention to Wittgenstein's *Lectures on Religious Belief* reveals that the opposition between *belief* and *knowledge* that he identifies may be between religious belief and scientific knowledge (that is, knowledge gained by the methods of empirical science). What Wittgenstein sees regarding knowledge is, I think, analogous to what he detects regarding evidence: the attitudes tied to committed religious belief are at loggerheads with the investigative attitude required by scientific evidence-gathering and coming to knowledge by the methods of empirical science. If this is right, then Wittgenstein's focus, like Kierkegaard's, is on enquiry-attitudes, not knowledge per se.

Buber too, I think, is at least in part objecting to approaching God with enquiry-attitudes. He associates attaining knowledge with analysing the object to be known, categorising it, and adding it to our store of knowledge. But, for Buber, if we treat God as an object of knowledge in this way, we end up making God into an It, a thing among things, that we use in 'the project of finding [our] way in the world'. However, for Buber, the contrast to the effort to gain such knowledge is 'the act of beholding'.[30] Beholding is the mode of seeing that we find in the Psalms. The Psalmist beholds the works of the Lord in His creation, and he is moved thereby. In wonder, and in fear and trembling, he finds that he is in God's presence. Buber would say that he *encounters* God and deny that he meets God in his *experience*. I think that we need not worry overmuch about whether beholding is or is not a kind of experiencing. In any case it is not the kind of experiencing that is involved in analysing, categorising, noting aspects of, gathering data about, and so on. In this way beholding can bring with it knowledge (just not categorising or use-oriented knowledge). And so, given this construction of Buber's animadversions of knowledge, when one beholds God's presence in making the religious discovery one can come to knowledge of God's presence and of one's relationship to God.

Still there is something right about the perception of the indifference of knowledge: knowledge often is indifferent. And there is something right about the perception that knowledge can be received with such profoundly non-religious attitudes as curiosity or merely theoretical interest. Religious knowledge, if there be such, should necessarily not be indifferent – as faith in God, as opposed to the bare existence-belief of Malcolm's atheist, is necessarily not indifferent. Also religious knowledge should not admit of a non-religious reception. We need a distinction similar to that between levels of understanding. Once more the needed distinction is to be found in religious reflection. In fact the distinction that we need is found in one form or another in the works of many religious writers. The terms employed in drawing the distinction vary, but the essential or core distinction, I think, is the same in each case: a distinction between life-affecting religious knowledge religiously received and non-religious knowledge that may be indifferently or wrongly received even though its object is religious.

Let us look at several instances of this distinction, starting with St. Paul and his first letter to the Corinthians. Paul in his letter denounces knowledge and wisdom. Knowledge 'puffs up' (8.1) and makes us boastful or proud. While it can thus affect us, it does not religiously affect us. The wisdom he denounces is the wisdom of the wise and of the world (1.18–.20). But, he says, 'among the mature we impart . . . a secret and hidden wisdom of God' (2.6–.7). For Paul knowledge puffs up, and for Paul human wisdom belongs to the 'wise', the intellectual, but the hidden wisdom of God is from God and given to the 'foolish', the unpretentious, the pure in heart who turn toward God's love. In this way Paul at once distinguishes a wrong kind of knowledge from a right kind and characterises the way of attainment of a right knowledge, or secret wisdom, of God.

After Paul this distinction recurs often in devotional and mystical literature, for instance in the *Imitation* and in Bonaventura's *The Mind's Road to God*. In the seventeenth century we find it in the writings of the Cambridge Platonist John Smith. Smith in his discourse 'The true Way or Method of attaining to Divine Knowledge',[31] following Paul, distinguishes between knowledge that puffs up and Divine Knowledge. The former is the knowledge of 'Systems and Models', the 'aiery knowledge' of speculation and of 'Syllogisms'. Even the most sublime speculations on the Deity can be 'empty froath' if not 'impregnated with true Goodness'. Divine Knowledge of the Truth is not a matter of breaking through the 'Shell of words & phrases that house it up' or of 'Logical Analysis' or of tracing the niceties of the dogmas of any sect. For Smith Divine Knowledge is got not by 'Notions', but 'Action': 'he that is most Practical in Divine things, hath the purest and sincerest Knowledge of them'. And Smith connects Divine Knowledge to 'Purity of heart'. The best and truest knowledge, he says, is not 'wrought out by the labour and sweat of the Brain', but is 'kindled within us by an heavenly warmth in our Hearts'. Smith develops the purity of heart theme in his own Neo-Platonic way: as the eye must be sunlike to behold the sun, so the soul must be Godlike to behold God. And it is a matter of beholding for Smith. It is also a matter of 'Sensation', as opposed to 'Speculation'. He quotes Psalm 34: 'taste and see how good the Lord is'. (The Soul, he says, has its sense, as does the body.) Vice, however, twists the reason and makes some 'question that Truth which to Good men shines as bright as the Sun at noon-day'.

Because Smith appeals to Plotinus as much as to the Psalmist there are strongly Neo-Platonic elements in his discourse on Divine Knowledge. Thus he is drawn to the idea that it is our souls' being contaminated by 'Sense and Passion' that keeps us from Divine Knowledge, and he speaks sympathetically of 'Mathematical Contemplations' as a means whereby we might lessen our dependency upon sense. Also for Smith Divine Knowledge is innate and so already within us, though much darkened. Nevertheless, his Neo-Platonism notwithstanding, there is in Smith's discourse an elaboration of the core distinction we seek.

The same distinction, in a signal form, is found in Cardinal Newman's *Grammar of Assent*. In that work Newman elaborates his well-known distinction between *notional assent* and *real assent*. Initially this may not seem to be a distinction between knowledge and knowledge, for assenting to a proposition seems to be on a different logical footing from coming to know that a proposition is true. However Newman is in agreement with Aquinas that knowledge is a kind of assent, namely 'a firm assent'.[32] Newman says that when the proposition assented to is as absolutely true as the assent pronounces it to be, then 'the proposition or truth [is] a *certainty*, or thing known . . . and to assent to it is to *know*'.[33] Both notional and real assent can be a firm assent to a true proposition, and so, for Newman, each assent can amount to a kind of knowledge.

In making notional assents we contemplate abstractions – notions – as opposed to things themselves vividly recalled in our imagination.[34] Notional assent, Newman allows, is sufficient to enable us to converse sensibly on such subjects as history, politics, philosophy, and art, though without personal knowledge of their objects. And religion too, for Newman, can be made a subject of notional assent. Notional assent is not to be despised; it is properly at home in theology. But religion, for Newman, should be a matter of real assent grounded in real apprehension.[35] Real assent requires a personal apprehension, an impression of the object vividly presented in the imagination.

Newman finds the required reservoir of personal experience in our moral conscience. Through our 'feeling of conscience' we can gain an image of God and give a real assent to the proposition that He exists.[36] These experiences of conscience 'impress upon the imagination . . . the picture of a Supreme Govenor, a Judge, holy, just, powerful, all-seeing, retributive'.[37]

The importance that Newman here gives to our conscience is not unlike the importance given to moral consciousness by Baillie, and some, like H. D. Lewis, who criticise Baillie on this score might also criticise Newman. Also Neman commits himself to psychological views about the role of the imagination in real assent that he may be able to do without. In any case we find in his religious thought, correlated with his distinction between notional and real assent, a form of the distinction between knowledge and knowledge that we are seeking. And it is, for our purposes, a particularly significant form.

This is true in part because Newman's background concerns are not unrelated to some of the concerns of this book, and in part because the grammar of assent that Newman develops is in places very like the grammar of the Third Perspective. There are several points worth noting here. To begin with, Newman was concerned with the right of simple faith to be certain and with the deeper, experiential foundations of faith; both of which we have explored. Second, Newman's distinction between notional and real assent applies both within and outside religion, as does the model of discovery that fits the religious discovery. Third, his distinction allows that the very same religious proposition can be given a notional assent or a real assent; and it allows that a real assent, with religious knowledge, can, upon the attainment of personal experience, replace a notional assent with its – at best – theological knowledge. Each of these elements parallels the grammar of the Third Perspective. Fourth, Newman's account of real assent and its religious knowledge, as he says, leaves open how much there is implied a special divine aid, or grace.[38] This point too can be made about the logic of the religious discovery. Finally his emphasis on 'personal knowledge', 'real apprehension', and 'experience' is in itself in accord with the religious discovery, although the general and religious epistemology that he goes on to develop, with its dependence on 'concrete' inference and the 'illative sense', is enquiry-oriented and thus radically different from the realisation-epistemology of the religious discovery.

I shall add one further instance, this time drawing upon a contemporary religious thinker in order to present the distinction in one of its contemporary forms. Paul Holmer in *The Grammar of Faith*, in discussing the nature of theology, draws a distinction between *knowledge of God* and *knowledge about God*. It is knowledge *of* God that is truly religious knowledge, for Holmer. Theology starts in the '"about" mood', he says, but since 'theology must be more than a sum of truths', it must move from *about* to *of*.[39] In fact unless it does it is not really about God.

> Theology, to the extent that it becomes knowledge of God, has to have the form of personal appropriation built in. Otherwise, it is not about God at all but is only a history of someone's thoughts. For to have knowledge of God you must fear him and you must love him.[40]

Holmer goes on to relate knowledge of God to purity of heart:

> Theology is certainly taught, and often under that very name. But the knowledge of God is also given to the pure in heart, to the fools for Christ's sake, and even to professors in theological seminaries and pastors and laity in unlikely churches.[41]

Knowledge of God is not closed to theologians, but they do not have it by virtue of their learning or by virtue of their theological knowledge about God. For them as for everyone,

> Knowing God . . . is a matter of coming to know him in prayer, worship, praise, and much else that makes up the religious life.[42]

We thus find a fairly wide spectrum of religious thinkers who in one way or another posit the kind of distinction that we need between knowledge and knowledge. Many others could have been cited, including, besides the author of *The Imitation of Christ* and St. Bonaventura, John Calvin, and, among contemporary thinkers,

John Hick, Emil Brunner, and Martin Buber. Again, not all of these thinkers understand the distinction in the same way. Some may even be at odds with others. Yet each at its core is informed by the same insight, I think. In each case religious knowledge is not a matter of reasoning, analysis, or, broadly, any mode of enquiry. It rather requires our own individual religious experience. Religious knowledge engages the affections and is embodied in the religious person's life, the affections not so much responding to the knowledge as in their engagement representing one side of the knowledge itself.

How does this distinction relate to the Third Perspective? In just this way: if one should make the religious discovery, the knowledge that one would come to *of necessity* would be, in accord with this distinction, *religious knowledge*. I do not claim that all the religious writers I have cited would give a place to the religious discovery as the way one comes to religious knowledge. Nevertheless the religious discovery is a very strong candidate for *a* way to the attainment of this religious knowledge. For all of the following are true: (i) making the religious discovery brings one to knowledge as much as making other realisation-discoveries does, (ii) the knowledge it brings one to is not attained through enquiry, (iii) the religious discovery, as a realisation-discovery, of necessity is made in and through seeing the significance of one's own experience, and (iv) its knowledge, partly because it comes as a realisation and partly because it comes as the realisation of the Divine significance of all that is, including one's life, and thus of one's own relationship to the Divine, is necessarily affective. It involves the inwardness of subjectivity (though not by virtue of uncertainty) as well as the inwardness of intent and disposition spoken of in the *Imitation of Christ* and alluded to by Paul, and in this way it moulds and is expressed in the individual's practice of belief. Moreover there is no reason to deny that the religious knowledge attained is certain knowledge (allowing that there can be uncertain knowledge). Those in the Third Perspective who understand themselves as having made the discovery of God's presence are certain in their minds and hearts and view what they have discovered as being as certain as their own lives.

But now let me turn to an aspect of religious knowledge that I have so far not addressed, namely, the role of choice and decision, the role of will. As we have seen, making the religious discovery importantly involves the will, for not-seeing, or religious blindness, for the Third Perspective, is a matter of willfully not understanding and, if self-deception is present, the result of willfully refusing to see. The Third Perspective is not alone in sensing the importance of the moral dimension in religious belief, but for the Third Perspective human will and willfulness are deeply woven into religious cognitivity. If religious blindness is overcome, if our eyes are opened, then if we see what is there to be seen, we shall, for the Third Perspective, discover the presence of God and so come to know that there is a God, that we are in His presence, and that we are in a life-claiming relationship to Him. If our eyes are opened by God, and by God's grace alone, then our discovery, our first seeing God, is not by our decision. Rather God has made something happen which lets us, or even makes us, see His presence. (In secular realisation-contexts people analogously may speak of the truth unexpectedly dawning on them.) On the other hand, if we participate in opening our eyes, if there was an endeavour to see, then to some extent our will is involved. Among those who believe that they have discovered God's presence, some are conscious of how little they have done and of how something happened to them almost in spite of themselves to make them see. At the same time others are conscious of disciplining themselves and struggling to see God, or of struggling not to and of their shuddering decision to surrender their resistance. Believers of the first sort must give no or little role to the will. Believers of the second sort cannot deny a role to the will. The logic of the religious discovery, by itself and theologically unadorned, allows that the discovery may be made in either way. It seems then that making the religious discovery can, on one account, occur without one's willing, or wishing, to see God. Yet, on either account, there is a necessary role for the will; and there is in two ways. First, it remains that the will is involved in *not* seeing God; and, second, it is involved in *continuing* to see God. (i) It is our willing not to see (our refusing to see or willing not to understand), our willing to look away, that prevents our seeing. Generally in realisation-contexts, especially if self-deception is involved, not coming to know is wilful. Perhaps this is the germ of truth in what Kierkegaard saw when he said that we doubt by an act of will.[43] Better, for the Third-Perspective, we will not to see, and so doubt and deny. (ii) After we have seen, it is our willing not to look away that allows us to continue to see (to make again and again the discovery of God's presence and not after time to deny our discovery).[44]

At this point I think that we are in a position to address a dilemma that relates to the conflicting roles of choice and certainty in faith: Either faith can be accompanied by religious knowledge and certainty or it can embody the commitment of choosing to believe, but not both. If faith is the certain faith of Abraham and Job, then faith allows and even requires knowledge; but there is no choosing, for one does not choose to *know* or to be *aware* of what is certain and one sees to be certain. If faith is the uncertain faith of the *Postscript*, then faith allows and even requires choosing to believe; but there is no knowledge, for the very uncertainty that necessitates choosing to believe against all odds rules out knowledge.

The resolution of the dilemma, at least within the Third Perspective, I think, is this: choice is necessary, but the necessary choice is not choosing to believe and, a fortiori, it is not choosing to know, or to be aware of what is certain. Having opened their eyes, or their eyes having been opened, believers must will not to look away. And of course if believers participate in the opening of their eyes by choosing to cease looking away, then the will plays a role there too. At the same time, having come to see, having made the religious discovery of God's presence, believers have the certainty of religious knowledge. This resolution, I believe, derives wholly from the logic of realisation-discoveries and does not trespass on theological matters. At least it leaves alone the theological question of whether one's own efforts to open one's eyes are necessary, are sufficient, or are neither, for coming to see God's presence.

Also the Third Perspective is in a position to address another issue regarding religious belief, the issue of conceptual change. When religious belief is what might be called *absolute belief* a kind of conceptual change seems to be involved in belief. For instance, for religous persons with the absolute belief that all that happens to them, being from God, is for their *good*, much that many will not count as good will be so counted and God will be thanked. So too for other key concepts, like *love* and *mercy* in the absolute belief that God is loving and merciful. Those holding this belief as an absolute belief will count much as love or mercy that many others would not. Now there are two very different ways to understand absolute belief and the conceptual change that goes with it. One way, toward which the First Perspective is sympathetic, construes the conceptual change as a *connotative change*: the believer who has an absolute belief *resolves* to believe, or is *captivated* by belief, and gives a new religiously internal sense to the affected concepts. The other way, toward which the Second Perspective is more sympathetic, construes the conceptual change as a *denotative change*: believers with an absolute belief come to the *recognition* that more than they had thought is in the affected concepts' reference.

Very often the belief of Third-Perspective believers is absolute belief with its conceptual change. For the Third Perspective absolute belief is a matter of recognition, as opposed to resolving to take up belief or being captivated by belief; and so the Third Perspective must regard the conceptual change invovled as what I have called a 'denotative change'. But if it does, then it must be acknowledged that it is faced with an epistemological problem: What justifies Third-Perspective believers in counting as good, love, or mercy what others do not and what, it may well be, they themselves in the recent past did not regard as good, love, or mercy? This problem does not address itself to the other construction of absolute belief; for, according to it, when individuals come to hold absolute beliefs about, for instance, God's goodness, they do not come to see that more than they had thought is good in the sense of 'good' that holds in ordinary discourse; rather they acquire new religious concepts that give this term and others new meanings internal to religion.[45] I do not wish to imply that within the Third Perspective this epistemological problem is felt as a problem. It is not, and the reason it is not is that the question that poses the problem is implicitly and completely answered by the grammar of the Third Perspective. The religious discovery, in various forms, can be precisely the discovery, or recognition, that more than one had thought is in the reference of a significant religious concept. If in making the religious discovery one discovers God's presence by discovering that the familiar bespeaks God's goodness, then one thereby recognises that many things not before seen as manifestations of goodness are just that. In the same way, if one makes the religious discovery by discovering that the familiar manifests God's love or mercy, then one thereby recognises that many things not seen as embodiments of love or mercy are just that. Alternatively the religious discovery of God's presence may lead to the secondary recognition, or a series of secondary recognitions, that these concepts contain more in their reference than had been thought; for, after one has made the religious discovery one will see that since the God whose presence has been discovered all about one is a God of goodness, love, and mercy, much more than one had thought manifests His goodness, love, and mercy. It may go either way, but either way the religious discovery grounds the recognition of the wider extension of the key religious concepts affected.

In these ways the Third Perspective can address both the dilemma of choice and certainty in religious belief and knowledge and the issue of the nature of absolute belief and its conceptual change. That it can do so is a strength, I think. At the same time it respects the strengths of the First and Second Perspectives. With the Second it can understand religious knowledge claims to be full-fledged knowledge claims. It does not sever the certainty that religious believers may have from grounded knowledge; and so it runs no danger of attributing religious certainty to irrationality. However, at the same time the Third Perspective speaks to First-Perspective concerns with knowledge. The knowledge affirmed by the Third Perspective is *religious* knowledge. It is knowledge that necessarily engages our emotions. And it is knowledge that does not contain the 'attitude of knowledge' (since that is an enquiry-attitude). Moreover, here too the Third Perspective, like the First Perspective, is alive to the moral dimension of religion: religious knowledge, being the fruit of the religious discovery, requires a role for the will and hence has a moral dimension. So, while the Third Perspective, with the Second, affirms religious knowledge, at the same time the Third Perspective shares with the First Perspective some deep instincts about the possible indifference of knowledge, the 'attitude of knowledge', and the moral dimension of faith. In this way, once again, the Third Perspective provides a middle ground whereupon the First and Second Perspectives can draw closer to one another.

III   FINAL COMMENTS

These remarks, though they are concluding remarks, are not a conclusion. I have no general conclusion to draw. Certainly I would not draw the conclusion that the Third Perspective is *the* true, or even best, perspective that applies to religious belief; nor, at another level, would I draw the conclusion that some have in truth made the religious discovery. The first I would not argue for if I could; the second, I believe, cannot be established by argumentation. Nevertheless some final comments are in order. In this book I have tried to address the issue that I identified in the introduction, the issue of the cognitivity of religion. This issue is one that can make religious believers, or believers of certain sorts, feel that they do not know their way about – that something is not quite right in the tug and pull of their reflections on their own religiousness. The issue of cognitivity is, in one way, defined by the opposite tendencies of the First and Second Perspectives. Neither of these perspectives may seem altogether right, and yet each may to an extent seem to be very right. The resulting tension – that is, the issue of cognitivity – thus forms a philosophical problem that is also a personal problem for individual believers (and perhaps non-believers too) and, as well, a theological problem. I have tried to resolve this issue by stilling, or at least slowing, the pendulum swing between the First and Second Perspectives. This I have tried to do by consulting the tradition of religious realisation, which I labelled the 'Third Perspective'. In the Western theistic heritage this is the tradition of the Psalmist (or one in which he stands), although others too stand in this tradition; nor is it limited to the Western heritage.

This perspective, the Third Perspective, I believe and have tried to show, can accommodate the strengths of the other two perspectives. At the heart of the Third Perspective is the religious discovery, but we need not agree that the religious discovery is indeed a discovery in order to see how the Third Perspective can respect and systematically account for the strengths of the first two perspectives. It can given only the logic of its central religious discovery and the grammatical structure generated by that logic, as we have seen in this chapter.

By way of a summary, instead of listing again the strengths of the first two perspectives on each of the five subissues accommodated by the Third Perspective (see the concluding paragraphs of sections (1)–(5) above for that), I shall try to give a composite, retrospective picture of the Third Perspective's ability to accommodate the strengths of the first two perspectives. In general the First Perspective emphasises the non-cognitive values of religion (and it sees a tension between those values and the various dimensions of cognitivity). On the other hand, the Second

Perspective sees clearly the aspect of religion in which it regards itself as deeply reflecting reality, and so possessing an essential cognitivity (but the Second Perspective slights the non-cognitive values of religion). The Third Perspective goes between the two, or rather, constructs a bridge between the two. Thus, while the Third Perspective implicitly maintains the rationality of religious belief, the rationality it would proclaim is not the enquiry-rationality rightly objected to by the First Perspective. And though it recognises the cognitivity of religious belief in its own tradition, it does not thereby make belief into hypotheses of any sort. It perceives that the very passion of religion is not just compatible with, but requires the cognitivity of belief. Again the Third Perspective heeds both the essential cognitivity of religious belief and the moral dimension of religion as it relates to understanding, certainty, and knowledge. It sees with the Second Perspective that there is a level at which religious belief can be understood, believed, and even known to be true by virtue of merely intellectual endeavour (as at least some with the Second Perspective hold), and it sees with the First Perspective (as at least some with the First Perspective hold) that true understanding and belief require a turning of the will. For the Third Perspective it is not that religion's moral dimension merely coexists with religion's cognitivity; rather, the cognitivity of religion, which for the Third Perspective is a realisation-cognitivity, is deeply interwoven with the will and willfulness. The Third Perspective sees both the importance for honesty of tracing, or not denying, the logical implications of belief and how, finally, having religious truth is not so much a matter of tracing the implications of belief as it is a matter of having religious understanding of what is believed. Though for the Third Perspective religion is deeply cognitive, the essence of religion is not holding to be true cognitive beliefs. Third-Perspective belief is tied to the religious discovery of a relationship to the Divine or God. However, the Third Perspective can grant that for one to discover a relationship to Reality (which is a personal God for the Psalmist) it is not necessary to have a right conception of Reality, and that to be in an abiding relationship to Reality it is not even necessary to believe that one is. At the same time, religious believers who are in the tradition of the Psalmist not only may be described as being in a relationship to God, but in their own self-understanding they recognise that they are, know that they are, cannot deny that they are; and they religiously understand that relationship to be informed by God's love and goodness and to be a relationship in which they are to participate through their own love, trust, and obedience. For the Third Perspective a relationship to God or to Reality awaits the discovery of each and all. The evidence of God's presence is manifest. But it is not enquiry-evidence (in accord with First-Perspective intuitions). It is not that those who have not found God have not yet seen enough, it is closer to it that they have seen too much and having seen too much have seen nothing. This is not quite right either. The fault is not in what we can or cannot see of the stars, the fault is in ourselves. With the religious discovery comes religious knowledge, for (as the Second Perspective appreciates), there is or can be religious evidence (of a kind) and religious knowledge (of a kind).

I shall end by quoting and then commenting on what a member of a Benedictine monastery has said about his spiritual discipline:

> The Bible calls the responsive listening of obedience 'living by the word of God', and that means far more than merely doing God's will. It means being nourished by God's word as food and drink, God's word in every person, everything, every event.
>
> This is a daily task, a moment by moment discipline. I eat a tangerine and the resistance of the rind, as I peel it, speaks to me, if I am alert enough . . .
>
> But a calamity is also word of God when it hits me . . .
>
> The clue lies in the fact that any given moment confronts us with a given reality. But if it is given, it is gift. If it is gift, the appropriate response is thanksgiving. Yet, thanksgiving where it is genuine, does not primarily look at the gift and express appreciation; it looks at the giver and expresses trust. The courageous confidence which trusts in the Giver of all gifts is faith. To give thanks when we cannot see the goodness of the gift, trusting in the goodness of the Giver – to learn this is to find the path to peace of heart . . .
>
> In a lifelong process the discipline of listening teaches us to live 'by *every* word that proceeds from the mouth of God' without discrimination. We learn this by 'giving thanks in *all* things' . . . [46]

I think that the reverberations of the Psalmist's tradition are unmistakable. This is so even though the author makes spiritual *listening* central to what he says. But if we may speak of seeing God in all that He does and gives, we may also speak of hearing God in all that is His word and His gift. As for the author, so for the Third Perspective: all things daily may lead to the renewed realisation of God (the nourishment of God's word), even calamity. At times believers may not be able to hear the word of God in what occurs, see God's goodness in what overtakes them. Though God's goodness cannot be seen, still thanks is to be given in accord with the absolute belief in God's goodness, in trust, and perhaps also in the hope that God's goodness will be seen. And, it may be, by giving thanks in all things, the goodness of God will be seen in all things. Thanking God can bring us to see God's goodness in all things as much as anything else.

Notes

INTRODUCTION

1. Most often I shall use the words 'religion' and 'religious' to refer to religious belief in God or especially to religious belief in God. Given that my concern arises within Western religion, within the Judaeo-Christian tradition in particular, this quasi-technical use of 'religion' will avoid repetition. I do not mean it to imply anything about what might or might not appropriately be called religious. In fact at times I myself shall use the term to refer to religions outside the Western theistic heritage.
2. Dionysius, *The Mystical Theology*, ɪ; *Dionysius the Areopagite*, trans. C. E. Rolt (London: SPCK, 1940) p. 194. And *Summa Theologica*, ɪ, q.2, a.2.
3. St. Bonaventura, *The Mind's Road to God*, trans. George Boas (Indianapolis and New York: Bobbs-Merrill, 1953).
4. Tertullian, who said that the Son of God died is to be believed because it is absurd and that He was buried and rose again is certain because it is impossible, made both of these defiantly fideistic proclamations in *On the Flesh of Christ*. Elsewhere, however, he does not hesitate to use the very skills of dialectic that he seems to renounce in this celebrated passage.
5. *Summa Theologica*, ɪɪ–ɪɪ, q.2, a.1.
6. John Calvin, *The Institutes*, ch. 2 of the 1535 edition; *John Calvin: Selections from His Writings*, ed. John Dillenberger (Garden City, N.Y.: Anchor books, 1971) p. 274.
7. All references to the Bible, unless otherwise indicated are to the Revised Standard Version.
8. On the cognitivist side are, for instance, Basil Mitchell and John Hick; on the non-cognitivist side are, for instance, R. B. Braithwaite and R. F. Holland. See Basil Mitchell, his contribution to 'Theology and Falsification', *New Essays in Philosophical Theology*, ed. Antony Flew and Alasdair MacIntyre (London: SCM Press, 1955); John Hick, 'Theology and Verification', reprinted in *The Existence of God*, ed. John Hick (New York: The Macmillan Company; London: Collier-Macmillan Limited, 1964); R. B. Braithwaite, 'An Empiricist's View of the Nature of Religious Belief', reprinted in Hick's *The Existence of God*; and R. F. Holland, 'Religious Discourse and Theological Discourse', *The Australasian Journal of Philosophy*, vol. 34 (1956).
9. Let me say exactly how I shall use 'grammer' and 'grammatical' (and, at times 'logic' and 'conceptual nature'). I shall use them in accord with sec. 371 of the *Philosophical Investigations*, where Wittgenstein says that '*essence* is expressed by grammar' (his emphasis), and sec. 373, where, clarifying this

comment, he says that 'grammar tells what kind of object anything is'. In this sense, then, a grammatical question is a question about the 'essence' of something, that is, a question about the kind of 'object' or thing it is. I shall take it as given that there can be disagreements about the grammar of religious belief and other religious 'objects', as quite evidently there are, even if these disagreements are too deep to be merely differences of opinion.

CHAPTER 1   TWO PERSPECTIVES ON MODERN ISSUE OF COGNITIVITY

1. Søren Kierkegaard, *Fear and Trembling* and *Sickness unto Death*, trans. Walter Lowrie (Princeton University Press, 1941) pp. 47 and 51.
2. Kierkegaard was aware of this difference. In his papers he wrote: '. . . it is one thing to believe by virtue of the absurd . . . and [another] to believe the absurd. The first expression is used by Johannes de Silentio [in *Fear and Trembling*], the second by Johannes Climacus [in the *Postscript*]', *Søren Kierkegaard's Papirer*, x^6 B 80. This translation is from *Søren Kierkegaard's Journals and Papers*, tr. Howard V. Hong and Edna H. Hong (Bloomington and London: Indiana University Press, 1967) I, serial entry number 11.
3. Søren Kierkegaard, *Concluding Unscientific Postscript*, trans. David F. Swenson and Walter Lowrie (Princeton University Press, 1941) pp. 182 and 188.
4. Pretty clearly, it seems to me, this is the way Kierkegaard's thinking about faith goes in the *Postscript*. Faith is a continuous enbracing of the absolute paradox. 'If I wish to preserve myself in faith I must constantly be intent upon holding fast the objective uncertainty', Kierkegaard says (*Concluding Unscientific Postscript*, p. 182).
5. M. O'C. Drury, 'Some Notes on Conversations with Wittgenstein', *Acta Philosophica Fennica*, vol. 28 (1976) pp. 32–3, repr. in Rush Rhees (ed.), *Ludwig Wittgenstein: Personal Recollections* (Totowa, New Jersey: Rowan & Littlefield, 1981).
6. Ludwig Wittgenstein, 'A Lecture on Ethics', *The Philosophical Review*, vol. 74 (1965) pp. 8–12.
7. Kai Nielsen, 'The Challenge of Wittgenstein: an Examination of his Picture of Religious Belief', *Studies in Religion/Sciences Religieuses*, vol. 3 (1973) pp. 36–7. And see Rush Rhees, 'Some Developments in Wittgenstein's View of Ethics', *Philosophical Review*, vol. 74 (1965) pp. 17–21; and W. D. Hudson, *Wittgenstein and Religious Belief* (London and Basingstoke: Macmillan, 1975) pp. 78ff.
8. Wittgenstein once said to M. O'C. Drury, 'I am not a religious man but I cannot help seeing every problem from a religious point of view', M. O'C. Drury, 'Some Notes on Conversations with Wittgenstein', p. 25.
9. Ludwig Wittgenstein, *Lectures on Religious Belief* in *Lectures and Conversation on Aesthetics, Psychology and Religious Belief*, compiled from notes taken by Yorick Smythies, Rush Rhees, and James Taylor, edited by Cyril Barrett (Berkeley: University of California, 1966).
10. Wittgenstein, *Lectures and Conversations on Aesthetics, Psychology and Religious Belief*, pp. 57–8.

11. D. Z. Phillips, *Faith and Philosophical Enquiry* (New York: Schocken Books, 1971) pp. 17ff.

12. D. Z. Phillips, *Religion without Explanation* (Oxford: Basil Blackwell, 1976) p. 7.

13. Phillips, 'Religion and Epistemology: Some Contemporary Confusions', *Faith and Philosphical Enquiry*, p. 124.

14. Cf. Phillips, 'Philosophy, Theology and the Reality of God', *Faith and Philosophical Enquiry*, p. 7.

15. See for instance *Religion without Explanation*, pp. 7–8 where Phillips speaks of religious belief as a 'human activity'.

16. He has especially in *The Idea of a Social Science and its Relation to Philosophy* (London: Routledge & Kegan Paul, 1958); and in 'Understanding a Primitive Society', *American Philosophical Quarterly*, vol. 1 (1964), repr. in *Religion and Understanding*, ed. D. Z. Phillips (Oxford: Blackwell, 1967).

17. MacIntyre's article appears in *Faith and the Philosophers*, ed. John Hick (New York: St. Martin's Press, 1964).

18. Winch, 'Understanding a Primitive Society', *Religion and Understanding*, pp. 12–13 and 30–1.

19. Winch, 'Understanding a Primitive Society', *Religion and Understanding*, p. 21.

20. Winch, 'Understanding a Primitive Society', *Religion and Understanding*, pp. 15 and 35.

21. Cf. Kai Nielsen, 'Wittgensteinian Fideism', *Philosophy*, vol. 42 (1967) p. 207.

22. Winch, 'Understanding a Primitive Society', *Religion and Understanding*, p. 15.

23. St. Francis de Sales, *Treatise on the Love of God*, trans. Henry Benedict Mackey (Westport, Conn.: Greenwood Press, 1971) Bk. xi, ch. 1, p. 466.

24. Peter Geach, 'Causality and Creation', *God and the Soul* (London: Routledge & Kegan Paul, 1969) p. 85.

25. Geach, *God and the Soul*, pp. 100–17.

26. Alvin Plantinga, *God and Other Minds* (Ithaca, N.Y.: Cornell University Press, 1967) pp. vii and 271.

27. Alvin Plantinga, *The Nature of Necessity* (Oxford: Clarendon Press, 1974) p. 221.

28. Cf. Thomas McPherson, *Philosophy and Religious Belief* (London: Hutchinson University Library, 1974) pp. 22–3.

29. *Dialogues Concerning Natural Religion*, Part xii.

30. *In Memoriam*, xcvi, 11. 1995–6.

31. *In Memoriam*, xcvi.

32. *In Memoriam*, lv and lvi. See Basil Willey, *More Nineteenth Century Studies* (New York: Columbia University Press, 1956) p. 91.

33. Cf. Paul Edwards, 'Kierkegaard and the "Truth" of Christianity', *Philosophy*, vol. 46 (1971) p. 98.

34. H. H. Price, 'Faith and Belief', *Faith and the Philosophers*, ed. John Hick (London: Macmillan; New York: St. Martin's Press, 1964) p. 16.

35. H. H. Price, *Belief* (London: Allen & Unwin; New York: Humanities Press, 1969) pp. 481–8. This volume consists of Price's 1960 Gifford Lectures.

36. John King-Farlow and William Christensen, *Faith and the Life of Reason* (Dordrecht, Holland: D. Reidel, 1972) pp. 2–18.

37. James's comments on rationality, or what is 'lawful' in belief, and his

arguments for a more pragmatic conception of rationality are found in more than one work. However, it is generally felt that the best expression of his view remains 'The Will to Believe', in *Essays in Pragmatism*, ed. Albury Castell (New York: Hafner Publishing Company, 1948).

38. See his *Belief in God: a Study in the Epistemology of Religion* (New York: Random House, 1970); and his introduction to *The Rationality of Belief in God*, ed. George Mavrodes (Englewood Cliffs, N.J.: Prentice-Hall, 1970). However, in 'Rationality and Religious Belief – a Perverse Question', *Rationality and Religious Belief*, ed. C. F. Delaney (Notre Dame and London: University of Notre Dame Press, 1979), Mavrodes says that the question of *religion's* rationality may be 'not a very important question' (p. 28).

39. 'Rationality and Religious Belief – a Perverse Question', *Rationality and Religious Belief*, pp. 40–1. Mavrodes has made this point or one similar to it in various places. See for instance pp. 11–15 in *Belief in God: A Study in the Epistemology of Religion*.

40. We shall look at John Hick's views on the importance of religious experience for belief, and the possible role of religious experience as evidence for belief, later in this chapter when we turn to the issue of religious evidence (the fourth subissue).

41. In the *Postscript* Kierkegaard speaks of faith or inwardness as infinite passion (p. 182). On p. 540 he makes explicit the connection between the greatest faith and the greatest objective uncertainty, the absurd, the 'absolute paradox'; 'Faith is the objective uncertainty due to the repulsion of the absurd held fast by the passion of inwardness, which in this instance is intensified to the utmost degree.'

42. Kierkegaard, *Concluding Unscientific Postscript*, pp. 179–80.

43. Cf. *Concluding Unscientific Postscript*, p. 540, where Kierkegaard says: 'The thing of being a Christian is not determined by the *what* of Christianity but by the *how* of the Christian. This *how* can only correspond with one thing, the absolute paradox' (Kierkegaard's emphasis).

44. In *Concluding Unscientific Postscript* Kierkegaard says: 'Christianity is no doctrine concerning the unity of the divine and the human, or concerning the identity of subject and object; nor is it any other of the logical transcriptions of Christianity.' 'Christianity', he says, 'is not a doctrine, but the fact that God has existed' (pp. 290–1).

It is interesting to compare Geach and Kierkegaard on idolatry. For Kierkegaard it is not the idol worshipper who is idolatrous, even though his eyes rest upon the image of an idol; it is the other, for he 'prays falsely to the true God, and hence worships in fact an idol' (*Concluding Unscientific Postscript*, p. 180). For Geach idolatry is treating an object as God – which we do when our conception of God is wrong enough and our worship is misdirected (see section (1) above). For Kierkegaard idolatry is treating God as an object – which we do even with a true concept of the true God, if we pray in a 'false spirit'. Geach and Kierkegaard seem a universe apart. Yet, interestingly, they come to a point of agreement. Geach says that 'if a man comes to worship a God because the true God "calls and draws him," then certainly this worship will be directed towards the true God, *however inadequately conceived*' ('On Worshipping the Right God,' *God and the Soul*, p. 112; my emphasis). Geach reluctantly concedes this. Kierkegaard rushes to embrace it.

45. Kierkegaard, *Fear and Trembling* and *The Sickness unto Death*, p. 46.

46. See Norman Malcolm, *Ludwig Wittgenstein: a Memoir* (London: Oxford University Press, 1958) pp. 70–1, for the personal importance Wittgenstein attached to these feelings.

47. Wittgenstein, 'A Lecture on Ethics', pp. 8–10.

48. Rudolf Carnap, 'Autobiography', in *The Philosophy of Rudolf Carnap*, ed. Paul Schilpp (LaSalle, Illinois: The Open Court Publishing Co., 1964). Portions are reprinted in *Ludwig Wittgenstein: the Man and His Philosophy*, ed. K. T. Fann (New Jersey: Humanities Press; Chichester: Harvester Press, 1967), where the pertinent pages are pp. 35–6.

49. Nielsen makes this observation in 'The Challenge of Wittgenstein: An Examination of his Picture of Religious Belief', p. 37.

50. It should be noted, though, that if Stuart Brown is right, even the later Wittgenstein would have regarded religious *claims* (for instance that there is a God or a Last Judgment) to be cognitive nonsense. Brown reasons that Wittgenstein would regard claims that God exists, say, as cognitive nonsense because he regarded it as illegitimate to try to derive substantive truths from the 'arbitrary' rules of grammar. As Brown shows us, there are passages in Wittgenstein that support this interpretation (such as *Philosophical Investigations*, I, sec. 372.) Stuart C. Brown, 'Religion and the Limits of Language', *Reason and Religion*, ed. Stuart C. Brown, Royal Institute of Philosophy Conference, 1975 (Ithaca and London: Cornell University Press, 1977) pp. 233n and 240–1. Interestingly, Wittgenstein once said in conversation with Freidrich Waismann that religion does not require speech at all. F. Waismann, 'Notes on Talks with Wittgenstein', *The Philosophical Review*, vol. 74 (1965) p. 16.

51. Phillips, 'Philosophy, Theology and the Reality of God', *Faith and Philosophical Enquiry*, p. 12; and 'Faith, Scepticism, and Religious Understanding', *Faith and Philosophical Enquiry*, p. 31.

52. Phillips, 'Religious Beliefs and Language-Games', *Faith and Philosophical Enquiry*, pp. 101–6. Cf. Wittgenstein, *Lectures and Conversations on Aesthetics, Psychology and Religious Belief*, p. 59.

53. Phillips, 'Religion and Epistemology: Some Contemporary Confusions', *Faith and Philosophical Enquiry*, pp. 127–8.

54. Norman Malcolm, 'Is it a Religious Belief that "God Exists"?', *Faith and the Philosophers*, ed. John Hick (New York: St. Martin's Press, 1964), pp. 103ff. Phillips cites Malcolm in 'Faith, Scepticism, and Religious Understanding', *Faith and Philosophical Enquiry*, p. 14.

55. Phillips, 'Faith, Scepticism, and Religious Understanding', *Faith and Philosophical Enquiry*, p. 17. Cf. Alasdair MacIntyre, 'The Logical Status of Religious Belief', *Metaphysical Beliefs*, ed. A. MacIntyre, 2nd edn (London: SCM Press, 1970) p. 193.

56. See Phillips, 'Religious Belief and Philosophical Enquiry', *Faith and Philosophical Enquiry*, p. 71, and 'Religious Beliefs and Language-Games', *Faith and Philosophical Enquiry*, pp. 85–6.

57. Phillips, *Religion without Explanation*, pp. 176–7; and Rush Rhees 'Religion and Language', *Without Answers* (London: Routledge & Kegan Paul, 1969) pp. 131–2.

58. 'Wisdom's Gods', *Faith and Philosophical Enquiry*, pp. 170–203.

59. Phillips, 'Religious Beliefs and Language-Games', *Faith and Philosophical Enquiry*, p. 100.
60. Phillips, 'Belief and Loss of Belief', *Faith and Philosophical Enquiry*, p. 117.
61. Phillips, 'Religious Beliefs and Language-Games', *Faith and Philosophical Enquiry*, p. 97.
62. Cf. Stuart Brown on the second condition. Stuart Brown, 'Religion and the Limits of Language', *Reason and Religion*, pp. 245–7. Brown argues that both Phillips' and Winch's accounts of religious belief make the truth of religious beliefs consist in people being able to live by them.
63. Phillips, *Religion without Explanation*, p. 188; 'Faith, Scepticism, and Religious Understanding', *Faith and Philosophical Enquiry*, p. 17; and 'Religion and Epistemology: Some Contemporary Confusions', *Faith and Philosophical Enquiry*, p. 131.
64. Phillips, 'Religious Beliefs and Language-Games', *Faith and Philosophical Enquiry*, p. 87.
65. Plantinga, *God and Other Minds*, pp. 115ff. For Mackie's 'natural atheology' see his 'Evil and Omnipotence', rept. in *God and Evil*, ed. Nelson Pike (Englewood Cliffs, N.J.: Prentice Hall, 1964). For McCloskey's see his 'God and Evil', also reprinted in *God and Evil*.
66. The challenge addressed by Mitchell and Hick is Antony Flew's falsification challenge in 'Theology and Falsification', *New Essays in Philosophical Theology*. For Mitchell's reply see his contribution to 'Theology and Falsification'. For Hick's reply see his 'Theology and Verification', *The Existence of God*, or ch. 8 of his *Faith and Knowledge*, 2nd edn (Ithaca, N.Y.: Cornell University Press, 1966). For an updated version of his reply see his 'Eschatological Verification reconsidered', *Religious Studies*, vol. 13 (1977).
67. R. Bambrough, *Reason, Truth and God* (London: Methuen, 1969) p. 37.
68. Terrence W. Tilley, *Talking of God* (New York, Ramsey, and Toronto: Paulist Press, 1978) p. 109.
69. Kai Nielsen, *Scepticism* (London: Macmillan; New York: St. Martin's Press, 1973) p. 28 (Nielsen's emphasis).
70. Calvin, *The Institute*, ch. 2 (Dillenberger, *Selections*, p. 274).
71. Roger Trigg should be mentioned here. See his *Reason and Commitment* (Cambridge University Press, 1973) pp. 74ff.
72. Wittgenstein, *Lectures and Conversations on Aesthetics, Psychology and Religious Belief*, p. 55.
73. Wittgenstein, *Lectures and Conversations on Aesthetics, Psychology and Religious Belief*, pp. 59 and 71.
74. Wittgenstein, *Lectures and Conversations on Aesthetics, Psychology and Religious Belief*, pp. 55–62.
75. D. Z. Phillips, *Death and Immortality* (London: Macmillan; New York: St. Martin's Press, 1970) p. 76.
76. Phillips, 'Faith, Scepticism, and Religious Understanding', *Faith and Philosophical Enquiry*, p. 29.
77. Stuart C. Brown, *Do Religious Claims Make Sense?* (New York: Macmillan, 1969) p. xviii.
78. Brown, *Do Religious Claims Make Sense?* p. 174.
79. Brown, *Do Religious Claims Make Sense?* pp. 17–18.
80. Patrick Sherry remarks regarding Brown's view: 'There seems to be an

inconsistency in claiming that understanding and belief go hand in hand and yet admitting that a man may reject religious beliefs because he finds them sufficiently intelligible to know what it would be for them to be false', *Religion, Truth and Language-Games* (New York: Barnes & Noble, 1977) n.15, p. 208.

Sherry's point seems to be right if 'understanding' means *any* understanding, but not if it means substantive understanding.

81. Phillips, *Death and Immortality*, pp. 72–7.
82. Phillips, *Death and Immortality*, pp. 72–3. Phillips is quoting from Nielsen's 'Wittgensteinian Fideism', p. 196.
83. Phillips recently has wished to distance himself from the view that one must be a religious believer to understand religious belief. See 'Belief, Change, and Forms of Life: the Confusions of Externalism and Internalism', *The Autonomy of Religious Belief*, ed. Frederick Crosson (Notre Dame and London: University of Notre Dame Press, 1981) p. 88. Phillips reminds us that in 1966 in 'God and Ought' he said:

> These problems [problems which occur in our relationships with others and from which prayer for forgiveness arises] can be appreciated by the religious and the non-religious alike. Because of such connections between religious and non-religious activity, it is possible to convey the meaning of religious language to someone unfamiliar with it, even if all one achieves is to stop him from talking nonsense.

However, Phillips goes on to say on the next page of 'God and Ought' in a passage of which he does not remind us: 'What I do want to stress is that despite the existence of connections between religious and non-religious discourse, the criteria of sense and non-sense in the former are to be found *within* religion'. *Faith and Philosophical Enquiry*, p. 231 (Phillips' emphasis).

As I have indicated, though, Phillips' view is complex and, as he maintains, it is not identical with the view that religious belief can only be understood by religious believers.

84. Alasdair MacIntyre, 'Is Understanding Religion Compatible with Believing?', *Faith and the Philosophers*, ed. John Hick (New York: St. Martin's Press, 1964) pp. 115–16.
85. MacIntyre of course is not alone in seeing a problem here. Sherry raises it, regarding loss of faith specifically, in connection with his discussion of Brown's view, *Religious Truth and Language-Games*, p. 142.
86. Brown, *Do Religious Claims Make Sense?*, p. 146. The quotation is from *Dogmatics in Outline*.
87. Phillips, 'Faith, Scepticism, and Religious Understanding', *Faith and Philosophical Enquiry*, pp. 29–33.
88. Nielsen, *Scepticism*, pp. 26–7.
89. John King-Farlow, 'Cogency, Conviction, and Coercion', *International Philosophical Quarterly*, vol. 8 (1968) p. 464.
90. Trigg, *Reason and Commitment*, pp. 84–6.
91. Trigg, *Reason and Commitment*, p. 166.
92. Cf. Trigg, *Reason and Commitment*, p. 50.
93. Not surprisingly, D. Z. Phillips expresses this very view in 'On the Christian Concept of Love', *Faith and Philosophical Enquiry*, p. 246.

94. Trigg's subject in the context where he draws this distinction is the issue of understanding and belief, and his difference with Wittgenstein and Phillips on this issue; however he does not use the distinction to address the problem I have raised for the Second Perspective. *Reason and Commitment*, pp. 50–3.

95. This distinction is made by W. D. Hudson in his discussion of the sense in which an unbeliever can contradict a believer. *Wittgenstein and Religious Belief*, pp. 192–3.

96. The Danish word '*Tro*' can be translated as either 'faith' or 'belief'.

97. Kierkegaard, *Concluding Unscientific Postscript*, p. 189.

98. Cf. Gregor Malantschuk, *Kierkegaard's Thought*, ed. and trans. Howard V. and Edna H. Hong (Princeton University Press, 1971), p. 256.

99. Kierkegaard, *Concluding Unscientific Postscript*, p. 182.

100. Kierkegaard, *Concluding Unscientific Postscript*, p. 155.

101. Wittgenstein, *Lectures and Conversations on Aesthetics, Psychology and Religious Belief*, p. 57.

102. I take this to be the import of Wittgenstein's point about the religious use of "believe" in *Lectures on Religious Belief*. *Lectures and Conversations on Aesthetics, Psychology and Religious Belief*, pp. 57 and 59–60.

103. Wittgenstein, *Lectures and Conversations on Aesthetics, Psychology and Religious Belief*, p. 57.

104. Wittgenstein, *Lectures and Conversations on Aesthetics, Psychology and Religious Belief*, pp. 60–1.

105. Wittgenstein, *Lectures and Conversations on Aesthetics, Psychology and Religious Belief*, p. 56.

106. Wittgenstein, *Lectures and Conversations on Aesthetics, Psychology and Religious Belief*, p. 61.

107. Phillips, 'Wisdom's Gods', *Faith and Philosophical Enquiry*, pp. 197–8.

108. Phillips, *Religion without Explanation*, pp. 6–7.

109. Phillips, 'Faith, Scepticism, and Religious Understanding', *Faith and Philosophical Enquiry*, p. 13.

110. Phillips, 'Wisdom's Gods', *Faith and Philosophical Enquiry*, p. 202.

111. Norman Malcolm, 'The Groundlessness of Belief,' *Thought and Knowledge* (Ithaca and London: Cornell University Press, 1977) p. 208. Malcolm's essay in an earlier and shorter version appears in *Reason and Religion*, ed. Stuart C. Brown, along with a reply by Colin Lyas, remarks by Basil Mitchell, and a postscript by Malcolm.

112. Malcolm, 'The Groundlessness of Belief', p. 213.

113. There may, however, be a difference between what Malcolm and Phillips have in mind as evidence within or internal to religious belief. For Malcolm internal evidence relates to doctrinal issues within belief. For Phillips internal evidence can be reasons for belief in God as a whole, but such reasons hold only within faith and so would not provide evidence in support of belief for someone outside belief.

114. Malcolm, 'The Groundlessness of Belief', p. 201. Cf. Wittgenstein in *On Certainty*, eds G. E. M. Anscombe and G. H. von Wright, trans. D. Paul and G. E. M. Anscombe (Oxford: Basil Blackwell, 1969) paras 163 and 166, which Malcolm cites.

115. Malcolm, 'The Groundlessness of Belief', p. 216.

116. Malcolm, 'Is it a Religious Belief that "God Exists"?', p. 106.

117. Malcolm, 'The Groundlessness of Belief', p. 215.

118. Norman Malcolm, 'Anselm's Ontological Arguments', *Knowledge and Certainty* (Englewood Cliffs, N.J.: Prentice-Hall, 1963).

119. Malcolm, 'Anselm's Ontological Arguments', p. 161.

120. In *New Essays in Philosophical Theology*.

121. MacIntyre, 'The Logical Status of Religious Belief', p. 190.

122. MacIntyre, 'The Logical Status of Religious Belief', p. 195.

123. MacIntyre, 'The Logical Status of Religious Belief', p. 191.

124. MacIntyre, 'The Logical Status of Religious Belief', p. 199.

125. In the translation of *The Brothers Karamazov* by David Magarshack (Baltimore, Maryland: Penguin Books, 1958), see I, p. 294 and cf. p. 299.

126. John Hick, 'Sceptics and Believers', *Faith and the Philosophers*, pp. 245–6. See also his introduction to *The Existence of God* (New York: Macmillan; London: Collier-Macmillan, 1964) pp. 15–18; and his discussion note 'Faith and Coercion', *Philosophy*, vol. 42 (1967) pp. 272–3. For a full discussion of Hick's view see his *Faith and Knowledge*, esp. ch. 6, 'Faith and Freedom'.

127. Hick, *Faith and Knowledge*, pp. 139–40.

128. Hick, 'Sceptics and Believers', p. 245. Cf. *The Existence of God*, p. 17.

129. Hick, *Faith and Knowledge*, pp. 141ff.

130. Hick, 'Sceptics and Believers', p. 239, and *The Existence of God*, pp. 9–10.

131. Hick, 'Sceptics and Believers', p. 246.

132. Hick, *Faith and Knowledge*, pp. 209–10.

133. Robert Herbert, *Paradox and Identity in Theology* (Ithaca and London: Cornell University Press, 1979) p. 67 (Herbert's emphasis).

134. Herbert, *Paradox and Identity in Theology*, pp. 67–8.

135. Herbert, *Paradox and Identity in Theology*, pp. 52–3.

136. Herbert, *Paradox and Identity in Theology*, p. 71. The Kierkegaard quotation is from the *Papirer*, VIII, A 7, also in Hong and Hong, *Journals and Papers*, I, 778.

137. George Schlesinger, *Religion and Scientific Method* (Dordrecht and Boston: D. Reidel, 1977) p. 201.

138. Schlesinger, *Religion and Scientific Method*, pp. 182–3.

139. Schlesinger, *Religion and Scientific Method*, p. 5.

140. Schlesinger, *Religion and Scientific Method*, p. 182.

141. Schlesinger's argument that Theism is the most adequate, or simplist, hypothesis turns on Theism's being the hypothesis 'selected with the aid of the only useable guiding rule', *Religion and Scientific Method*, pp. 185–92, and see p. 163.

142. Richard Swinburne, *The Concept of Miracle* (New York: St. Martin's; London: Macmillan, 1970) p. 11. While this is a Humean definition, Hume himself said more simply that 'a miracle is a violation of the laws of nature'. Hume in *An Enquiry Concerning Human Understanding* directed his energies toward showing that there could be no such thing, or at least that there could be no good reason for thinking that such a thing had occurred. Since he thought that his efforts were successful he never turned to the issue of what would be evidence that a violation was due to God's intervention.

143. Swinburne, *The Concept of Miracle*, p. 26.

144. Swinburne, *The Concept of Miracle*, p. 32.
145. Swinburne, *The Concept of Miracle*, p. 33. A fourth kind of historical evidence is given by Swinburne: 'our contemporary understanding of what things are physically impossible or improbable'. But, as he says, this fourth kind is really only a corrective to the other three.
146. Swinburne, *The Concept of Miracle*, pp. 58–9. Cf. Schlesinger, *Relgion and Scientific Method*, p. 173.
147. Swinburne, *The Concept of Miracle*, p. 66.
148. Price, *Belief*, pp. 481–6; see also Price's 'Faith and Belief', pp. 16–19.
149. Price, 'Faith and Belief', pp. 19–20.
150. Bambrough, *Reason, Truth and God*, p.103.
151. Bambrough, *Reason, Truth and God*, p. 46.
152. Reprinted in John Wisdom, *Philosophy and Psycho-analysis* (Oxford: Basil Blackwell, 1964).
153. Bambrough, *Reason, Truth and God*, p. 57.
154. Bambrough, *Reason, Truth and God*, p. 91.
155. Bambrough, *Reason, Truth and God*, p. 66.
156. H. D. Lewis, *Our Experience of God* (London: Allen & Unwin Ltd.; New York: Macmillan, 1959) pp. 13 and 59.
157. Lewis, *Our Experience of God*, pp. 14–15.
158. Lewis, *Our Experience of God*, p. 59.
159. Lewis, *Our Experience of God*, p. 59.
160. Lewis, *Our Experience of God*, pp. 65–6.
161. Lewis, *Our Experience of God*, p. 56.
162. Lewis, *Our Experience of God*, p. 107.
163. Lewis, *Our Experience of God*, p. 111.
164. Lewis, *Our Experience of God*, pp. 126–7.
165. Lewis, *Our Experience of God*, p. 110.
166. Lewis, *Our Experience of God*, pp. 61 and 284. Although he does not mention it, Lewis on this point also differs with Friedrich Schleiermacher and Rudolf Otto.
167. Lewis, *Our Experience of God*, p. 53.
168. Lewis, *Our Experience of God*, pp. 287–8.
169. Stephen T. Davis, *Faith, Skepticism, and Evidence* (Lewisburg: Bucknell University Press; London: Associated University Presses, 1978) pp. 26ff and 214ff.
170. Davis, *Faith, Skepticism, and Evidence*, p. 26.
171. Davis, *Faith, Skepticism, and Evidence*, p. 28.
172. Malcolm, 'Is it a religious Belief that "God exists"?', p. 108 (Malcolm's emphasis).
173. Davis, *Faith, Skepticism, and Evidence*, p. 27.
174. Davis, *Faith, Skepticism, and Evidence*, p. 220.
175. There are other differences as well. See Davis, *Faith, Skepticism, and Evidence*, pp. 170ff for Davis on James's 'right to believe' doctrine.
176. Kierkegaard, *Concluding Unscientific Postscript*, p. 189 (Kierkegaard's emphasis).
177. Kierkegaard, *Concluding Unscientific Postscript*, p. 182.
178. Kierkegaard, *Concluding Unscientific Postscript*, p. 512.
179. Kierkegaard, *Concluding Unscientific Postscript*, p. 507.

180. Kierkegaard, *Concluding Unscientific Postscript*, p. 280 (my emphasis).

181. At one point in the *Postscript* Kierkegaard does seem to allow that there is a kind of knowledge compatible with faith. This is where he allows that there is 'essential' or 'subjective' knowledge. But 'essential knowledge' does not 'signify . . . that knowledge corresponds to something as its object' (*Postscript*, p. 177). 'Essential Knowledge', in short, is not knowledge *of* anything. It is, rather, a subjective response to the concern of individual existence, to use Kierkegaard's terms.

182. Søren Kierkegaard, *Philosophical Fragments*, trans. David F. Swenson, trans. revised Howard V. Hong (Princeton University Press, 1962) p. 103.

183. Kierkegaard, *Philosophical Fragments*, pp. 103–4.

184. Søren Kierkegaard, *Training in Christianity*, trans. Walter Lowrie (Princeton University Press, 1944) p. 28.

185. Kierkegaard, *Training in Christianity*, p. 36.

186. Kierkegaard, *Training in Christianity*, p. 36 (Kierkegaard's emphasis).

187. The perception of an opposition between faith and knowledge is also to be found in contemporary analytic philosophy. See Raziel Abelson, 'The Logic of Faith and Belief', *Religious Experience and Truth*, ed. Sidney Hook (New York University Press, 1961) pp. 122–4.

188. Miguel de Unamuno, *The Agony of Christianity and Essays on Faith*, trans. Anthony Kerrigan (Princeton University Press, 1974) p. 175.

189. Martin Buber, *I and Thou*, trans. Walter Kaufmann (New York: Charles Scribner's Sons, 1970) p. 90.

190. Buber, *I and Thou*, p. 162.

191. Wittgenstein, *Lectures and Conversations on Aesthetics, Psychology and Religious Belief*, pp. 59–60.

192. Wittgenstein, *Lectures and Conversations on Aesthetics, Psychology and Religious Belief*, p. 57.

193. Phillips, 'Religion and Epistemology: Some Contemporary Confusions', *Faith and Philosophical Enquiry*, p. 132.

194. Phillips, 'Religion and Epistemology: Some Contemporary Confusions', *Faith and Philosophical Enquiry*, p. 29.

195. Phillips, 'Religion and Epistemology: Some Contemporary Confusions', *Faith and Philosophical Enquiry*, p. 21. Later in the essay, as we have seen, he modifies his thesis slightly to allow for forms of belief not characterised by love.

196. Phillips, 'Faith, Scepticism, and Religious Understanding', *Faith and Philosophical Enquiry*, p. 32 (my emphasis).

197. Phillips, 'Religion and Epistemology: some Contemporary Confusions', *Faith and Philosophical Enquiry*, p. 123.

198. Phillips, 'Religion and Epistemology: Some Contemporary Confusions', *Faith and Philosophical Enquiry*, p. 143. The quotation is from Winch's *The Idea of a Social Science* (Winch's emphasis).

199. Phillips, 'Religion and Epistemology: Some Contemporary Confusions', *Faith and Philosophical Enquiry*, p. 132.

200. Cf. Joseph Butler, *The Analogy of Religion*, Part. II, Ch. 1, para. 7.

201. Emil Brunner, *Revelation and Reason*, trans. Olive Wyon (Philadelphia: The Westminster Press, 1946) p. 305.

202. Brunner, *Revelation and Reason*, p. 13.

203. Brunner, *Revelation and Reason*, p. 21.
204. Brunner, *Revelation and Reason*, pp. 27–8.
205. Brunner, *Revelation and Reason*, pp. 29–30.
206. Brunner, *Revelation and Reason*, pp. 16–17.
207. Brunner, *Revelation and Reason*, pp. 340–1. Brunner echoes Buber in the sense that Buber wrote the prelude to *Eclipse of God*, in which he makes the same point Brunner makes, in 1932, several years before the publication of *Revelation and Reason*.
208. John Ballie, *Our Knowledge of God* (New York: Charles Scribner's Sons, 1939) p. 132.
209. Ballie, *Our Knowledge of God*, p. 143.
210. Ballie, *Our Knowledge of God*, pp. 181–2.
211. Ballie, *Our Knowledge of God*, pp. 6–7.
212. Lewis, *Our Experience of God*, pp. 273–4.
213. Ballie, *Our Knowledge of God*, p. 178.
214. Ballie, *Our Knowledge of God*, see, e.g. pp. 132 and 183.
215. Hick, *Faith and Knowledge*, esp. ch. 5 'The Nature of Faith' and ch. 9 'Faith as Knowledge'. And cf. Hick's *God and the Universe of Faiths*, ch. 3 'Religious Faith as Experiencing-as' (London: Macmillan, 1973).
216. Hick, *Faith and Knowledge*, p. 123.
217. Hick, 'Sceptics and Believers', *Faith and the Philosophers*, p. 239. See pp. 237–41 for Hick's criticisms of the Neo-Wittgensteinian 'autonomist' position.
218. In *Fear and Trembling* Kierkegaard says of Abraham that if he had doubted, then he would not have had faith (pp. 36–7). That is, the knight of faith must see himself as certain, as knowing, as opposed to believing by an act of will in the face of uncertainty.
219. *Philosophical Investigations*, p. 352. Patrick Sherry has pointed out that there are two strands, a conventionalist and a non-conventionalist strand, in Wittgenstein's thought; see his 'Is Religion a "Form of Life"?', *American Philosophical Quarterly*, vol. 9 (1972) pp. 164–6. And if Renford Bambrough is right, Wittgenstein's thought as it applies to religion is much more cognitivist than many Neo-Wittgensteinians would allow; see his introduction to *Reason and Religion*, pp. 14 and 18–19.

CHAPTER 2   THE THIRD PERSPECTIVE

1. I shall refer to 'the Psalmist' in the traditional manner, although the Psalms were written by several authors over a period of time. Whether the Psalms were written by one or several authors does not affect our concern.
2. James, 'The Sentiment of Rationality', *Essays in Pragmatism*, p. 27.
3. King-Farlow and Christensen, *Faith and the Life of Reason*, p. 189.
4. James says: 'Since belief is measured by action, he who forbids us to believe religion to be true, necessarily also forbids us to act as we should if we did believe it to be true'. 'The Will to Believe', p. 108, n. 4.
5. Davis, *Faith, Skepticism, and Evidence*, pp. 171–3.
6. Davis, *Faith, Skepticism, and Evidence*, p. 171.

7. Raphael Demos, 'Religious Faith and Scientific Faith', *Religious Experience and Truth*, pp. 130–6.

8. William James, *The Varieties of Religious Experience*, lectures IV and V.

9. Alvin Plantinga, 'Is Belief in God Rational?', *Rationality and Religious Belief*, pp. 7–27 and Alvin Plantinga, 'Is Belief in God Properly Basic?', *Noûs*, vol. 15 (1981) pp. 41–51.

10. Plantinga, 'Is Belief in God Rational?', *Rationality and Religious Belief*, pp. 12–13.

11. Plantinga, 'Is Belief in God Properly Basic?', p. 47.

12. Plantinga, 'Is Belief in God Properly Basic?', p. 44.

13. Plantinga, 'Is Belief in God Rational?', *Rationality and Religous Belief*, p. 26.

14. Plantinga, 'Is Belief in God Properly Basic?', p. 48 (Plantinga's emphasis).

15. Plantinga, 'Is Belief in God Properly Basic?', p. 48.

16. Plantinga, 'Is Belief in God Properly Basic?', p. 50.

17. Plantinga, 'Is Belief in God Properly Basic?', p. 50 (Plantinga's emphasis).

18. Plantinga, 'Is Belief in God Rational?', *Rationality and Religious Belief*, p. 27 (Plantinga's emphasis).

19. Plantinga, 'Is Belief in God Properly Basic?', p. 46.

20. Plantinga, 'Is Belief in God Properly Basic?', p. 46.

21. In 'Gods' Wisdom, in discussing various techniques for settling issues after all the data are known, in effect draws to our attention various types of issue-settling discoveries. See Chapter 1, section (4) for a description of Wisdom's issue-settling techniques.

22. For the sake of convenience I shall use this title to refer to this specific realisation discovery-type. However we should bear in mind that there are other kinds of realisations as well, e.g. the kind Bambrough discusses in *Reason, Truth and God*, pp. 119–20.

23. Phillips, 'From World to God?', *Faith and Philosophical Enquiry*, p. 54 (Phillips' emphasis).

24. I quoted the passage earlier (Chapter 1, section (4)). It is from Malcolm's 'The Groundlessness of Belief'.

25. Cf. Phillips, 'Faith, Scepticism, and Religious Understanding', *Faith and Philosophical Enquiry*, p. 13.

26. Romans 1.20.

27. Richard of St. Victor, *The Twelve Patriarchs, The Mystical Ark*, and *Book Three of the Trinity*, trans. and intro. Grover A. Zinn (The Classics of Western Spirituality. New York: Paulist Press, 1979) p. 129.

28. Richard of St. Victor, *The Twelve Patriarchs, The Mystical Ark*, and *Book Three of the Trinity*, p. 131.

29. St. Bonaventura, *The Mind's Road to God*, trans. George Boas (New York: Bobbs-Merrill, The Library of Liberal Arts, 1953) p. 13.

30. St. Bonaventura, *The Mind's Road to God*, p. 13.

31. St. Bonaventura, *The Mind's Road to God*, p. 9.

32. St. Bonaventura, *The Mind's Road to God*, p. 28.

33. St. Bonaventura, *The Mind's Road to God*, p. 39.

34. Examples could be taken from the writings of, for instance, John Calvin and Johann Arndt. An example from Jewish mysticism is to be found in the writings of the Jewish mystic and rabbi Abraham Isaac Kook. And, ranging beyond the Judaeo-Christian heritage, examples are to be found in Sufism.

See John Calvin, *The Institutes*. I, v, 1 and 2 (Dillenberger, *Selections*, pp. 333–35); Johann Arndt, *True Christianity*, trans. and intro. Peter Erb (The Classics of Western Spirituality. New York: Paulist Press, 1979) p. 118; Abraham Isaac Kook, *The Lights of Penitence, The Moral Principles, Lights of Holiness, Essays, Letters,* and *Poems*, trans. and intro. Ben Zion Bokser (The Classics of Western Spirituality. New York: Paulist Press, 1978) p. 223; and Abū Hāmid al-Ghāzalī, 'The Revivification of Religion', *Readings from the Mystics of Islam*, trans. Margaret Smith (London: Luzac, 1950), p. 59.

35. The episode occurs in Book Six in the section entitled 'Recollections of Father Zossima's Adolescence and Manhood while He was Still in the World. The Duel', F. Dostoyevsky, *The Brothers Karamazov*, trans. David Magarshack (Baltimore: Penguin Books, 1958) I, 352.

It is arguable that another example occurs in the *Rime of the Ancient Mariner* when the Mariner's desperation was broken and he looked upon the creatures of the sea that he had seen as loathsome and 'blessed them unaware'.

36. Arndt, *True Christianity*, p. 42; St. Bernard of Clairvaux, *On the Necessity of Loving God* in *The Wisdom of Catholicism*, ed. Anton C. Pegis (New York: Random House, 1949) p. 255; St. Bonaventura, *The Mind's Road to God*, p. 7.

Denial of self is not found in the Judaeo-Christian tradition alone. John Hick in a recent work has shown how this theme is deeply involved in various religious traditions. See his *Death and Eternal Life* (New York: Harper & Row, 1976) ch. 21 'Moksha, Nirvana and the Unitive State'.

37. Quoted earlier in Chapter 1, section (4).

38. Also there may be a structural similarity between the religious discovery of God's presence and a moral realisation-discovery of the sort that Josiah Royce calls 'the moral insight' in *The Religious Aspect of Philosophy*. In 'The Death of God and the Death of Persons', *Religious Studies*, vol. 16 (1980), I try to show the symmetrical relationship between these two discoveries.

39. See for instance Hick's *God and the Universe of Faiths*, ch. 10 'The New Map of the Universe of Faiths'.

40. Friedrich Nietzsche, *The Antichrist*, secs. 55 and 46, in *The Portable Nietzsche*, ed. and trans. Walter Kaufmann (New York: The Viking Press, 1954) pp. 639–40 and 625.

41. Sigmund Freud, *The Future of an Illusion*, trans. W. D. Robson-Scott, revised James Strachey (Garden City, N.Y.: Anchor Books, 1964) pp. 48–9.

42. Freud, *The Future of an Illusion*, pp. 34–5.

43. Freud, *The Future of an Illusion*, pp. 70–1.

44. William Alston, 'Psychoanalytic Theory and Theistic Belief', *Faith and the Philosophers*, p. 76.

45. Freud, *The Future of an Illusion*, pp. 48–52.

46. Freud, *The Future of an Illusion*, p. 52. We should note that Freud did not deny that religion has social value. The projected father-figure proclaims the rules of culture and so helps to restrain anti-social instincts. But ideally for Freud human beings should have no illusions, no beliefs motivated by wish-fulfilment. They should clearly see the need for rules of culture to restrain their instincts and give them a social justification based on a scientific and pragmatic outlook.

47. Friedrich Nietzsche, *Thus Spoke Zarathustra*, First Part, 'On the After-worldly'; in Kaufmann, *The Portable Nietzsche*, p. 143.

48. Perhaps the best known discussion is Herbert Fingarette's *Self-Deception* (*Studies in Philosophical Psychology*, ed. R. F. Holland. New York: Humanities Press, 1969); see Fingarette's bibliography, pp. 163–4, for works about or relevant to self-deception that were published before 1969. Other discussions published after Fingarette's book are: Terence Penelhum, *Problems of Religious Knowledge* (New York: Herder & Herder, 1972), appendix A, 'Self-Deception', pp. 149–55; Amelie Oksenberg Rorty, 'Belief and Self-Deception', *Inquiry*, vol. 15 (1972); Alan Drengson, 'Critical Notice: Herbert Fingarette, *Self-Deception*', *Canadian Journal of Philosophy*, vol. 3 (1974); John Turk Saunders, 'The Paradox of Self-Deception', *Philosophy and Phenomenological Research*, vol. 35 (1975).

49. This is John Turk Saunders' distinction. It is meant to apply to both awareness *of* and awareness *that*, and it will apply to self-deception generically if 'awareness' is understood in a nonachievement sense, such that 'I am aware that P' does not entail 'P is true.' Although the distinction between implicit and explicit awareness does little to *explain* self-deception, still the distinction is useful, and I shall make use of it and 'aware' in Saunders' nonachievement sense.

In his book Fingarette makes an effort to resolve the paradox of self-deception by providing an analysis, not in terms of consciousness and knowing, but in terms of 'spelling out'. However, as John Turk Saunders points out in his paper, Fingarette's account of self-deception as a refusal to spell-out requires a necessary reference to consciousness and knowing.

50. Penelhum, *Problems of Religious Knowledge*, p. 152 (his emphasis). Penelhum's discussion of what self-deception is not is helpful, and I have freely drawn upon it in what follows.

51. Fingarette, *Self-Deception*, pp. 28 and 67 (emphasis deleted).

52. Drengson, 'Critical Notice: Herbert Fingarette, *Self-Deception*', p. 482.

53. Rorty, 'Belief and Self-Deception', p. 395.

54. Saunders, 'The Paradox of Self-Deception', p. 564.

55. Terence Penelhum, 'Pleasure and Falsity', *Philosophy of Mind*, Stuart Hampshire, editor (New York: Harper & Row, 1966) p. 259. Reprinted from *American Philosophical Quarterly*, vol. 1 (1964).

56. H. D. Lewis says that the 'consciousness of the transcendent tends to set up some form of resistance to itself'. For, he observes, 'it makes exacting demands upon us . . . by requiring certain mental or spiritual adjustments'. When God's 'ultimate mystery comes into human life', human beings are apt to feel crushed: 'the God of love is also the God of terror' (*Our Experience of God*, pp. 88–9.)

57. Phillips, 'Wisdom's Gods', *Faith and Philosophical Enquiry*, p. 202.

58. Alasdair MacIntyre, 'Freudian and Christian Dogmas as Equally Unverifiable', *Faith and the Philosophers*, p. 111. MacIntyre's discussion note is a reply to both Alston's 'Psychoanalytic Theory and Theistic Belief' and Malcolm's 'Is it a Religious Belief that "God Exists"?'

59. Hick, *Faith and Knowledge*, ch. 8 'Faith and Verification'; and *God and the Universe of Faiths*, p. 147.

60. Hick, *Faith and Knowledge*, p. 194. Eschatological verification, Hick says, remains relevant to the 'function for which it has been advanced – namely,

establishing the factual character of theistic belief in response to questions raised by contemporary philosophy'. This, of course, is another matter.

61. Nielsen, *Scepticism*, p. 21.
62. M. O'C. Drury, 'A Symposium: Assessments of the Man and the Philosopher, II', *Ludwig Wittgenstein: The Man and His Philosophy*, ed. K. T. Fann (New Jersey: Humanities Press; Sussex: Harvester Press, 1967) p. 70.

Kierkegaard in his papers wrote: 'It is specifically the task of human knowing to understand that there is something it cannot understand and to understand what that is' (See Hong and Hong, *Journals and Papers*, III, 3089 and 3090).

CHAPTER 3 THE FRAMEWORK OF THE THIRD PERSPECTIVE

1. Chapter 1, section (1). Henceforth in this chapter if an earlier discussion is cited it will be in the corresponding section of Chapter 1 unless otherwise indicated.
2. Price, 'Faith and Belief', pp. 19–20.
3. Phillips, *Religion without Explanation*, p. 190.
4. It is tempting in philosophy of religion to argue against various constructions of religious belief with which one does not agree by citing what 'the religious' (or 'the truly religious' or 'the impressively religious,' etc.) say, do, or believe. Always, though, there will be other believers who do not favour one's case but count themselves among the religious, or at least there will be the possibility of such believers developing. I recall how I learned this lesson, or rather how it was brought home to me, for of course we all know it in a sense. I had been arguing for a certain view of religious faith, at each crucial step citing what 'religious persons' say. And Frank Ebersole, with that penetration that so often marks his philosophical comments, asked me simply: 'Where did you meet these religious persons – in Africa?' (I had been in Africa for the previous two years.) I had no reply.
5. Phillips, *Religion without Explanation*, pp. 175–7.
6. Trigg, *Reason and Commitment*, p. 75.
7. Cf. Stuart C. Brown, 'Religion and the Limits of Language', *Reason and Religion*, p. 252, where Brown is commenting on Peter Winch's First-Perceptive thesis that religious awe and wonder do not require any mention of beliefs. Winch advances this thesis in 'Meaning and Religious Language' in the same volume. See esp. p. 198.
8. Geach, 'Praying for Things to Happen', *God and the Soul*, p. 86.
9. D. Z. Phillips, *The Concept of Prayer* (New York: Schocken Books, 1966) p. 121. (His emphasis.)
10. My emphasis.
11. Phillips, *The Concept of Prayer*, pp. 113ff.
12. St. Francis de Sales, *Treatise on the Love of God*, Book VI. ch. I, p. 232.
13. See John Smith, 'Faith, Belief, and the Problem of Rationality', *Rationality and Religious Belief*, p. 55.
14. Simone Weil, *Gravity and Grace* (London: Routledge & Kegan Paul, 1963)

p. 40, quoted by Phillips in *Death and Immortality*, p. 54; St. Bernard of Clairvaux, *On The Necessity of Loving God*, ch. x, in *The Wisdom of Catholicism*, ed. Anton C. Pegis (New York: Random House, 1949) pp. 254–7.

15. This example is from *The Sickness unto Death*. *Fear and Trembling* and *The Sickness unto Death*, p. 152.

16. Cf. Brown on Winch's view of belief and practice: 'Religion and the Limits of Language', *Reason and Religion*, p. 254.

17. Kierkegaard, *Fear and Trembling* and *The Sickness unto Death*, pp. 218–27.

18. Kierkegaard, *Philosophical Fragments*, p. 139.

19. See *Notes from Underground* and *The Grand Inquisitor*, trans. Ralph E. Matlaw (New York: E. P. Dutton, 1960) p. 19.

20. Kierkegaard, *Concluding Unscientific Postscript*, p. 332.

21. On the relationship between speculation and faith in Kierkegaard's thought, especially in the *Postscript*, see Bretall's introduction to *A Kierkegaard Anthology*, xxiii–xxiv and M. J. Charlesworth, *Philosophy of Religion: the Historic Approaches* (New York: Herder & Herder, 1972) p. 130. For Kierkegaard himself see *Concluding Unscientific Postscript*, pp. 51–5.

22. Malcolm, 'The Groundlessness of Belief', *Thought and Knowledge*, p. 216.

23. Herbert, *Paradox and Identity in Theology*, p. 71.

24. Phillips, 'From World to God?', *Faith and Philosophical Enquiry*, p. 54.

25. Norman Kemp Smith says, 'Potentially any situation may yield an immediate awareness of the Divine; actually there is no situation whatsoever which invariably yields it'. 'Is Divine Existence Credible?' *The Credibility of Divine Existence: the Collected Papers of Norman Kemp Smith*, eds A. J. D. Porteus, R. D. Maclennan, and G. E. Davie (London: Macmillan; New York: St. Martin's Press, 1967) p. 393.

26. The distinction between *having a reason* and *being able to give a reason* is discussed by George Mavrodes in *Belief in God* (see pp. 11 and 88–9). Mavrodes suggests that sometimes when we have a reason we still may not be able to give a reason because the 'web' of our experience may be too complex for our analysis. This of course is not what prevents Third-Perspective believers from giving a reason: their not being able to give reasons to others does not derive from the complexity of their experiences or the difficulty of the analysis of their experiences. In fact they can articulate such sentences as 'God's goodness is everywhere', but such utterances do not *give reasons* in the sense I identified.

27. *The Imitation of Christ*, Book 1, chs 1, 2, 3; Book 3, chs 31, 43.

28. St. Bonaventura, *The Mind's Road to God*, pp. 4–5.

29. See the *Postscript*, p. 51, where Kierkegaard's objections are to the indifference of the 'speculative philosopher' who would 'contemplate Christianity'; p. 118, where he objects to the 'objective tendency' to make everyone into an 'observer'; and p. 512, where he criticises the 'objective interpretation of Christianity' for conceiving 'that by learning to know objectively what Christianity is (as an investigator learns it by the way of research, scholarship, learning) one thereby becomes a Christian . . .'.

30. Buber, *I and Thou*, pp. 90–1. The German word translated as 'behold' by Kaufmann is *Schauen*. See p. 61, n. 6.

31. John Smith, *Select Discourses*, ed. John Worthington (London: printed by F. Flesher for W. Morden, 1660) pp. 1–21; reprinted in a facsimile edition by

Garland Publishing, New York and London, 1978, in their series British Philosophers and Theologians of the 17th and 18th Centuries, ed. René Wellek.

32. *Summa Theologica*, II–II, q.2, a.1.
33. John Henry Newman, *A Grammar of Assent* (Notre Dame and London: University of Notre Dame Press, 1979) p. 162. (Newman's emphasis.)
34. Newman, *A Grammar of Assent*, p. 76.
35. Newman, *A Grammar of Assent*, p. 62.
36. Newman, *A Grammar of Assent*, pp. 95–101. Cf. pp. 304ff., where Newman discusses other 'Evidences of Religion' important for our experience, such as the order of the universe. But 'conscience', he says, 'is nearer to me than any other means of knowledge'.
37. Newman, *A Grammar of Assent*, p. 101.
38. Newman, *A Grammar of Assent*, p. 105.
39. Paul L. Holmer, *The Grammar of Faith* (San Francisco: Harper & Row, 1978) pp. 24–5.
40. Holmer, *The Grammar of Faith*, p. 25.
41. Holmer, *The Grammar of Faith*, p. 31.
42. Holmer, *The Grammar of Faith*, p. 203.
43. Kierkegaard, *Philosophical Fragments*, p. 102. Kierkegaard's concern is not with the religious discovery of course. He is arguing that since doubt is an act of will, and not from knowledge, belief, which overcomes doubt, is not a form of knowledge, but also an expression of will.
44. Cf. Hick, 'Faith and Coercion', p. 273: 'the dawning religious sense of existing in God's presence is such that we can either welcome it and permit it to grow upon us, or repress and reject it'.
45. Thus Phillips, who regards absolute belief's conceptual change as connotative in accord with his First-Perspective intuitions, sees the religious response to evil as one that admits 'the sheer pointlessness' of natural evil. That is, for Phillips, the religious belief in God's goodness severs the normal connection between being good and having a good purpose. Phillips, 'The Problem of Evil', *Reason and Religion*, p. 120.
46. Brother David Steindl-Rast, 'My Spiritual Discipline', *Mystics and Scholars*, ed. Harold Coward and Terence Penelhum (SR Supplement/3), pp. 20–1 (emphasis in the original).

Bibliography

1. R. Abelson, 'The Logic of Faith and Belief', in *Hook* (55).
2. W. Alston, 'Psychoanalytic Theory and Theistic Belief', in *Hick* (48).
3. St. Thomas Aquinas, *Summa Theologica*.
4. Johann Arndt, *True Christianity*, trans. and intro. P. Erb (New York: Paulist Press, 1979).
5. J. Baillie, *Our Knowledge of God* (New York: Charles Scribner's Sons, 1939).
6. R. Bambrough, *Reason, Truth and God* (London: Methuen, 1969).
7. St. Bernard of Clairvaux, *On the Necessity of Loving God*, in *The Wisdom of Catholicism*, ed. A. C. Pegis (New York: Random House, 1949).
8. St. Bonaventura, *The Mind's Road to God*, trans. George Boas (Indianapolis and New York: Bobbs-Merrill, 1953).
9. R. B. Braithwaite, 'An Empiricist's View of the Nature of Religious Belief', reprinted in *Hick* (45).
10. R. Bretall (ed.), *A Kierkegaard Anthology* Princeton University Press, 1946).
11. S. C. Brown, *Do Religious Claims Make Sense?* (New York: Macmillan, 1969).
12. S. C. Brown (ed.), *Reason and Religion* (Ithaca and London: Cornell University Press, 1977).
13. S. C. Brown, 'Religion and the Limits of Language', in *Brown* (12).
14. E. Brunner, *Revelation and Reason*, trans. O. Wyon (Philadelphia: The Westminster Press, 1946).
15. M. Buber, *I and Thou*, trans. W. Kaufmann (New York: Charles Scribner's Sons, 1970).
16. J. Calvin, *The Institutes*, in *Dillenberger* (25).
17. R. Carnap, 'Autobiography', in *The Philosophy of Rudolf Carnap* ed. Paul Schilpp (LaSalle, Illinois: The Open Court Publishing Co., 1964).
18. A. Castell (ed.), *Essays in Pragmatism* (New York: Hafner Publishing Company, 1948).
19. M. J. Charlesworth, *Philosophy of Religion: the Historic Approaches* (New York: Herder & Herder, 1972).
20. H. Coward and T. Penelhum (eds), *Mystics and Scholars* (SR Supplement/3).
21. F. Crosson (ed.), *The Autonomy of Religious Belief* (Notre Dame and London: University of Notre Dame Press, 1981).
22. S. T. Davis, *Faith, Skepticism, and Evidence* (Lewisburg: Bucknell University Press; London: Associated University Presses, 1978).
23. C. F. Delaney (ed.), *Rationality and Religious Belief* (Notre Dame and London: University of Notre Dame Press, 1979).
24. R. Demos, 'Religious Faith and Scientific Faith', in *Hook* (55).

25. J. Dillenberger (ed.), *John Calvin: Selections from His Writings* (Garden City, NY: Anchor Books, 1971).
26. Dionysius, *The Mystical Theology*, in *Rolt* (120).
27. F. Dostoyevsky, *The Brothers Karamazov*, trans. D. Magarshack, 2 vols (Baltimore, Maryland: Penguin Books, 1958).
28. F. Dostoyevsky, *Notes from Underground* and *The Grand Inquisitor*, trans. R. E. Matlaw (New York: Dutton, 1960).
29. A. Drengson, 'Critical Notice: Herbert Fingarette, *Self-Deception*', *Canadian Journal of Philosophy*, vol. 3 (1974).
30. M. O'C. Drury, 'Some Notes on Conversations with Wittgenstein', reprinted in *Rhees* (117).
31. M. O'C. Drury, 'A Symposium: Assessments of the Man and the Philosopher, II', in *Fann* (33).
32. P. Edwards, 'Kierkegaard and the "Truth" of Christianity', *Philosophy*, vol. 46 (1971).
33. K. T. Fann, *Ludwig Wittgenstein: the Man and His Philosophy* (New Jersey: Humanities Press; Chichester: Harvester Press, 1967).
34. H. Fingarette, *Self-Deception* (New York: Humanities Press, 1969).
35. A. Flew, 'Theology and Falsification', reprinted in *Flew and MacIntyre* (36).
36. A. Flew and A. MacIntyre, *New Essays in Philosophical Theology* (London: SCM Press, 1955).
37. S. Freud, *The Future of an Illusion*, W. D. Robson-Scott, rev. J. Strachey (Garden City, NY: Anchor Books, 1964).
38. P. Geach, 'Causality and Creation', reprinted in *Geach* (39).
39. P. Geach, *God and the Soul* (London: Routledge & Kegan Paul, 1969).
40. P. Geach, 'On Worshipping the Right God', in *Geach* (39).
41. P. Geach, 'Praying for Things to Happen', in *Geach* (39).
42. R. Herbert, *Paradox and Identity in Theology* (Ithaca and London: Cornell University Press, 1979).
43. J. Hick, *Death and Eternal Life* (New York: Harper & Row, 1976).
44. J. Hick, 'Eschatological Verification Reconsidered', *Religious Studies*, vol. 13 (1977).
45. J. Hick (ed.), *The Existence of God* (New York: Macmillan; London: Collier-Macmillan, 1964).
46. J. Hick, 'Faith and Coercion', *Philosophy*, vol. 42 (1967).
47. J. Hick, *Faith and Knowledge* (2nd ed; Ithaca, NY: Cornell University Press, 1966).
48. J. Hick (ed.), *Faith and the Philosophers* (New York: St. Martin's Press, 1964).
49. J. Hick, *God and the Universe of Faiths* (London: Macmillan 1973).
50. J. Hicks, 'Sceptics and Believers', in *Hick* (47).
51. J. Hick, 'Theology and Verification', reprinted in *Hick* (45).
52. R. F. Holland, 'Religious Discourse and Theological Discourse', *The Australasian Journal of Philosophy*, vol. 34 (1956).
53. P. L. Holmer, *The Grammar of Faith* (San Francisco: Harper & Row, 1978).
54. H. V. Hong and E. Hong, (eds and trans.), *Søren Kierkegaard's Journals and Papers*, 7 vols (Bloomington and London: Indiana University Press, 1967–78).
55. S. Hook (ed.), *Religious Experience and Truth* (New York: New York University Press, 1961).

56. W. D. Hudson, *Wittgenstein and Religious Belief* (London: Macmillan, 1975).
57. D. Hume, *Dialogues Concerning Natural Religion*.
58. D. Hume, *An Enquiry Concerning Human Understanding*.
59. *The Imitation of Christ*.
60. W. James, 'The Sentiment of Rationality', in *Castell* (18).
61. W. James, 'The Will to Believe', in *Castell* (18).
62. W. Kaufmann (ed. and trans.), *The Portable Nietzsche* New York: The Viking Press, 1954).
63. S. Kierkegaard, *Concluding Unscientific Postscript*, trans. D. F. Swenson and W. Lowrie (Princeton: Princeton University Press, 1941).
64. S. Kierkegaard, *Fear and Trembling* and *Sickness unto Death*, trans. W. Lowrie (Princeton; Princeton University Press, 1941).
65. S. Kierkegaard, *Philosophical Fragments*, trans. D. F. Swenson, trans. revised H. V. Hong (Princeton: Princeton University Press, 1962).
66. S. Kierkegaard, *Training in Christianity*, trans. W. Lowrie (Princeton: Princeton University Press, 1944).
67. J. King-Farlow, 'Cogency, Conviction, and Coercion', *International Philosophical Quarterly*, vol. 8 (1968).
68. J. King-Farlow and W. Christensen, *Faith and the Life of Reason* (Dordrecht, Holland: D. Reidel, 1972).
69. Abraham Isaac Kook, *The Lights of Penitence, The Moral Principles, Lights of Holiness, Essays, Letters*, and *Poems*, trans. and intro, B. Z. Bokser (New York: Paulist Press, 1978).
70. H. D. Lewis, *Our Experience of God* (London: Allen & Unwin; New York: Macmillan, 1959).
71. A. MacIntyre, 'Freudian a d Christian Dogmas as Equally Unverifiable', in *Hick* (48).
72. A. MacIntyre, 'Is Understanding Religion Compatible with Believing?', in *Hick* (48).
73. A. MacIntyre, 'The Logical Status of Religious Belief', *Metaphysical Belief*, ed. A. MacIntyre (2nd ed; London: SCM Press, 1970).
74. J. L. Mackie, 'Evil and Omnipotence', reprinted in *Pike* (111).
75. G. Malantschuk, *Kierkegaard's Thought*, ed. and trans. H. V. and E. Hong (Princeton: Princeton University Press, 1971).
76. N. Malcolm, 'Anselm's Ontological Arguments', *Knowledge and Certainty* (Englewood Cliffs, NJ: Prentice-Hall, 1963); also in *Hick* (45).
77. N. Malcolm, 'The Groundlessness of Belief', *Thought and Knowledge* (Ithaca and London: Cornell University Press, 1977); also in *Brown* (12).
78. N. Malcolm, 'Is it a Religious Belief that "God Exists"?', in *Hick* (48).
79. N. Malcolm, *Ludwig Wittgenstein: a Memoir* (London: Oxford University Press, 1958).
80. G. Mavrodes, *Belief in God: a Study in the Epistemology of Religion* (New York: Random House, 1970).
81. G. Mavrodes, 'Rationality and Religious Belief—A Perverse Question', in *Delaney* (23).
82. G. Mavrodes (ed.), *The Rationality of Belief in God* (Englewood Cliffs, NJ: Prentice-Hall, 1970).
83. H. J. McCloskey, 'God and Evil', reprinted in *Pike* (111).

84. T. McPherson, *Philosophy and Religious Belief* (London: Hutchinson University Library, 1974).

85. B. Mitchell, 'Theology and Falsification', reprinted in *Flew and MacIntyre* (36).

86. J. H. Newman, *A Grammar of Assent* (Notre Dame and London: University of Notre Dame Press, 1979).

87. K. Nielsen, 'The Challenge of Wittgenstein: an Examination of his Picture of Religious Belief', *Studies in Religion/Sciences Religieuses*, vol. 3 (1973).

88. K. Nielsen, *Scepticism* (London: Macmillan; New York: St. Martin's Press, 1978).

89. K. Nielsen, 'Wittgensteinian Fideism', *Philosophy*, vol. 42 (1967).

90. F. Nietzsche, *The Antichrist*, in *Kaufmann* (62).

91. F. Nietzsche, *Thus Spoke Zarathustra*, in *Kaufmann* (62).

92. T. Penelhum, 'Pleasure and Falsity', reprinted in S. Hampshire (ed.), *Philosophy of Mind* (New York: Harper & Row, 1966).

93. T. Penelhum, *Problems of Religious Knowledge* (New York: Herder & Herder, 1972).

94. H. H. Price, *Belief* (London: Allen & Unwin; New York: Humanities Press, 1969).

95. H. H. Price, 'Faith and Belief', in *Hick* (48).

96. D. Z. Phillips, 'Belief, Change, and Forms of Life: the Confusions of Externalism and Internalism', in *Crosson* (21).

97. D. Z. Phillips, 'Belief and Loss of Belief', reprinted in *Phillips* (100).

98. D. Z. Phillips, *The Concept of Prayer* (New York: Schocken Books, 1966).

99. D. Z. Phillips, *Death and Immortality* (London: Macmillan; New York: St Martin's Press, 1970).

100. D. Z. Phillips, *Faith and Philosophical Enquiry* (New York: Schocken Books, 1971).

101. D. Z. Phillips, 'Faith, Scepticism, and Religious Understanding', reprinted in *Phillips* (100).

102. D. Z. Phillips, 'From World to God', reprinted in *Phillips* (100).

103. D. Z. Phillips, 'God and Ought', reprinted in *Phillips* (100).

104. D. Z. Phillips, 'On the Christian Concept of Love', reprinted in *Phillips* (100).

105. D. Z. Phillips, 'Philosophy, Theology and the Reality of God', reprinted in *Phillips* (100).

106. D. Z. Phillips, 'The Problem of Evil', in *Brown* (12).

107. D. Z. Phillips (ed.), *Religion and Understanding* (Oxford: Blackwell, 1967).

108. D. Z. Phillips, *Religion without Explanation* (Oxford: Blackwell, 1976).

109. D. Z. Phillips, 'Religious Beliefs and Language-Games', reprinted in *Phillips* (100).

110. D. Z. Phillips, 'Wisdom's Gods', reprinted in *Phillips* (100).

111. N. Pike, *God and Evil* (Englewood Cliffs, NJ: Prentice-Hall, 1964).

112. A. Plantinga, *God and Other Minds* (Ithaca, N.Y.: Cornell University Press, 1967).

113. A. Plantinga, 'Is Belief in God Properly Basic?', *Nous*, vol. 15 (1981).

114. A. Plantinga, 'Is Belief in God Rational?', in *Delaney* (23).

115. A. Plantinga, *The Nature of Necessity* (Oxford: Clarendon Press, 1974).

116. R. Rhees, 'Some Developments in Wittgenstein's View of Ethics', *The Philosophical Review*, vol. 74 (1965).

117. R. Rhees (ed.), *Ludwig Wittgenstein: Personal Recollections* (Totowa, NJ: Rowman & Littlefield, 1981).

118. R. Rhees, *Without Answers* (London: Routledge & Kegan Paul, 1969).

119. Richard of St. Victor, *The Twelve Patriarchs*, *The Mystical Ark*, and *Book Three of the Trinity*, trans and intro. G. A. Zinn (New York: Paulist Press, 1979).

120. C. E. Rolt (trans.), *Dionysius The Areopagite* (London: SPCK, 1940).

121. A. O. Rorty, 'Belief and Self-Deception', *Inquiry*, vol. 15 (1972).

122. St. Francis de Sales, *Treatise on the Love of God*, trans. H. B. Mackey (Westport, Conn.: Greenwood Press, 1971).

123. J. T. Saunders, 'The Paradox of Self-Deception', *Philosophy and Phenomenological Research*, vol. 35 (1975).

124. G. Schlesinger, *Religion and Scientific Method* (Dordrecht and Boston: D. Reidel 1977).

125. P. Sherry, 'Is Religion a "Form of Life"?', *American Philosophical Quarterly*, vol. 9 (1972).

126. P. Sherry, *Religion, Truth and Language-Games* (London: Macmillan; New York: Barnes & Noble, 1977).

127. J. Smith, 'Faith, Belief, and the Problem of Rationality', in *Delaney* (23).

128. J. Smith, 'The True Way or Method of attaining to Divine Knowledge', *Select Discourses* (London: printed by F. Flesher for W. Morden, 1660; reprinted by Garland, New York and London, 1978).

129. M. Smith (trans.), *Readings from the Mystics of Islam* (London: Luzac, 1950).

130. N. K. Smith, *The Credibility of Divine Existence: the Collected Papers of Norman Kemp Smith*, ed. A. J. D. Porteous and others (London: Macmillan: New York: St. Martin's Press, 1967).

131. N. K. Smith, 'Is Divine Existence Credible?', in *Smith* (130).

132. Brother David Steindl-Rast, 'My Spiritual Discipline', in *Coward and Penelhum* (20).

133. R. Swinburne, *The Concept of Miracle* (London: Macmillan; New York: St. Martin's Press, 1970).

134. Alfred, Lord Tennyson, *In Memoriam*.

135. Tertullian, *On the Flesh of Christ*.

136. T. W. Tilley, *Talking of God* (New York, Ramsey, and Toronto: Paulist Press, 1978).

137. R. Trigg, *Reason and Commitment* (Cambridge: Cambridge University Press, 1973).

138. M. de Unamuno, *The Agony of Christianity and Essays on Faith*, trans. A. Kerrigan (Princeton: Princeton University Press, 1974).

139. F. Waismann, 'Notes on Talks with Wittgenstein', *The Philosophical Review*, vol. 74 (1965).

140. S. Weil, *Gravity and Grace*, (London: Routledge & Kegan Paul, 1963).

141. B. Willey, *More Nineteenth Century Studies* (New York: Columbia University Press, 1956).

142. P. Winch, *The Idea of a Social Science and Its Relation to Philosophy* (London: Routledge & Kegan Paul, 1958).

143. P. Winch, 'Meaning and Religious Language', in *Brown* (12).

144. P. Winch, 'Understanding a Primitive Society', reprinted in *Phillips* (107).

145. J. Wisdom, 'Gods', *Philosophy and Psycho-analysis* (Oxford: Blackwell, 1964).

146. L. Wittgenstein, *Lectures and Conversations on Aesthetics, Psychology and Religious Belief*, ed. Cyril Barrett (Berkeley: University of California Press, 1966).

147. L. Wittgenstein, 'A Lecture on Ethics', *The Philosophical Review*, vol. 74 (1965).
148. L. Wittgenstein, *On Certainty*, ed. G. E. M. Anscombe and G. H. von Wright, trans. D. Paul and G. E. M. Anscombe (Oxford: Blackwell, 1969).
149. L. Wittgenstein, *Philosophical Investigations*, trans. G. E. M. Anscombe (New York: Macmillan, 1953).

Index